I0828555

PRAISE FOR *WINNING WITHOUT PERSUADING*

"Many years in YPO have taught me that leadership is ultimately a series of people-puzzles. We reach people by being curious enough to tell stories that resonate and inspire. Esther Choy offers an insightful and immediately usable path to greater connection. This is powerful beyond business. And it's an entertaining read too!"

—Scott Mordell, former global CEO of YPO, current board director and CEO advisor

"You're already surrounded by the stories you need to lead. Let Esther Choy be your guide to unlock your inner storyteller and take your company on the path to success."

—David Risher, CEO of Lyft

"As leaders, we often assume that having all the answers—and convincing others to adopt them—is the hallmark of great leadership. Esther Choy offers a powerful, transformative alternative. She shows how curiosity can open doors that persuasion cannot. I used a few of her insights—like Crazy Good Questions—at our recent off-site and the impact was extraordinary. Engagement skyrocketed, every voice found space, and our team left energized and aligned!"

—Sylvia Kwan, PhD, CEO of Ellevest Wealth Management

"In *Winning Without Persuading*, Esther Choy fundamentally reshaped how I understand the role of story in leadership. I once believed my own authentic stories were primarily tools to inspire and engage. Choy reveals a far more powerful truth: Leaders win by practicing authentic curiosity to discover, facilitate, and empower the stories of others. With clear insights and practical guidance, she shows how curiosity can become a disciplined leadership craft—one capable of unlocking the transformative power of story across an entire organization."

—Kent Johnson, CEO of Highlights for Children

"A call to arms for reticent storytellers, like me, to share more of ourselves without feeling like self-promoters, to honor our own unique perspectives. As Esther Choy says, our stories often reveal themselves in subtle ways—that's what makes them so fun and meaningful to discover. Building shared bonds through group storytelling can be transformative. We simply need to ask the questions—and truly listen."

—Paul Lussow, CEO of TIFIN Give, Inc.

"In *Winning Without Persuading*, Esther Choy charts a path for leading with curiosity. Through that lens, organizations uncover stories that reveal new possibilities once thought out of reach. She challenges leaders to continually seek what they don't yet know and reminds them that progress depends on hearing and elevating other voices. In today's complex business environment, that kind of shared leadership builds truly connected teams of teams."

—Jon Selame, CEO of Wilkins Media

"Esther Choy delivers a true gift you will use again and again—an immersive, pragmatic guide to making your worlds better through the generative power of curiosity. In a time plagued by toxic certainties, she brings to life the power of discovery in evocatively presented vignettes paired with systematic frames for scaffolding novel insights. You will find many opportunities to think again, as you see new angles through the lenses she offers to uncover ways of winning with authentic stories that will refresh you as much as your audience."

—Amir Pasic, PhD, Eugene R. Tempel Dean
at Indiana University Lilly Family School of Philanthropy

"I'm incredibly energized after reading Esther Choy's *Winning Without Persuading*! As a board chair and a family business owner, I always seek ways to help leaders see the bigger picture. The tools in this book are coupled with real-life scenarios that quickly build an understanding of how to successfully implement them. I can't wait to start using Crazy Good Questions to pull out missing stories that highlight unseen opportunities, increase engagement, and accelerate innovation."

—Kimberly Paxton-Hagner, co-owner
and board chair, KLC Holdings, Ltd.

"Timing for this book could not be more relevant for the challenges family enterprises are facing. Families communicate through stories and the ability to uncover, understand, communicate, and utilize those stories more effectively is essential."

—Matt Allen, PhD, professor and executive director, John L. Ward Center for Family Enterprises, Kellogg School of Management, Northwestern University

"This book is so insightful and actionable that I read it twice in a month. Esther Choy shows how to uncover powerful stories with courageous curiosity in ourselves and in the people we lead. That empathy fuels connection and inspires genuine commitment. It is a guide to deepening trust and elevating leadership through the joy of empowering others."

—Adam Farver, chairman of the board, Pella Corporation

"What moves and persuades us to act is not data and numbers, but vivid stories that inspire and move us to action. This book offers a story about stories, how to develop them and use them for optimal impact on others. I found it so useful and clear. A learning guide to keep handy!"

—Dennis Jaffe, PhD, senior research fellow, BanyanGlobal Family Business Advisors

"If you believe, as I do, that leadership is crucially connected to innovation, Esther Choy's new book, *Winning Without Persuading*, will resonate deeply. The essential idea motivating the book is that 'leaders must help others discover what they don't yet realize they know,' and Choy shows how we can do this by combining curiosity and story discovery. She encourages us to draw out stories—'understanding the who'—from ourselves and others, a creative process that, inevitably, is accompanied by *surprise*, because what emerges from the process are 'stories that you didn't realize you need to hear.' This book is full of compelling ideas, compellingly told, and the cumulative effect of those ideas is inspiring."

—D. Gordon Smith, JD, Ira A. Fulton Chair, BYU Law School

"In storytelling expert Esther Choy's newest book, *Winning Without Persuading*, she goes deeper than merely influencing someone. For Choy, storytelling is *discovery and facilitation*—a transformational mindset of curiosity and presence that helps leaders make deeper connections to their purpose, their people, and themselves. Leaders who have seen the power of storytelling in their lives *and* want to build more trust with their people should definitely read this book."

—Erica Keswin, bestselling author, speaker, and workplace strategist

"*Winning Without Persuading* is as revealing as it is refreshing. Esther Choy invites us beyond the game board of leadership into the human stories that shape how we connect, decide, and lead. Honest, vulnerable, and unexpectedly fun, this book redefines persuasion as discovery—and leadership as purpose in action."

—Dr. Rod Berger, author of *The Narrative Edge: Authentic Storytelling That Meets the Moment*

"Esther Choy has a rare ability to pull you in with vivid detail and make you feel not only like you know the people in her stories, but like you are seen in them. Her insights on when to lead from the front and when to guide from the side are powerful, practical, and deeply human. It's the kind of work that continues to shape the leader I'm becoming and the stories I want to tell."

—Casey Foss, chief commercial officer, West Monroe

"Curiosity—the drive to keep asking, exploring, and learning—is a leadership fundamental. Esther Choy understands this deeply, and her passion for elevating curiosity as a cornerstone of great leadership is at the core of her latest book."

—Malin Leschly, chief design officer, Logitech International S.A.

"Every page in *Winning Without Persuading* proves that when you lead with curiosity and listen without agenda, the world hands you its best stories. This book left my heart sparked and my mind wide open, offering both illuminating and practical insight after insight that I'll want to carry into every conversation."

—Jackie Wei Green, Americas head of communication, Arup Group Limited

"A leader inspires others to do what they might not have done on their own—and nothing sparks that inspiration more powerfully than a good story. So how do we, as leaders, find the stories that truly connect and motivate people to achieve? In *Winning Without Persuading*, Esther Choy hands leaders the keys to discover and harness the authentic stories within their teams—and in doing so, unlock genuine excitement and shared purpose."

—Glenn Hollister, VP of sales strategy & effectiveness, United Airlines

"In *Winning Without Persuading*, Esther Choy shows how to turn everyday moments into unforgettable stories that inspire trust and action. With her deep expertise and practical framework, she gives modern leaders a guide to connect more deeply and lead with greater impact."

—Christine Hsu Evans, president of Headspace, Inc.

"Esther Choy's approach charts us a masterful path to take many basic leadership skills we know are important—listening, asking great questions, nurturing your teams' talents . . . and weaves them (through engaging stories) to provide a fresh perspective. This book provides me with a renewed spirit to recognize the value of *facilitating* teams to achieve great things."

—Lisa Fry, chief strategy and innovation officer, SCP Health

"Using her signature blend of mastery, insight, and intrigue, Esther Choy draws readers into an illuminating exploration of how to discover the stories of others. A gifted teacher, Choy makes transformative storytelling techniques feel effortless to learn and apply, helping leaders spark empathy, deepen relationships, and transform the way we connect . . . one authentic story at a time."

—Sandi Bragar, chief client officer and partner, Aspiriant Wealth Management, and cohost of the podcast *Money Tales*

"In leadership, stories matter—and results matter. Esther Choy's new book is a master class in showing leaders how to turn strategy into clear, compelling narratives that people can believe in and execute. *Winning Without Persuading* should be on every leader's desk."

—Ray Rothrock, venture capitalist and philanthropist

"*Winning Without Persuading* has flipped the script on influence. Esther Choy shows how to shift the spotlight away from yourself and onto your audience, how curiosity beats certainty, and how empathy and dialogue are the real factors in triggering action. This book is a powerful reminder about the impact of listening with intent."

—Andy Crestodina, cofounder and chief marketing officer, Orbit Media Studio, Inc.

"Esther Choy has written the leadership book I didn't realize I'd been waiting for. I've read plenty on strategy, communication, and performance—but she names and unlocks the missing element: how inviting others to tell their stories transforms how we lead. This book is a powerful reminder that great leaders don't just tell compelling stories—they create the conditions for others to be fully seen, heard, and understood. Esther shows exactly how to do that with clarity, heart, and practical wisdom."

—Stephanie Ellis-Smith, founder and CEO of Phīla Engaged Giving

"Esther Choy reminds us that being truly seen and heard is transformative—and that leaders create this transformation not by speaking more, but by noticing more. *Winning Without Persuading* is a generous, wise book that will make you a better colleague, advisor, and human being. Its message is perfect for this day and age."

—John A. Warnick, JD, AEP, founder of the Purposeful Planning Institute

"Esther Choy has done it again! Her first book, *Let the Story Do the Work*, fundamentally transformed how my team at Sawyer communicates and leads. Now, in *Winning Without Persuading*, she shows how curiosity and story discovery can make us better leaders and better humans. Her approach continues to guide how we lead with purpose. A required reading for anyone searching for ways to lead effectively in the age of AI."

—Kurt Avery, founder and president, Sawyer Products

"Great leaders don't just persuade—they illuminate. Esther Choy shows us how the stories we've gathered throughout our lives can become powerful tools to clarify vision, inspire teams, build trust, and create genuine connection. This book is an essential guide to unlocking the narrative power every leader already carries."

—ADM Lisa Franchetti, USN (Ret.), 33rd chief of naval operations

"Storytelling genius Esther Choy brings to life the value of curiosity, story, and human decision-making. With prudent insights like, 'In brainstorming sessions . . . silence is oxygen,' this book is filled with unforgettable lessons."

—Amy Lee Boonstra, PhD, executive director, Roman Family Center for Decision Research, University of Chicago Booth School of Business

winning without persuading

winning without persuading

esther choy

A New Framework for Leading with Curiosity and Story Discovery

HarperCollins Leadership

An Imprint of HarperCollins

Winning Without Persuading

Published by HarperCollins Leadership, an imprint of HarperCollins Focus LLC, 501 Nelson Place, Nashville, TN 37214, USA.

ISBN 978-1-4002-5279-4 (ePub)
ISBN 978-1-4002-5277-0 (HC)

HarperCollins Publishers, Macken House, 39/40 Mayor Street Upper, Dublin 1, D01 C9W8, Ireland (https://www.harpercollins.com)

Library of Congress Control Number: 2025947480

Art direction and design: Ron Huizinga
Cover illustration: Irina Kiro
Interior Design: Neuwirth & Associates, Inc.

Printed in the United States of America

26 27 28 29 30 LBC 5 4 3 2 1

For Dad
The best storyteller I know.

For Mom
My fiercest protector.

a word about names

Why did it take me nine years to write another book?

Because I'm a classic introvert. I only speak up when I have something of real substance to say. Time has a way of elevating perspective, and mine is no exception. What's deepened my point of view on storytelling is the range of clients I've been lucky enough to work with in these intervening years. Fully aware this edges into humble-brag territory, I mention it only because there's no other way to explain how I came to see that leaders must be both a guide on the side *and* a sage on the stage. Those lessons, gathered client by client, are what fill the pages of this book, *Winning Without Persuading*.

As much as possible, I use real names—the names of clients generous enough to let their stories be shared here. Because their stories have taught me so much, I believe they will leave a mark on you too. In the rare case I couldn't use a name for privacy reasons, I use only a first name. Regardless of real or pseudonym, every event, every challenge, every recognition and turning point you'll read is true.

My hope is that through these stories you'll find your imagination sparked, your heart opened, and your mind inspired to lead with curiosity—and that, through curiosity, you'll discover stories that lead to possibilities once thought impossible.

contents

foreword by Gregory Warner xix
introduction xxiii

the *why* section
chapter 1: The Power of Curiosity and Story Discovery 3
chapter 2: Spotting and Snatching the Best Stories 17
chapter 3: Excavating the Unspoken 33
chapter 4: Beyond the Trumpet 51

the *what* section
chapter 5: Opportunities Abound 67
chapter 6: Leading Through Curiosity and Story Discovery 89
chapter 7: Winning Without Persuading (Yes, Again) 111

the *how* section
chapter 8: Winning with Crazy Good Questions 143
chapter 9: Winning with Story Refining 163
chapter 10: Winning with Leadership Storytelling 183

appendix 201
acknowledgments 207
notes 213
index 223
about the author 233

foreword

The folding chairs were all set out, neat rows facing a podium with a hand-lettered sign: *Listening Session #3: Bridging the Divide.* The coffee urn steamed beside untouched cookies. The clock ticked, but no one was showing up.

The university had organized a series of listening sessions to ease polarization on campus. They were expensive events with big-name guests. But they were becoming a joke. A punch line about how empathy had a funeral and no one came.

I got a call about this particular event from a college administrator who was a listener to my podcast on NPR. *Rough Translation* was a show I created to explore how ideas travel across cultures—and what gets lost or gained in translation. The show treated foreignness as a kind of superpower, a way of stepping outside your comfort zone that could teach you to perceive the world differently.

Our listeners included executives managing international teams, officers at the State Department, immigrants trying to navigate American workplaces, and, apparently, at least one college administrator trying to encourage students to listen to one another. She wanted to know "How do we get students to show up?"

Maybe, I thought, you need to start by not treating listening like homework.

I gave her what pointers I could, but her question haunted me. Everywhere I've reported—from Kyiv to Kansas—the moments that changed people's minds started with a question, not a statement. They began when someone decided to listen with curiosity instead of certainty. So why do so many good-faith efforts at listening—on campuses, in companies, in public life—fail?

I didn't find the answer until I met Esther Choy.

I first met Esther through *Rough Translation*. Esther's life was a sort of *Rough Translation* tale of its own. As an immigrant navigating American business schools and boardrooms, she'd learned to use her outsiderness as an advantage.

She started small—helping applicants write business school essays that actually sounded like themselves. That led to coaching executives to communicate with humanity and curiosity.

"I can't do what you do," she told me once. "But I can take what you do and turn it into steps anyone can learn."

I've watched her do it. And I've watched a room tilt toward her even as she cast the spotlight away from herself and, instead, channeled her curiosity squarely on her audience.

It was in talking with her that the puzzle from that university story finally clicked into place. Those administrators had framed listening as a duty: hear the other side, be civil, stay polite. And that's how most of us are taught about listening, right? *Wait your turn. Pay attention when someone else is speaking.*

That's not exactly wrong. We should consider other people's perspectives. But do we owe others our attention, like a tax that must be forked over to the gods of civil discourse? Perhaps. But good luck convincing people to pay.

The case for listening is easier to make when you look at the benefits. As I've learned from *Winning Without Persuading*, good listeners aren't just better companions—they're better parents, partners, managers, leaders. Curiosity about others can reduce your own anxiety. People who feel deeply understood can become more open to criticism and to reconsidering their own biases. Listening changes minds.

Reading this book also helped me see what went wrong in those university listening sessions when they framed listening as a courtesy instead of a creative act. If that college administrator called me today, I'd send her a copy of *Winning Without Persuading*.

If you're holding this book, you probably already sense that something's missing in the way we communicate. Maybe you lead a team and feel that every meeting produces more words but fewer insights. Maybe you're a manager whose employees nod along but rarely speak up. Maybe you've been told you need to "tell your story" and wondered what that even means.

You're not alone.

I've spent much of my professional life asking questions for a living. I've been lucky enough to interview people in war zones, in marketplaces, in laboratories. And for most of my life, I was the shyest person you'd ever meet. Shyness, I've realized, is training for this work. It teaches you to observe, to sense the mood in a room, to notice when someone's words don't match their eyes.

The truth is, curiosity isn't a personality type. It's a craft. And like any craft, you can practice it, refine it, and get better at it.

In business, that craft can feel risky. Success is often measured by your ability to persuade—to win the pitch, close the deal, lead the room. Curiosity, by contrast, can feel like exposure: what if, when you're the one in charge, asking questions makes you look incompetent? What if, in a heated argument, taking time to discover the other person's story makes you look weak?

Esther's answer is simple: The cost of not being curious is higher.

She teaches that curiosity isn't passive, it's strategic. Asking the right question isn't about giving up control. It's about creating conditions where new information—and new trust—can emerge.

And we need that now more than ever.

Expertise is under assault. Institutions are distrusted. Algorithms can out-answer us. Artificial intelligence can now analyze your quarterly report and write your résumé. But it can't yet notice the flicker in someone's eyes when something doesn't fit. It can't feel when a story is about to take an unexpected turn.

The skill of asking the right question—of knowing where your colleagues, your customers, your bosses are coming from—is what will keep the rest of us in the game.

The insights and techniques in these pages will make you better at your job. They'll also make you better at being a person. They'll help you lead meetings that don't drain the life out of people. They'll help you build teams that feel seen, customers who feel understood, and relationships that can withstand disagreement. They might even help you talk to your sullen teenager.

And maybe, if enough of us practice what Esther teaches, they'll help heal the wider world too.

We measure success by who we convince. Esther reminds us that real success is in who we understand.

Gregory Warner
Peabody award-winning journalist and
host of the podcasts *The Last Invention*
and NPR's *Rough Translation*

introduction

I have two friends. They move through the world in different keys, yet the same melody runs underneath.

David can't pinpoint when competition became oxygen for him; he only knows it's essential. Barely in his late thirties, he'd already broken into the inner circle of one of the world's most elite private equity firms, taking on roles usually held by people with far more gray hair. He didn't need the Chartered Financial Analyst designation, but he sat for it anyway—three grueling exams—as a personal challenge. In study groups and on daily quizzes, he chased the top score among thousands; anything less gnawed at him for the rest of the day. And still, that wasn't the full picture.

He's an avid cyclist and jumps into races whenever he can. He met a romantic partner who rides, too, and whose competitive streak matches his. One day, they decided on a two-hundred-mile route through mountains and valleys. No prizes. No podium. Just bragging rights. Late the night of the race, David pulled ahead and kept going—no lights on either bike, no glances back. Did he worry about her safety? He can't recall. Did he consider what that choice might do to their relationship? He'd like to think so, but he isn't sure. They both made it home safely. She didn't speak to him for two months. He told me the story years later, equal parts regret and reflection. He simply needs to win.

And then there's my other friend, Dado.

Dado is a gentle giant—at least eighteen inches taller than me—and every time we meet I feel as welcomed and safe as I do with family.

We met when he was twenty-five. As my MBA admissions client, he walked me through the major events of his life and work, hoping I could help him tell his stories in ways that were true and compelling. I listened in awe: sorrow for what he'd endured as a child; optimism for what felt possible for him next. A dual master's—Northwestern and Harvard—followed, and his career took off like a rocket. Then we lost touch for thirteen years, swept up in our own lives. When we finally reconnected over coffee in downtown Chicago one spring afternoon, Dado wanted to make sure I heard one thing.

"Much of what you helped me shape through our early interactions was getting to know myself," he said, twisting his water glass left and right. Without looking up, he added, "Which was the basic building block for the rest of it."

"The rest of it" is his life now: a jet-setting career the boy he once was couldn't have imagined and the ability to care for his single mother the way she deserves. We sat quietly. I didn't expect that kind of tenderness and couldn't find words worthy of it. Silence—me watching his thumb and middle finger turn the glass—felt like the most respectful response. When I finally looked up, he was wiping away tears.

But here's the thing: David and Dado are the same person.

When we first met, he went by David Slezak. Dado is his given name in Slovakia and the one he's used since graduate school. The fiercely competitive David and the deeply introspective, tender-hearted Dado live in the same person. Temperaments that seem to pull in different directions coexist. How does he navigate those ways of being? He mentioned that getting to know himself was the early building block for his success. But how? How does anyone do that work? And why does it matter to you?

If those questions draw you in, you're the reader I wrote this book for—you're willing to lead with curiosity.

You may not yet have a feel for "story discovery." For nearly twenty years bookstores everywhere have been crowded with advice on how storytelling helps you win. I added to that in 2017 with *Let the Story Do the Work: The Art of Storytelling for Business Success.* It was praised for its practicality and encouragement—even Stephen Dubner of *Freakonomics* called it out by name.

Story discovery is something else. What does it ask of you? What does it unlock?

THE MIRROR, THE FOUNDATION.

Thirteen years ago, Dado initially came to me for what he thought was a practical task: positioning his MBA applications so he would be admitted to the top-tier US business schools. He expected what most people expect: researching schools with the best personal fit, streamlining his résumé entries into tighter lines, crafting a neat arc of "I did this, then I achieved that."

What he didn't expect was the mirror.

As he put it later: "You pushed me past the surface level. Here's what I did, here's the result—that's résumé talk. You pushed me two, three, four levels deeper, to understand who I was. It was the first time I looked at myself in the mirror and understood how my own behaviors shaped what came next."

That mirror startled him. Until then, he had been successful, especially given his modest background, but mostly based on momentum: do the work, aim for the next rung, repeat. He had not stopped to ask why certain choices carried him forward or why others seemed to stall him. He had not traced the thread of his own actions, reactions, strengths, or blind spots.

It was these moments of recognition that turned into the beginning of everything else.

This is the difference between story*telling* and story *discovery.* Storytelling, as most business books describe it, furthers what we think the world wants to hear. But these stories are mostly anticipated episodes turned into mediocre performance. They focus on how the tellers can stand out and win. They give little, if any, attention to what the audiences' stories might be. Discovery does something harder.

It requires sitting in the mirror long enough to notice not just what happened but who you were in the middle of it: what impulses carried you forward, what costs accompanied the wins, what truths lingered behind the convenient surface. You will see its power for one person, but as you read the rest of Dado's story, imagine the exponential impact that this power can create for teams, for organizations, for community.

For Dado, the mirror became his lifelong foundation.

AMBITION'S COSTS AND DOORS

Ambition, Dado admitted, had always been his engine. It drove him from a boy in borrowed sneakers to scholarships abroad, from Northwestern and Harvard to the top of private equity. But ambition also has a cost.

"When you're ambitious," he told me, "you open some doors, but you may be closing others. Especially early in your career, you want everyone to know the idea was yours. Yes, that might win you the promotion. But it doesn't create a community around you."

He remembered times when he insisted on recognition, when credit felt like survival. The win came, but at a cost: colleagues left behind, trust weakened. Over time, he learned the alternative. Give credit where credit was due. Let others shine, and in turn build supporters who wanted to see him succeed.

Far from faking sincerity, it was about recognizing that careers are not built on solitary brilliance. They're built on constellations of people, each one capable of lifting or blocking your path. Ambition can blaze ahead on its own for a while, but it burns out faster. What lasts is the community you weave around you.

SMALL BUT BIG DIFFERENCE IN LEADERSHIP

If community was one revelation, another came later, when Dado found himself playing in the same league with the most powerful people in finance. At first glance, they seemed superhuman. Names like Schwarzman—"the Michael Jordan of finance," Dado called him. But watching closely, he realized something.

"Their edge," he told me, "isn't that they're massively smarter than everyone else. It's the small differences. How you carry yourself in a meeting, when you speak and when you hold back, whether you leave people drained or renewed after working with you. That's what makes all the difference."

Success, of course, requires hard work, intellect, determination, timing, luck, and all the expected ingredients. These factors matter a great deal, but it's not what separates the successful from those at the very top. It takes attentiveness. Precision in timing. The discipline to notice what others ignore, and to act on it.

For Dado, this was both humbling and liberating. The gulf between himself and the Michael Jordans of his field came down less to innate brilliance and more to cultivating a different kind of awareness—attunement to what moments ask of you and what people around you need.

What people need from you are often subtle, unspoken, unclear, and sometimes self-contradicting. But with acute curiosity, you can find it.

Not long ago, while working on an acquisition, he decided to be intentional about staying connected with senior leaders who might otherwise forget his name. Not with a barrage of asks but with gestures that placed no burden on them: a relevant article, a short note once a year, a thought that might be useful to them, without expectation of reply. When the deal closed, one of those leaders remembered. "Why don't you join us?" he asked. There was no job description yet, only the recognition that he had been thoughtful, creative, worth pulling in. That conversation led him to the seat he holds today.

And what a seat it is. Dado now is an executive vice president of a firm that works at the center of an undertaking almost impossible to fathom: building the energy infrastructure to fuel the AI revolution. Some of his projects require doubling the electricity capacity of entire regions—what took a century to build, now demanded in less than two years. It is a scale that strains everything: the technology, the capital, the human imagination. The mandate is staggering, but the leadership principle of curiosity is the same: Refined attentions accumulate. A note remembered, a gesture carried forward: one small difference can multiply in big ways.

FROM SCARCITY TO SCALE

Dado's seat today could not be further from where he began. He grew up in Slovakia, the child of a single mother, in a house where money was scarce and violence close at hand. An older cousin he looked up to was murdered in their home. Everyone in his family worked before finishing school; university was a dream no one in his circle had reached. Even basketball—his great escape—he played in a jersey repurposed from old pillow cases, in borrowed sneakers. Every trip outside his city felt like a luxury.

It was in this setting that he noticed a certain worldview, one he later described as "conditions." Success, people told themselves, depended on what you were given: the gym you trained in, the shoes on your feet, the country you were born into. By that logic, there was always a ceiling.

But cracks of light kept breaking through. A scholarship to Austria, then another that carried him to North Dakota State University, then Northwestern and Harvard. Each step widened his horizon—and each step confirmed that conditions were never the whole story.

Through reflection, he came to see the difference. "You are more successful," he said, "when you stop waiting for the right conditions and start focusing on what you can do with what's already in front of you. Maybe you didn't go to the best school, but you still have access to the best books. You still have choices."

That recognition—turning away from excuses, toward agency—tied his past to his present. The boy in borrowed sneakers is now charged with building what has never been built: energy infrastructure at a scale and speed to fuel the AI revolution. The conditions will never be perfect. The timelines will never be comfortable. And yet, the work must be done.

STORIES AS A CATALOG

That turn toward agency reshaped more than his career. It reshaped how he thought about his own life. What once felt like a torrent of stress—deals, litigations, family challenges—became something else when he paused to reflect. "These are experiences I'm collecting," he said. "They're stories I can pull on later."

It was the same mirror I first held up years ago, now woven into his daily rhythm. Long rides on his bike, hours on foot, became moving classrooms where he replayed the day's events: What did I do? How did it land on others? Where did I miss, and why? In his words, every day became a practice of looking again—seeing himself, his actions, his impact. Over time, that practice blossomed into habit. The mirror was no longer something I held up for him. It was something he carried himself.

And that is the foundation of this book: story not as performance but as discovery.

BOOK OUTLINE

What Dado's story reveals is what I've seen again and again in my work with leaders. Story becomes a way of perceiving, of noticing what others overlook, of making sense of moments that might otherwise blow past—both in our individual self, as well as our collective selves. Once you practice this way of working, the mirror is always with you—not just for your own growth but for helping others see themselves more clearly, to become a better version of themselves that they didn't realize possible.

This book shows you how to win without persuading.

In the chapters ahead, I'll map the path in three parts: first, why story discovery matters more than ever; second, what leaders are listening for; and third, how to practice the habits that turn story into leadership.

THE WHY SECTION

Chapter 1: The Power of Curiosity and Story Discovery
Why Leaders Must Be the Sage and the Guide
The higher leaders rise, the more they risk shutting the door on discovery. To last, they must be elite without becoming elitist: Ambitious yet attuned, accomplished yet still curious. At times a sage on the stage, at times a guide on the side—always willing to seek out what they don't yet know.

Chapter 2: Spotting and Snatching the Best Stories
Why Presence—Not Eminence—Reveals the Best Stories
Great stories rarely arrive fully formed. They hide in the ordinary, waiting for someone present enough to notice. In this chapter, I show you how to spot them, snatch them, and help others do the same.

Chapter 3: Excavating the Unspoken
Why Leaders Must Seek to Hear the Hidden Stories Now
The stories leaders most need are often the ones no one volunteers—and the cost of missing them is greater than we think.

Chapter 4: Beyond the Trumpet
Why Leaders Can't Afford to Miss the Richest Possibilities of Story
Too often, leaders treat story as a trumpet—loud, polished, self-serving. But when we reduce it to performance, we miss its deeper power: culture, shared memory, imagination, possibility, and connection across generations.

THE WHAT SECTION

Chapter 5: Opportunities Abound
What Hidden Skills Separate Good Leaders from Great Ones

Great leaders shine at the front of the room. But they also listen for the story waiting to be found. Because in every gathering, there is a story that could change everything.

Chapter 6: Leading Through Curiosity and Story Discovery
What Mindset Leaders Possess Shapes What They Find
Story discovery turbocharges strategy. Leaders skilled in narrative excavation uncover insights that no report or dashboard could ever reveal.

Chapter 7: Winning Without Persuading (Yes, Again)
What Great Facilitators Know That Most Leaders Miss
Facilitation is a quieter power. Leaders who practice it move farther, faster—creating progress without the constant strain of persuasion.

THE HOW SECTION

Chapter 8: Winning with Crazy Good Questions
How Curiosity Becomes the Most Powerful Voice in the Room
Asking Crazy Good Questions transforms ordinary conversations into turning points—shaping decisions, surfacing truths, and unlocking possibility.

Chapter 9: Winning with Story Refining
How to Strategically Sequence Facts and Emotions and Win
With a deliberate story architecture, leaders connect data with emotion—bridging logic and meaning to move groups forward.

Chapter 10: Winning with Leadership Storytelling
How Curiosity and Story Discovery Create the Conditions for Transformation
This is where curiosity meets craft: scene, summary, and reflection are more than storytelling tools. In the hands of leaders, they become

habits of attention—ways to notice, shape, and share meaning that people remember and act on.

THE T² APPROACH: TRANSACTIONAL X TRANSFORMATIONAL

After he hadn't stayed in touch for thirteen years, what prompted Dado to reach out was a profile piece about him in *Forbes* Slovakia, an "American dream" story his younger self in borrowed sneakers could never have imagined. Near the end of his email he wrote, "And I just want to keep expressing my gratitude for that."

Gratitude—for the mirror I first held up, for the curiosity it piqued for him, for the practice of discovery that grew from it. But also for the way story has continued to carry him, not only through his career but into the work he leads now.

That's what this book is about. Storytelling in my practice is never just transactional—never just about winning a pitch, securing an investment, or delivering a memorable keynote. Yes, those matter, of course, in fact a great deal. But when story is discovered and facilitated with care, it also becomes transformational. It reshapes how leaders see themselves, how they listen to others, and how they create conditions for the impossible to become possible. *That's the T² approach: transactional outcomes multiplied by transformational change.*

Which brings me to you. If you lead today, you are operating in a time when trust is brittle, attention is fractured, and AI and automation are redrawing the boundaries of what human communication even means. Leaders cannot afford to wait until they are onstage or under pressure to begin. They cannot afford to treat story as decoration or delay the work of discovery for a "better time."

This book is written for now—for the leaders who recognize that every conversation holds more than content, every team carries more than metrics, every moment could be the mirror.

winning without persuading

the *why* section

chapter 1

THE POWER OF CURIOSITY AND STORY DISCOVERY

why leaders must be the sage and the guide

What does a health care policy expert and a travel guide celebrity have in common?

At the end of 2024, Ezekiel Emanuel—a physician, political philosopher, and one of the most influential voices in US health care policy—set an unusual goal for the new year. At sixty-seven, with authority already secure, he wasn't aiming for another title or position. Instead, he wanted to become more empathetic: "To understand how people get to where they are . . . what challenges they've confronted, how they've overcome them." He noticed that getting to know other people's stories "really made a difference to them."[1]

Rick Steves, meanwhile, has spent four decades becoming America's best-known guide to Europe. Millions follow his books, shows, and tours. Yet what he prizes most isn't being the expert in the spotlight. "On my ideal tour, I'm not the teacher," he says. "I'm the facilitator."[2] Of the thousands of trips he's led, his favorite moments come in the evening "Reflection Times" when travelers trade stories and sift meaning together.

Emanuel and Steves are worlds apart—one shaping health systems, the other shaping travel experience. But both model something rare. They've reached the top of their fields without closing the door on discovery. They are good at being the sage on the stage. But they also embrace the role of the guide on the side.

And that is what this book will show you: leaders who win not by persuading louder or performing harder but through curiosity and story discovery—making space for others' voices to surface.

THE SAGE AND THE GUIDE—TWO SIDES OF THE SAME COIN

We often picture great leaders as those who step into the spotlight: charismatic, articulate, visionary, commanding attention. They have a vision for the future, and they can convince others to believe, trust, and follow. When they speak, the rest of us listen.

But leadership, as most of us experience it now, is something else. As we rise, we stop being doers and start amplifying others' ability to do and lead—often better than they thought possible. The role shifts from center stage to facilitation, from sage to guide. Although mastery is still relevant, the type of mastery you embody is even more important, and more urgent.

"We always talk about being best in class." Tyson Voelkel, CEO of the Texas A&M University Foundation, put it this way in a conversation with me. "We want to be number one at what we do, because in our world, that means creating more impact and more opportunities. But if that turns into *We're so good we don't need to learn or evolve*, it seeps into leadership teams. That's when you become elitist. That's when you stop listening."

For Voelkel, the distinction is simple: Striving to be elite means being the best in what you do while staying curious, still learning, listening, and still wondering if there're other ways to be even better. Being elitist, on the other hand, means closing down—distancing yourself from most people whom you deem to be "not as good," "don't get it," or worse, "just plain wrong." Elitists crown themselves as superior to others, fool themselves into assuming their presumed superiority exempts them from the work of discovery.

But that curiosity, that openness to discovery, is exactly what twenty-first-century organizations are asking for. In a study of thousands of executive job descriptions over nearly two decades, researchers Raffaella Sadun and Joseph Fuller[3] found companies moving away from charismatic smooth talkers toward what they called "socially adept leaders." The leaders in demand are those who "listen empathetically, welcome input, and rally the workforce around a common goal."

The collective wisdom is clear: *The best way to get someone's attention is by giving them yours.*

WHAT MATTERS MOST? AND WHY?

One chilly Chicago afternoon in March 2023, I found myself on Zoom with psychologist Marc Schulz, a professor at Bryn Mawr College. His warmth came through the screen as he pointed out something so obvious I had been blind to it. Like many of my peers, I was raised to believe in self-reliance and achievement. Accomplish *X*, become *Y*, and happiness will follow.

Schulz had news for me.

THE HARVARD STUDY OF ADULT DEVELOPMENT

Since 1938, researchers at Harvard have tracked more than seven hundred participants—and later, their spouses and thirteen hundred descendants—in the longest-running study of human life. Across decades of data, the through line is unmistakable: *Positive, healthy relationships keep us happier and healthier, longer.*

And because work is where we spend most of our waking hours, Schulz—coauthor of *The Good Life*, a *New York Times* bestseller based on the study—made the connection explicit during an interview for one of my *Forbes* articles: "We want to be able to benefit from the connections we have at work—with colleagues, people in power above us, people who work for us, and those we serve. It's really important to figure out a way to get as much value as we can from those connections."[4]

That's easier said than done. Workplace norms complicate things: Be present, but don't comment on appearances. Be friendly, but don't ask about family status. Be confident, but don't brag. It's like reaching out with your right hand only to have your left slap it down.

Schulz's advice was refreshingly simple: "What people want at work is to be seen, heard, and understood."

That's the question for leaders. How do we create a workplace where people feel seen, heard, understood? And why should leaders invest scarce energy in a task that's not even in their job description? Because, as the data now shows, creating a workplace good for long-term health and well-being isn't just altruism. It strengthens the bottom line.

READING THE TEA LEAVES

Maybe a version of this has happened to you. You land what feels like a dream job—only to find the position you accepted isn't the role you're taking on.

That was me twenty years ago. On paper, it looked promising: a chance to learn from two leaders, outgoing and incoming, with different but overlapping mandates. In reality, those two rarely agreed on anything. I spent more time decoding their feuds than learning my job. A colleague who'd wanted my position made sure to question my every decision. And to everyone's surprise after a division reshuffle, my team was rewarded with bigger offices—an outward signal of confidence from senior leadership. I should have been thrilled. Instead, I wanted to quit. The metrics said our future was bright; my heart said otherwise.

GALLUP ON DISENGAGEMENT

I wasn't alone. According to Gallup's 2023 *State of the Global Workplace*, **low employee engagement costs the world $8.8 trillion annually—roughly 9 percent of global GDP.**[5] Engagement, defined as "the involvement and enthusiasm of employees in their work," impacts bottom line directly. Another Gallup study of 112,000+ business units[6] shows that teams in the top quartile of engagement deliver:

- **10 percent higher customer loyalty**
- **23 percent higher profitability**
- **18 percent higher productivity**

Clearly, workplace engagement delivers for organizations. Employees who are more engaged with leaders, colleagues, and customers are more willing to contribute. But there's more.

MAYO CLINIC ON BURNOUT

A *Mayo Clinic Proceedings* study adds another dimension: In high-stress fields like frontline health care, every one-point increase in leadership score yields a *3.3 percent drop in burnout and a 9 percent rise in job satisfaction.*[7]

Together, these findings underline what Marc Schulz told me in our earlier conversation: Strong leadership leads to strong employee engagement. Positive workplace relationships don't just make us healthier; they make organizations stronger, more competitive, better positioned to win.

Of course, desiring good relationships is easy. Building them—day after day, across teams and hierarchies—is the hard part. For one, engagement as a concept can feel vague and fragile because it hinges on relationships. More importantly, conflict is inevitable. In today's polarized climate, even one poorly received comment can ignite tension. Some clashes are inevitable—fights over resources, clashing personalities. But many others are hidden, festering in silence, never voiced. Those are the most dangerous because no one sees them coming until they unravel the fabric of the workplace.

This is where curiosity and story discovery begin: in the unspoken, the overlooked, the clues hiding in silence as much as in speeches and corporate slogans. Leaders who develop the ability to detect the unspoken, overlooked clues gain access to stories others miss—and to possibilities no metric can predict.

HE HAD NO IDEA

I could tell by the slant of his shoulders that something was off. This was before the pandemic normalized doing business in virtual environments. Back then, working with clients face-to-face was the protocol. Besides, while in the same room, I could pick up what wasn't said. And that day, though Jon's words were upbeat, his body language told a different story.

The transcript of our coaching session (shared with his permission) says it all:

Esther: What's bothering you?

Jon: What do you mean?

[Silence. A frown. More silence.]

Jon: Well, it's Mark.

Esther: Mark, your favorite director?

Jon: Yes. He's leaving, to join a competitor, after sitting out his time on the bench.

Esther: Did he know you had big plans for him? How much you valued him?

Jon: I thought it was obvious! But apparently, he had no idea.

Jon worked closely with Mark for almost two years and never realized the star in his team assumed he'd hit a ceiling. But Jon was hardly alone in misjudging.

That blind spot is common. Psychologist Nick Epley at the University of Chicago has shown that most of us consistently *overestimate our ability to read others' minds*. In one of his classic "perspective gap" studies,[8] volunteers predicted how much pain or discomfort others would feel in certain situations. Then he compared the guesses to people's actual reports. Again and again, the guesses fell short. We're not as accurate—or empathetic—as we assume.

I learned that lesson the hard way myself, years earlier as an MBA admissions officer. One year, applicants in Seoul filled chat rooms speculating about whether I'd "liked" them during interviews. Reading their threads later, I felt as if I hadn't even been in the same room. Their interpretations were that far off. Epley's research insight gave me the puzzle piece to solve the mystery: Most of us are poor mind readers, even when we're sure we're right.

So when Jon lost Mark, I reminded him: Confidence in our ability to "just know" isn't enough. Leaders need a different skill set.

OPEN ATTITUDE IS NOT ENOUGH

Remember the research that analyzed thousands of executive job descriptions? Across industries, companies are no longer seeking smooth-talking stars; instead, they're looking for empathetic listeners. The reason behind this pivot is quantifiable.

GETTING PEOPLE TO SPEAK UP SAVES MONEY

James Detert and Ethan Burris, professors of leadership and organizational behavior, studied a national restaurant chain in 2016. They found that when managers persuaded senior leaders to act on suggestions from frontline employees, turnover dropped by 32 percent—saving the company at least $1.6 million a year.[9]

The mechanism was simple but powerful: Employees share ideas only when they believe their voices will be heard.

WHAT KIND OF LEADERS DISCOVER STORY?

Detert and Burris compared two leadership styles (that I paraphrase):

- **Inspiring Leaders:** charismatic, articulate, energizing—excel at inspiring change.
- **Engaging Leaders:** quieter, less showy, but curious. They ask questions, listen closely, make space for others, and they act on their newly discovered story.

No surprise here. Engaging Leaders had the stronger, more consistent impact on employees' willingness to speak up—especially among the highest performers, who are often the most cautious about what they share.[10] The lesson is clear: Inspiration matters, but openness matters even more.

THE PINK ELEPHANT MISSING IN THE ROOM—CARING DEEPLY ABOUT THE *WHO*

Simon Sinek's Golden Circle—*why, how, what*—has reached millions. His TEDx Talk[11] still ranks among the top ten most viewed since 2009. But there's a missing piece, more important than any why.

It's the *who.*

Who are your people? What are their values? How have their lived experiences shaped their beliefs? What is their perception of you as their leader, their colleague? Do they know you are genuinely curious about their stories? Do they trust you to stand beside them—not just telling *your* story but helping them tell theirs?

Your team, family, tribe, and even adversaries are all made up of people. Nothing significant ever gets done without people. Do you know their stories? Are you curious about their stories? If so, do they know that you are?

WHAT ARE LEADERS, *REALLY*?

Evolutionary scholars define[12] leaders as those with disproportionate influence over group decision-making. That influence can cut both ways:

- **Costs:** If you don't do what your leaders say, there will be consequences.
- **Benefits:** Leaders' experience can help everyone move forward.

One untapped benefit? Helping others make sense of—and tell—their stories. Or as one adage puts it succinctly: "Managers make me feel like they're important. Leaders make me feel like *I am* important."

WHY EVEN ADVERSARIES MATTER

The people whose stories leaders need to hear aren't just direct reports. They're also peers, bosses, customers, clients, partners—and even adversaries. Why give the microphone to those who stand in your way? Because, as the Dalai Lama reminds us: "*The enemy is a very good teacher.*"

The **Ladder of Inference**[13] explains why. It shows how people climb from "raw data" to action:

1. Select which data to notice—colored by bias.
2. Interpret the data—skewed by personal experience.
3. Name or characterize what's happening—influenced by personal perspective.

4. Explain *why* it's happening—the beginning of forming internal stories.
5. Decide and act—the most visible to the outside world.

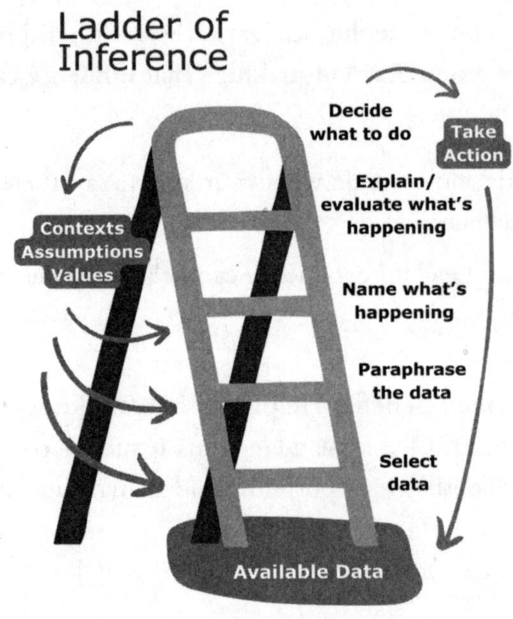

Image is re-created from https://thesystemsthinker.com/the-ladder-of-inference/.

What counts as "data"? Words, tone, gestures, as a starting point, but also invisible influences like upbringing, cultural norms, media consumed, or life-defining events. Everyone's ladder rests on a different foundation. Which means if you argue about the "right" action without understanding someone's ladder, you're fighting maps instead of walking the territory together.

Before leaders rush into planning or debating, persuading or deciding, they need to slow down long enough to discover the stories underneath. Otherwise, they're only arguing conclusions while missing the hidden ladders that carried people there. This is where empathy—tactical empathy, as Chris Voss, former FBI hostage negotiator and author of the *Wall Street Journal* bestseller *Never Split the Difference*, calls it—becomes indispensable. It doesn't mean agreeing or conceding. It means making someone feel thoroughly understood. That recognition alone can dissolve defensiveness and release potent forces for change.[14] Like a scalpel, empathy is neutral on its own; its impact depends on the hand that wields it. Story discovery is one of the surest ways leaders can practice this kind of empathy—helping people voice the data, experiences, and beliefs that shape their choices. Only then can a truly productive conversation begin.

OUR BIG BLIND SPOT WHEN IT COMES TO STORYTELLING

Leadership development often stresses balance: cultivating the self *and* focusing on others. But in storytelling, most business books tilt one way—toward self-promotion. From *Unleash the Power of Storytelling: Win Hearts, Change Minds, Get Results* by Rob Biesenbach (Eastlawn, 2018), *How to Tell a Story: The Essential Guide to Memorable Storytelling from The Moth* (Crown, 2023), or even my own *Let the Story Do the Work*, the emphasis is on: *my* brand, *our* case for change, *our* competitive edge.

What's missing is what this book is about. Curiosity, when paired with story discovery, is how leaders win without persuading. And the process that brings those two forces together has a name: *story facilitation*.

Story facilitation is the art of drawing stories out of others—helping them articulate the data, emotions, and meaning that usually stay unspoken. That's the gap this book fills. Because across psychology, sociology, anthropology, neuroscience, theater, literature, and even product design, the evidence converges: Understanding the who—their unmet needs, their lived realities, their unrealized potentials—is the gateway to connection, alliance, and lasting progress.

That's why story facilitation isn't a "nice to have." It's a critical leadership skill for the twenty-first century—and overdue for its place in the practice of leadership storytelling.

WHAT HAPPENS WHEN SOMEONE REALLY KNOWS YOU

One morning in 2023, Chris McAuley got a phone call from a work acquaintance out of the blue.

"My God," the caller blurted. "What did you *do*?"

The urgency came from what he'd just witnessed: the transformation of Barb, one of his colleagues. A month earlier, Barb had finished coaching with Chris, and now she seemed almost unrecognizable. Barb was thoughtful, curious—and painfully shy. Ironically, her role required frequent presentations, which terrified her. But even before coaching her, Chris suspected there was something powerful under that reserve: a steady inner voice, a quiet confidence. He just wasn't sure how to surface it.

As part of his discovery process, he led her through two exercises I teach in my facilitator training: *Passion DNA* and *Paired Introduction*. "I could hear it, I could see it, I could sense her power when she talked about her interests," Chris told me later.

From those conversations, he drafted a short narrative-based introduction of Barb—her story, drawn entirely from her own words. When he read it aloud, Barb was incredulous.

"Really? Are you serious? Is that me?"

Chris simply pointed back to her. "Yes. That's what *you* told me."

Something shifted. From that moment forward, Barb showed up differently. In meetings. Onstage. In presentations. Her manager—stunned by the change—was the one who called Chris to ask what magic he had worked. But there was no magic. Just the power of someone being seen, heard, and understood.

As columnist and cultural commentator David Brooks writes in his book *How to Know a Person*, "No one can fully appreciate their own beauty and strengths unless those things are mirrored back to them in the mind of another. There is something in being seen that brings forth growth. . . . If you see great potential in me, I will probably come to see great potential in myself."

Barb's story inspires warm feelings, of course, but the impact of her work with Chris, when multiplied by the thousands and millions, becomes measurable. In their research article "Does Happiness Promote Career Success?"[15] psychologists Julia Boehm and Sonja Lyubomirsky found that happiness precedes success; it doesn't follow it. Positive emotions lead to stronger workplace outcomes. In other words, when people feel joy, connection, and recognition, they perform better.

So let's ask the harder questions:

- If you can empower others to be happier at work—and therefore more successful—why wouldn't you?
- If you can help colleagues see and cultivate their own strengths, resolve conflicts more effectively, or know your clients better than they know themselves—why would you hold back?
- If you can lower burnout, increase engagement, and even extend the health and happiness of those you lead, why would you wait?

The answer is clear. Story discovery, through curiosity and facilitation, isn't a "nice to have." It's a leadership imperative. And the time to hone it is not someday.

It's now.

It starts with noticing stories that most people miss and developing the eyes, ears, and "sixth sense" to spot and snatch them. It starts with the next chapter.

chapter 2

SPOTTING AND SNATCHING THE BEST STORIES

Why Presence—Not Eminence—Reveals the Best Stories

It's the mid-1980s in Hong Kong. I was around nine years old, in third grade, still too short for my feet to touch the floor when I sat on a stool.

In our tiny living room—also our dining room—I braced myself. Reprimand or punishment. My palms cradled my chin, elbows resting on the edge of the foldable table where my family ate all our meals and my brother and I did homework. Mom sat across from me, staring at my report card. I stared at her staring.

In Hong Kong, even kindergartners got midterms and finals. I wasn't a good student—sitting still for four hours a day felt like walking backward with two left feet. But by third grade, I'd figured out how to fake it: gaze at the blackboard, rock in my seat quietly, avoid talking. As long as I didn't disrupt, teachers let me be.

Inside my mind, I was elsewhere. Admiring Lily's orange bow and wondering if I'd get invited to her birthday party. Trying to decipher the notes passed between my two best friends. Then, one day, my feet moved—on their own, it seemed. I floated across the classroom toward another row, toward two classmates working on something mysterious. I had to know what it was.

Then, silence.

"Hey! What do you think you're doing right now?" My homeroom teacher Mrs. Lee's voice cut through.

Was she talking to me?

Mom was still staring at the report card. She didn't look angry. We'd both seen the grades. Maybe she was hoping they'd change if she stared long enough. She finally spoke: "It says here you're brilliant and full of talents."

I was a B and C student, with the occasional A in PE, art, or music—subjects most parents saw as fringe. Our report cards came with comments about our character development and behavior. In that particular midterm, my homeroom teacher was generous enough to acknowledge my talent. But Mrs. Lee wrote, "She is also wasting her talents on nosing in other people's business."

No scolding followed. Just something worse—profound parental disappointment.

Wasting talents. That, in my parents' eyes, was a sin just shy of sacrilege. They had spent decades surviving scarcity—moving from Beijing to Hong Kong in the late 1970s, scraping by for years. Waste was intolerable. Waste food, and you got famine stories. Waste money, and you got lectures. But waste talent? That was so unthinkable they didn't even have a script for it.

What they couldn't foresee—what none of us could, decades ago—was that new careers would emerge. Roles no one had imagined. And the very things I was chastised for—curiosity, watchfulness, nosiness—would become my greatest strengths.

Even then, my young brain was scanning the room, always connecting dots between people and movements, weaving sense with moments. But in the mid-1980s, dangling my legs at that table, absorbing my mother's unspoken disappointment, I had no idea what was coming. I was stepping into the benevolent unknown: a country, the USA, that would open career paths unthinkable to my parents. My need to know—to really see people, understand them, dig gently into their lives—would become a form of empathetic curiosity. A skill.

Eventually, the people I "nose into" thank me.

I got the last laugh. I got a sixteen-year-and-running career doing what I feel like is my higher calling, helping others find and tell their stories so they can succeed in business and life.

JOIN ME, AND DISCOVER MORE STORIES

This chapter is about where great stories come from—and why most of us overlook them. Leaders often assume stories must be dramatic, heroic, sometimes tragic, or tied to major achievements. But in truth, the most compelling stories hide in ordinary moments: a comment from a child, a glance across a meeting table, a fleeting silence. What separates truly effective leaders from others isn't their eminence—their rank, résumé, or reputation—but their presence. Their ability to notice. To catch a story in the making before it slips past.

In the pages ahead, I have more stories to share. You'll see, very soon, how seemingly mundane, insignificant, or personal stories carry outsize significance in the professional arena. These stories will inspire you to start building your own story library you can return to again and again. When you begin to notice, you are not only discovering the stories that move others—you will begin to see yourself, your team, and your world more clearly.

WHERE DO COMPELLING STORIES COME FROM?

Has this ever happened to you?

You had the chance to say what you meant—and you said it. But moments later, the better version shows up. Then another. And another. All of them playing on a loop, but only in your head. That was me one afternoon in October, seated among eight hundred people waiting for the one and only Oprah Winfrey to appear. The

"Queen of Talk" was scheduled to close the 2024 Kellogg Global Women's Summit, and I was one of two dozen presenters at the conference. The crowd buzzed with energy and giddy anticipation that warmed up the building under the afternoon sun. We sat in the glass-encased Collaboration Plaza at Kellogg's Global Hub; Oprah would be here any minute. And yet—my mind was elsewhere.

Hours earlier, I had copresented a session called "High-Stakes Speeches: How to Share Memorable Leadership Stories" with my dear friend and colleague Gina Fong, the award-winning professor of consumer anthropology. I should've been basking in the enthusiastic response to our talk and the energy of the day. Instead, I kept replaying a moment from our session—one particular story I had shared. Or almost shared. Or should've shared. It looped in my mind, each version stronger than the last. And along with it, the question Gina and I posed to the audience kept echoing back:

Where do compelling stories come from?

At the time of this writing, I've spent more than sixteen years coaching and teaching classical storytelling to modern leaders. That question—where stories come from—has shown up in countless forms: How do I find stories worth telling? This project's still ongoing—how do I share it if there's no ending yet? My work is boring . . . is there even a story here? (Compliance. Risk management. GAAP—generally accepted accounting principles. The list is very, very long.) Sometimes, clients just say it outright: *"I don't have any stories. That's why I'm working with you!"* But the root question is the same: Where do I find good stories?

And maybe more importantly: Why does it matter that we know?

Because if you're mining for gold, but have no idea where the gold is, you'll come up empty, no matter how sophisticated your tools. Similarly, the best storytelling techniques, the most polished stage presence, the most advanced craft won't help you if you don't know where to look. So whether you're searching for your own stories or helping someone else uncover theirs, you need something more foundational: a sense for where the good stories live, a way of noticing, a presence attuned enough to snatch them before they slip past.

In a business context, a story—personal or professional—has to do more than just follow a conventional arc. A leader's story must carry authority with curiosity, tenacity with vulnerability, eminence with resonance. And the most effective leaders? They learn how to help others tell stories this way too.

SPOT AND SNATCH: BEING PRESENT ENOUGH TO NOTICE THE STORY

So, where do I find good stories?

When most people think about storytelling, they reach for the obvious: from their résumé, the official dossier of their professional highs of the highs. *I was the youngest person in my company to do X. I won Y and Z prestigious awards beating out thousands of others.* And yes, those moments are memorable, worth sharing, to be treasured. And some go to the other extreme—the lows of the lows. Illness. Loss. Business failures. The unexpected long detour. These are also powerful, and they often shape us deeply. So yes—tell those stories. But don't let them be your only source.

For most of us, the extraordinary—whether high or low—comes only once in a while. And we hold on to those stories so tightly that they become worn with repetition, familiar and predictable. Instead, I want to invite you to be present.

To notice what's happening around you—not just the events but what they mean. Sometimes your best stories aren't born in moments of triumph or tragedy. They're hiding in a car ride to work. A fleeting thought in between nonstop virtual calls. A glance from a colleague after a gaff. An awkward silence after making the ultimate ask. If you're present enough—attentive enough—you'll start to notice them.

And here's the beauty of this way of seeing: When you stop relying on the most "remarkable" events to find your story, you also stop elbowing others out of the way in the name of who's most outstanding. You beat cancer? I beat it twice. You closed a $5 million deal? Mine was eight. That kind of storytelling becomes a race with one lane and limited trophies.

But when you start from everyday moments—and draw out the meaning, the relevance, the connection—your stories become relatable and resonant. Your stories also become a community glue. No story will arrive fully formed in your lap. They'll need massaging. Interpretation. Craft. But if you're present enough, you'll spot them. And I hope you'll snatch them up.

And even if you have no idea yet what that story will be used for, you'll know there's just something to it, enough to hold on to it. Someday, it might become exactly the story someone else needs to hear.

TWO STORIES: ONE I CAUGHT, ONE CAUGHT ME

Here are two stories. One I was present enough to spot and snatch. And another—well, I was lucky. A complete stranger caught it for me.

STORY ONE

"Mommy, you look like a toddler every morning," my daughter blurted out one night as we sat down for dinner.

"Really?" I feigned surprise. But I knew what she meant.

First thing in the morning, I'm not exactly . . . friendly or presentable. Think: unbrushed hair, sleepy eyes, pajamas askew. And everyone in my family knows—don't approach Mom before her first cup of coffee. So it wasn't shocking that my daughter thought I resembled one of the playground toddlers in near meltdown mode every morning. But what she said next required a double take.

"When you walk into our room to wake us up," said Alina—she was eleven then, still sharing a bedroom with her younger sister, "you look like a toddler who just found all her presents on Christmas morning."

As I write this, Alina is seventeen. I don't even remember what I had for breakfast this morning so how do I remember what she said, word for word, all those years ago? Because I recorded it. A few hours after the impromptu observation of Mom-in-the-morning, I added it to my digital journal. Yes, I wanted to capture a tender moment. And yes, part of me wanted to relive a time when parenting felt simpler. But mostly, I wrote it down because that's how I build my story library.

Over the years, that library has grown to hundreds of entries—vignettes, overheard remarks, small exchanges with coworkers, good and bad surprises from clients, friends, family. At the time, I didn't know how I'd use them. But I know they're there, waiting. A treasure trove of meaning. A living archive of presence.

STORY TWO

I often ask people, "How do you usually spend your Saturday mornings?"

The summer of 2023, my Saturdays were for lake diving with my family. Now, not everyone in my household was equally thrilled about plunging into cold Lake Michigan. One daughter was all in. The other? She needed serious convincing. So, one July morning, the four of us made a pact: hold hands, take a breath, and leap in together. Just us. No cameras. No prep. And that was part of the magic—because if we'd paused to set up a tripod, our more hesitant daughter might've changed her mind. It was a now-or-never moment.

That's when a stranger stepped in.

A woman named Gunjan, sitting by the lake with her cousin, noticed us. Something about that moment—our family holding hands, counting down, laughing through the nerves—moved her. She pulled out her phone and filmed it. Then, after we climbed out of the water, she came over and asked if we wanted the video. Gunjan. A complete stranger. A total gift.

Our lives are made up of so many moments like that—short-lived, unassuming, full of feelings. But it takes someone like Gunjan to spot them. To be present enough to notice. To hit RECORD, to share, and to *not* wait for an invitation to record a story. We all have the power to capture these moments.

Don't let them slip by. Spot them. Snatch them.

Now, you might wonder what good these kinds of personal stories—mined from tuning into the everyday moment—could do in a leadership and business context. Well, sometimes the sky is literally the limit.

TOGETHER, WE GO FURTHER

A former client had a problem. The consulting firm that Alex Kruzel founded—Telesto Strategy—was at an inflection point. She was unsure how to open a talk she was giving at her company's annual off-site. Luckily, she has spotting and snatching in her muscle memory.

At the time, she was in the middle of a move—unpacking box after box in her new high-rise apartment. She was tired. Box fourteen had just about done her in. So she took a break. From the thirty-fourth floor, she looked out the window. That's when she noticed them: a flock of birds, gliding past, moving as one. She watched them—mesmerized, curious, then captivated—by the fluid choreography of their flight, the formation and rhythm. How they moved not as individuals but as a collective. She could've gone back to unpacking. But instead, she looked it up.

Why do birds fly in formation? What's the benefit? Turns out, when they do, they can fly up to 71 percent farther than they would alone. That became the opening of her off-site talk.

"Together, we go further."

The idea and the story didn't come from a TED Talk or a professional speech writer—but from a moment of daydreaming, from pausing long enough to notice something outside the window, playing out in the sky. That's where some of the best story ideas begin. But you also don't need to look far away for ideas. Often, the treasures are buried close by, so near that they're inside you.

TEN MINUTES THAT MADE THE DIFFERENCE

Everything in that room seemed to gleam: dark suits, polished shoes, stadium-style seatings designed to impress and intimidate. A major financial capital in Asia, late fall. Eight global firms had been invited to make their final pitch for a large institutional mandate to manage global investments on behalf of a sovereign wealth fund.

Only two finalists would be chosen.

My client was in his late thirties at the time, newly appointed head of his firm's Asia Pacific office and the lead of this major business pitch. He had ten minutes.

Technically, he had twenty—but half of that would be used for live translation by a junior analyst from a local office. It was his second major pitch as lead, and this time the stakes were geopolitical. Historic, even. This was the first time the client would entrust global investment management to foreign firms. On paper, my client's firm looked great: strong performance history, global footprint, contrarian thinking, rigorous analytical process. But so did everyone else in the room. The field was full of credentialed experts, armed with the same slide decks branded in different logos.

"How do I stand out?" he asked me.

His first instinct was to default to the familiar: Performance. People. Process. The PPP framework that investors know by heart. It's safe. It's respectable. And—it's forgettable. That's when I pivoted the conversation. I asked him to set aside the pitch deck, to forget about the historic opportunity for a moment. I asked him to tell me: Why do you care about this? Why does this mandate matter to you, not just your career or your firm?

He paused. Then, he told me about his grandmother.

She had run a small drugstore in Germany with his grandfather. They worked hard. Served their neighbors. Built a life. But around the time when conglomerate chain stores took over the market, his grandparents divorced, leaving his grandmother shouldering the business and family alone. She couldn't keep up. His grandmother had to close her business. And in retirement, she depended on the social security system to live. It was that system—structured, invisible, reliable—that allowed her to retain her dignity, to live with grace.

And so here he was, decades later, pitching to help manage another country's version of that same system. A social infrastructure meant to care for retirees—not just portfolios—through uncertainty. That became the emotional anchor of the pitch.

We practiced a few simple greetings in the local language to open. Then he would tell his grandmother's story. Personal. Honest. Unexpected. The bulk of the presentation would still cover the firm's strengths—but now, framed through the lens of meaning and trust. When you lead with why, you open the door for people to care.

He delivered the story before the pitch. Twenty minutes, split in two. And from what he later described, the clinical vibe in the room transformed into something much warmer and curious because the people in it could feel the legacy of a hardworking grandmother living within her grandson. The posture of the committee changed. Expressions softened. Arms unfolded.

They were selected as one of the two winning managers. And while performance metrics matter, what earned their attention and ultimate approval wasn't a better set of slides—it was a better connection.

WHEN TELLING YOUR STORY ISN'T ABOUT YOU

A lot of people I work with shy away from the spotlight. They quiver at the idea of the attention-seeking, me-me-me culture that social media has helped accentuate. But all work, jobs, careers have their autobiographical roots. So telling a personal story—when aligned with the right intention and audience-centric mindset—is not about the storyteller. My colleague Arlene Milon's story is an excellent example.

Arlene has a great story. But she didn't want to tell it.

She even paid out-of-pocket to join my certification program on story facilitation—a serious commitment for someone with a full-time job, a family, and a role as executive director of a faith-based nonprofit in Pittsburgh. She believed in the power of stories. She wanted the people around her to become better storytellers too. Despite her already full life, she carved out time and energy for the training.

But still, when it came to her own story, she resisted.

"But, Esther, it isn't about me," she protested.

Outside of the certification program, Arlene asked for my help preparing a welcome message for a Mass hosted by her organization. I encouraged her to build from a story that another participant had crafted for her, based on her background. In her training with me, she's learned plenty of exercises that help anyone uncover their own story quickly. That's when the pushback really began.

Nearly everyone stumbles over the deceptively simple "Tell me about yourself." Saying something brief, true, and memorable—without sounding boastful—feels so difficult that most people fall back on listing résumé items. There's also the fear of being judged. The risk of being misunderstood. So, in the very first assignment of my storytelling certification course, we dive into the deep end: Tell a story about yourself.

Arlene, like many of her peers, was personally drawn to stories and professionally motivated to use them to grow her organization. But when it came to sharing her own story, she balked.

"Esther," she said again, "this isn't about me. I want to help our couples tell their stories. I want to tell better stories about Renew the 'I do' Foundation so we can raise more money. I don't want to shift the focus onto me."

Her reasoning made sense. After all, the US marriage rate has been in decline. Healthy, joyful marriages are foundational to healthy families—but modern life places strain on even the strongest couples. Add parenting to the mix, and stress multiplies. Arlene's organization provides social, educational, and spiritual support to married couples across Pittsburgh. Given the scale of the challenges she's working to solve, it's easy to see why Arlene thought her story might be a distraction. But what she didn't realize was that she was stuck in her own point of view.

Most of us are, without even knowing it.

Telling a story of ourselves doesn't have to be about us. This is where the adage really applies: People don't care how much you know until they know how much you care.

And in today's world—one shaped by automation, information overload, and AI—knowledge is quickly becoming a commodity. But a well-told story? That signals care. It builds trust. And once trust is established, people are far more open to the information we have to share. After some nudging, Arlene finally agreed to revisit her story. Here's the beginning of the welcome message she shared at her organization's signature Valentine's Day event:

> Welcome! Happy Valentine's Day and World Marriage Week! So glad to have you here . . . and hello to all of the special people joining us on Zoom.
>
> I'm Arlene Milon. . . . I've always been a promoter at heart and have enjoyed promoting *big* things that bring joy to people!
>
> In high school, I loved booking cool bands and getting everyone to come. Then right out of college, I *officially* became a promoter with Ringling Bros. and Barnum & Bailey Circus, traveling across the country. It was an exhilarating first job and lasted throughout my twenties!
>
> Then I ran away *from* the circus to New York and worked at Madison Square Garden promoting big sporting events and new theater productions. My career then took me to Radio City Music Hall to lead the marketing team for national tours of the Radio City Christmas Spectacular starring the Rockettes. It was an awesome group of people to work with, and I loved almost every minute of it!

Then after hanging out with the Rockettes for twelve years, I still thought there could be something bigger . . . maybe that I could be *even more* passionate about promoting. I thought . . . Maybe my beloved Lehigh University? Or how about the United States of America? I *was* raised a very patriotic kid! Then . . . little did I know the best was yet to come![1]

What I didn't expect after my exciting years promoting big shows was that meeting and marrying my husband, Bill, and raising our two awesome kids, Luke and Kathleen, was going to be the biggest, most exciting, and joyful adventure of my life!

Now I'm happy to say that I am the executive director and cofounder of Renew the 'I do' Foundation. And it's *now* that I see that I'm doing the most important work of my life. . . . As a wife . . . and a mother . . . *and* now as my promoter gig, I get to *cheer on marriage*!

What could be bigger?!

What makes Arlene's story powerful is that it's *of* herself but *not about* herself. The story's concept—its DNA—is clear: Arlene Milon, a lifelong promoter of big things that bring people joy, is now dedicating her talents to promoting marriage, helping couples thrive in them. She could've just said that. Instead, she showed us. She walked us through her journey, from Ringling Bros. to Renew the 'I do.' She let us feel the transition—from promoting circuses to championing something more sacred. She told her story.

And in doing so, she showed her couples that she really, truly cares.

INHERITING OUTSIDERNESS

When I saw my mother over Christmas of 2024, I asked her if she remembered the report card incident—the embarrassing moment when she was told her child was wasteful of her talents by nosing into other people's business. She didn't.

Mom's in good health but also eighty-five years old. She couldn't possibly remember everything from my childhood. Just like the late psychologist and Nobel Prize winner of economics Daniel Kahneman observed in his 2010 TED Talk[2]: Out of the approximately six hundred million psychological moments in anyone's life, the vast majority of them are gone without a trace.

But I hold on to the report card moment. It means something to me.

I am an immigrant from Hong Kong, raising two American-born daughters. And I am the daughter of a Chinese mother who migrated from Indonesia to Hong Kong via mainland China. And my Chinese Indonesian mother is a daughter of an immigrant mother who moved with her husband (my grandfather) from southern China to Indonesia in the 1930s. I come from a long line of daughters of immigrant mothers, a four-generational story of relocations and new beginnings. A chain of unbelonging, as it was described back to me in 2024 during an interview with an award-winning journalist, the host of a popular NPR podcast, *Rough Translation*. Gregory Warner called it an inheritance of outsiderness in his Substack newsletter. Apparently, I have inherited the tendency of an outsider looking in. Gregory framed it: My ability to look at any situation and anyone as an outsider is my superpower.

What took Gregory all but an hour of conversation to figure out took me a lifetime to realize. But this is the ironic nature of seeing a person: It's "easy" and quick for the person who does the seeing, her talents, fears, gifts, emotional baggage, values, and, very simply, her story. But all these treasures can be completely invisible to the person carrying them. She might not even recognize these gems when you first draw their attention to her. I knew all the facts about my life, of course, but Gregory's framing shifted the way I looked at my gift. Although my multigenerational outsider status has prepared me to do the seeing, I couldn't do it for myself. Someone else, someone with respectful curiosity, someone—anyone—whose empathy, and a deep capacity to listen can do it for me, for all of us.

WHY LEADERS SHOULD BE A GUIDE ON THE SIDE *TOO*

This book isn't my first exploration of storytelling. My earlier book, *Let the Story Do the Work*, was a practical guide for leaders: how to craft compelling narratives, structure a pitch, deliver with confidence. It was about the how.

This one is different. This book is for those who hesitate to tell stories and for people who notice those who hesitate to tell their stories.

And yet, I wrote it because I believe they need it most. Because here's what I've seen, again and again: Leaders—especially those who lead other leaders—don't just need to tell great stories. They need to help others tell theirs. They need to be both the sage on the stage and the guide on the side. This book is about that second role. The quieter one. The harder one. The role that requires presence, curiosity, and the ability to see someone's story even before they do. It's about learning to listen beneath the surface: to spot the story hiding in the mundane, to catch the moment before it slips past.

Because the stories that reveal the most don't always announce themselves.

They come wrapped in contradiction. They carry weight and tenderness, ambition and doubt, grit and grace—all at once. And I didn't come to this from a script. I came to it from life. I came to it by noticing the way stories live quietly inside people who claim they have none. By tracing my own family line—not just through geography but through generations of migration, translation, reinvention. By realizing, far too late, that I'd been carrying a story that took someone else's insight to help me name.

And that's what this book is really about.

It's not about storytelling as performance. It's about storytelling as recognition. Once you learn to recognize a story—in yourself, in others—you stop waiting for brilliance to arrive fully formed. You start catching it in motion. In real time. In the pause before the answer. In the sideways glance. In the half-remembered anecdote that turns out to embody everything. Not just to help you tell your story. But to help you notice the moment when someone else's story begins to take shape. To help you stand beside them—with quiet confidence—and say: There it is. That's the one worth telling.

But there's a catch: The most important stories are rarely the ones people hand over freely. They're the hidden ones, waiting for someone curious enough to notice that they're missing, and skilled enough to draw them out. That's where we turn next.

chapter 3

EXCAVATING THE UNSPOKEN

Why Leaders Must Seek to Hear the Hidden Stories Now

Sarah and I see each other only once or twice a year. Gregarious, curious, and a natural storyteller, she can't walk a block in her neighborhood without stopping to greet someone. During one visit, as we rounded yet another corner (and paused again for her to greet a neighbor), I told Sarah I'd soon start writing another book—this one you're reading. Naturally animated, she asked, "What's it about?"

The manuscript was still in its infancy; I didn't have a polished elevator pitch. So, leaning into the spirit of our long friendship, where teasing is a love language, I gave her the best, slightly tongue-in-cheek answer I could think of: "It's a storytelling book . . . for people who don't want to tell stories." She froze midstep, eyebrows furrowed in confusion. "Uh . . . what? Who doesn't want to tell their stories?" she asked.

In her world, where telling stories is as natural as breathing among friends, colleagues, and even strangers, the idea that some people might not want to tell their stories sounded as strange as suggesting Neanderthals still walk amongst us. Sarah is an honest and generous friend. In her gentle yet direct way, she was also asking an obvious question: Who's going to buy your book?

I'm not offended, just amused. After all, Sarah's life is rich with what behavioral scientists call naïve realism: the tendency to assume that what's readily available to us—what we see, hear, and feel—represents the full picture.

In Sarah's orbit, everyone tells stories, so by extension, she assumed that was true everywhere. But there's a problem: we tend to believe our experience is universal, that there's nothing outside our frame. In reality, many find storytelling difficult, daunting, or even unthinkable due to external and internal reasons. Some desire to tell stories but face invisible walls. Others prefer not to share at all, out of caution, trauma, cultural values, or simply temperament. And speaking of temperament, I'm married to a man for twenty-four years and counting, and his former life motto was, "I aspire to be the most successful person no one has ever heard of." Truly, it was once his dream. He has always shied away from attention. So he used to wish to live in a world where he'd be free to work as hard as he could while having nothing to do with marketing, business development, or any self-oriented promotion. (I guess I changed his mind, eventually!)

My husband is far from alone. And if leaders and organizations fail to recognize this unseen group, they risk leaving entire reservoirs of insight untapped and whole communities of people unseen. The urgency to recognize them is not optional because we live in a world that moves fast and fragments faster, where noise rises, tempers flare, and truth feels like a moving target. The ground beneath us shifts constantly in what military strategists once named VUCA: volatile, uncertain, complex, ambiguous. The term may have been born in the fog of war; it's never felt more relevant than in our daily lives now.

Amid all this churn, the voices we most need to hear are often the ones keeping quiet and staying muffled. In an age of sharpened divisions and quick-fire opinions, theirs may be the calmest wisdom we have—but only if we learn to bring it forward. This chapter shows you why so many voices stay buried—through layers of culture, psychology, temperament, profession, and structure that conspire to keep them hidden.

WHY DON'T PEOPLE TELL THEIR STORIES?

What stands in the way, both outside and within?

There are five key reasons why people often hesitate to tell their stories, each powerful on its own but even more so in combination. These reasons are shaped by forces all around them: cultural, psychological, personal, professional, and structural. We'll explore each in depth, but here's a brief overview of the landscape we're stepping into.

1. CULTURAL

Unwritten rules weave through every community, telling us when it's safe to speak and when it's safer to stay small. In every tightly bonded group, standing out too much can feel less like success and more like walking around with a target on your back. Ask someone why they hold back, and you might get a puzzled smile—or simply, "That's just how it is." Cultures can teach us early that fitting in often matters more than being seen.

2. PSYCHOLOGICAL

Our minds are the greatest storytellers, but they often distort and depart far from reality. Biases and shortcuts often convince us that every stumble, every word, every hesitation is seared into others' memories. We carry an imagined audience on our shoulders, feeling the weight of eyes that aren't really there. And with it, it feels as though there's a spotlight trailing us everywhere we go.

3. PERSONAL

Before the world tells us who we should be, something subtler shapes who we are. Temperament weaves itself into the way we move, the way we listen, the way we keep or share our stories. Some voices grow restless to be heard. Others choose stillness without ever needing to be taught.

4. PROFESSIONAL

Every industry has its own unspoken rules—quiet signals that tell us what counts as credible and what should stay unsaid. Some fields prize precision above all. Others reward analysis, depth, control. In these spaces, personal voice can feel off script. Storytelling, even when welcomed in theory, rarely feels appropriate in practice.

5. STRUCTURAL

Some barriers are the hardest to recognize because they're the deepest woven.

Long before a story is told, the world signals which ones are welcome—and which are better left unsaid. As legal scholar Kenji Yoshino writes, many people don't hide who they are out of shame but out of strategy. Appearance, affiliation, belief, or identity—each can come with a cost. Institutions may speak the language of inclusion, but their unspoken social contracts often whisper something else.

Each of these barriers deserves closer attention—not just to explain why some stories remain untold, but to help us loosen the bondages so that those stories finally speak.

CULTURAL

There's a Japanese saying, "The nail that sticks out gets hammered down" (出る釘は打たれる, *deru kui wa utareru*). It's a vivid reminder that those who stand out—those who deviate from the group—are often pressured to conform or punished for their difference. While the phrase is distinctively Japanese, the sentiment behind it is not. Across cultures, variations of the same caution appear. In Chinese, a similar proverb warns, "The bird that sticks its head out gets shot" (枪打出头鸟, *qiāng dǎ chū tóu niǎo*). In Russia, an old saying goes,

"Initiative is punishable" (Инициатива наказуема)—a warning to those tempted to step out of line.

Even in highly individualistic cultures like the United States—where ambition and self-expression are supposedly celebrated—the reflex to punish conspicuous success remains stubbornly alive. Few figures illustrate this tension more vividly than Taylor Swift.

Today, Swift stands as one of the most successful entertainers in history—a mega pop singer whose Eras Tour shattered global records, grossing over $1 billion and becoming the highest-grossing concert tour of all time. She is *Time*'s 2023 Person of the Year, a self-made billionaire who reclaimed ownership of her music catalog, and a cultural force reshaping entire industries.

But when one of the most devastating moments happened at the 2009 MTV Music Video Awards, her current mega success seemed anything but inevitable. After Kanye West's "famous" controversy, Swift became the target of a global social media firestorm. The hashtag #TaylorSwiftIsOverParty trended worldwide, with millions participating in her public shaming—a campaign so intense it forced her into a painful, self-imposed retreat from public life.

My eldest daughter, Alina, the first Swiftie in our family, was born barely a year before this incident. Between learning the ropes of parenting and completing my second year in my full-time MBA program, I had barely paid attention to what was happening to Swift. But eventually, I caught up with the news and watched, along with millions of people worldwide, the horror of Tall Poppy Syndrome being unleashed on her. A social phenomenon most commonly associated with Australia and New Zealand, in which people who achieve notable success or stand out from the crowd are resented, criticized, or "cut down" by others. Kanye West led the most public cutting down of Swift in 2009. But it didn't stop there.

The backlash continued and took many forms. Swift's dating life was reduced to tabloid punch lines and award-show jokes, scrutiny rarely, if ever, applied to her male peers. When she defended her creative work or stood up for her intellectual property, she was called petty or greedy. When she stayed silent on political issues, she was labeled cowardly; when she spoke up, she was branded "too woke." Her most strategic achievements—reshaping the music industry's streaming models, rerecording her masters—were often downplayed as self-serving rather than visionary.

Meanwhile, online harassment surged: attacks on her authenticity, her body, her motives. Every success she built was treated as something suspect, a target to be chipped away. Swift's story is very representative. It shows how deeply Tall Poppy Syndrome runs even in cultures that claim to celebrate individual success. It shows how standing too tall, shining too brightly, often invites resentment.

The 2023 Tallest Poppy study[1] confirmed this pattern on a global scale: across more than a hundred countries, when nearly five thousand high-achieving women reported that standing out too much often led to burnout, social penalties, and withdrawal. Taylor Swift is hardly an isolated case. The cost of success was not simply the work it took to achieve it—it was the constant vigilance needed to survive it.

Tall Poppy Syndrome is a name originated in Australia and New Zealand, but it lives everywhere. It thrives even in the places that claim to reward ambition. When we fail to recognize these patterns, we dim collective progress. But culture is only part of the story. Even when external forces are absent, the real tug-of-war often happens much closer to home—within our own minds. Before a story ever leaves our lips, it must cross an invisible threshold shaped by psychology: by the mental shortcuts, biases, and internal calculations that govern when we speak up, and when we don't.

PSYCHOLOGICAL

If culture is the gatekeeper of the stories we can and cannot tell, psychology clouds how seen—and how exposed—we believe we'll be when we try to tell them.

Among the many invisible forces that muffle voices, the *spotlight effect* casts one of the longest shadows. First named by researchers

Gilovich, Medvec, and Savitsky in a landmark series of experiments, the spotlight effect describes our tendency to wildly overestimate how much others notice and remember our actions, words, or mistakes.[2]

We believe the world is watching closely, when, in truth, it is mostly looking inward at itself. The experiments were simple. Participants were asked to wear an embarrassing T-shirt—one emblazoned with the face of Barry Manilow—and then estimate how many people around them would remember it later. Those wearing the shirts thought nearly half the room would recall the image. In reality, barely a quarter did.

Similar distortions appeared in group discussions. People assumed their offhand comments, verbal stumbles, or even moments of silence would loom large in others' memories. But most of the time, others barely noticed. Attention, it turned out, was not a spotlight trained on the speaker—it was a flickering candle, swinging from one concern to another.[3]

The mechanism behind the spotlight effect is simple but persistent: egocentric bias.[4] We anchor so deeply in our own experience—how vivid, how cringeworthy, how unforgettable something feels to us—that we fail to adjust for the reality that others are much less focused on us. And the consequences are profound, especially when it comes to speaking up, telling our stories.

People under the influence of the spotlight effect often experience a heightened self-consciousness that makes every utterance feel perilous. In meetings, they hesitate to raise their hand, worrying a clumsy phrase will define them. In group discussions, they speak less frequently, convinced their every contribution will be dissected and remembered. In public forums, they stay silent altogether, feeling the imagined weight of every eye in the room.

Empirical studies confirm this dynamic: Individuals who experience the spotlight effect estimate that they talk more, make more mistakes, and leave a bigger impression than observers actually report. The internal pressure grows disproportionate to the actual risk. The effect is even more pronounced for those carrying additional burdens—social anxiety, minority status, underrepresented identities.[5] When you already feel different, the spotlight can feel merciless. And so, many voices never make it to the surface. Not because they have nothing to say, but because the imagined cost of saying it feels too high.

PERSONAL

Even deeper than culture or psychology lies the architecture of who we are. Our personalities—woven long before we find our voice—whisper when to speak and when to hold our stories close. Not every silence is learned. Some is simply lived. Modern psychology offers a powerful framework for understanding this inner terrain: the Big Five Personality Traits.[6] Across countless studies, five dimensions consistently shape how we move through the world:

1. **Openness** to new ideas and experiences.
2. **Conscientiousness** toward goals and responsibilities.
3. **Extraversion** in social energy.
4. **Agreeableness** in interpersonal warmth.
5. **Neuroticism** in emotional stability.

Each trait, as well as the interplay of the traits together, casts its own influence on how, when, and whether we speak.

I saw this unfold once during a storytelling workshop I led for emerging leaders at a global consulting firm. As we neared the end of the session, I invited participants to practice sharing a personal story they might someday weave into a client pitch.

A woman named Smita sat near the front, tapping her fingers lightly against her tablet. She leaned forward several times, ready to speak, but stayed silent as others volunteered first. When she finally raised her hand, she began with an apology:

"This probably isn't very relevant, but . . ."

What followed was a story about her grandfather's quiet ingenuity during the Green Revolution in India, an image so vivid, so quietly powerful, that the entire room stilled. Later, over coffee, Smita admitted she almost hadn't shared it.

"I'm usually the one who just supports the conversation," she said. "Not the one who tells the story."

It wasn't fear that held her back, nor was it for a lack of ideas. It was wiring: a lifetime of conscientiousness, agreeableness, and emotional carefulness that had taught her to weigh every word, to consider harmony before expression. Research confirms[7] what Smita's story showed so clearly: Those high in *extraversion* often find it easier to step forward—to share ideas and speak in groups. Even within extraversion, dominance and sociability, which is assertiveness paired with connection, predict leadership tendency and frequent speaking better than extraversion alone. *Openness* to experience also plays a role: Curious, imaginative people tend to engage more readily in storytelling, using narrative as a bridge across ideas. *Conscientiousness* brings drive and reliability—but also caution, a carefulness that can silence a voice before it even locates the right words. *Agreeableness* prizes harmony so deeply that highly agreeable individuals often hesitate to share stories that might disrupt or claim too much attention. And *neuroticism*, with its undercurrent of self-doubt, can magnify the perceived risks of visibility.

Personality does not necessarily dictate destiny. But it sketches the first map we carry—an operating model that tells us, long before anyone else does, how risky—or how safe—it feels to step into the spotlight. But even when personality opens the door to storytelling, professional culture often closes it. Some silences are taught, rewarded, and reinforced by the rules of the worlds we enter.

PROFESSIONAL

Even when personality opens the door to storytelling, professional culture often closes it. Years ago, I led an all-day training at a global pharmaceutical company. In the morning, I worked with the brand team. In the afternoon, the analytics team. The two halves of the day couldn't have been more different.

The brand team had folded my storytelling training into their annual off-site—nestled between campaign brainstorming and an evening of team building around the city. From the moment we began, the room buzzed. People laughed, took risks, tried out half-formed stories. One participant stood up—nervous but game—and shared something personal and raw in front of the EVP. He got a standing ovation. The room felt less like corporate training and more like a Super Bowl party.

Then came the analytics team. Same room, same materials. But it was as if someone had poked a slow leak into a giant balloon. The lively atmosphere flattened before I said a word. To be clear: They were smart, respectful, hardworking, deeply curious. But the questions they asked during the session—Why is this necessary? How does it help? What's the ROI of a story?—revealed something deeper. They weren't resisting out of cynicism. They were responding from within the norms of their profession: evidence first, emotion later—if at all.

During the break, one participant followed me as I tried to make a quick exit to the restroom. Why this? Why now? she asked. How would we use this in a regulatory review? How do we avoid undermining data integrity? Before I could answer all her questions, the break was over—and I resumed the session with a full bladder, and an even fuller sense of how deeply professional culture shapes the boundaries of storytelling.

In many fields—such as technical, legal, scientific, and investment just to name a few—professional identity is built on a foundation of objectivity, detachment, and precision. I have the privilege to work with clients across all these industries and beyond. From my observation over the decade and a half, it's clear that these cultures often view storytelling as an emotional indulgence, a soft skill, or, at worst, a threat to credibility.[8] In leadership and workplace studies, individuals in roles coded as "high stakes" or "technical" are often taught, explicitly or implicitly, that emotional expression diminishes authority.

The language of rigor becomes a shield. In academic publishing, in engineering specs, in quarterly earnings calls, facts are meant to stand alone. Feelings are seen as potential liabilities.

And yet, ironically, many similar studies show that the most successful leaders aren't simply rational—they're transformational. Those with greater psychological resources[9]—confidence, emotional awareness, a sense of self-efficacy—are more likely to motivate, inspire, and coach others into their best performance. They don't just manage facts. They build meaning. And meaning is built with story.

In contrast, leaders without those internal resources are more likely to avoid visibility, micromanage, or retreat into task-based roles. Not because they lack intelligence or discipline but because the professional cultures they inhabit have made story-sharing feel off script—risky, unserious. And that's why it's not unusual for me to spend up to one-third or even half of my coaching time with clients proving and persuading them that, contrary to their long-held belief, learning to tell better stories will help them enhance their executive presence, improve their leadership communication, and advance their career overall.

When professional norms define credibility narrowly, they leave little room for humanity.

And where there is no space for humanity, there is little space for the kinds of stories that create trust, and meaning. But even professional norms, powerful as they are, don't fully explain why so many voices stay quiet. Some silences are shaped by the organizations and the structural influences that envelop these entities. To understand those silences, we must zoom out.

STRUCTURAL

Some stories don't disappear. They're erased. Not all at once, but slowly. Smudged in the margins, misfiled in archives, buried under footnotes or anonymity. They are spoken, even written—but they fade anyway, in what curators of the Smithsonian American Women's History Museum's first digital exhibition, *Becoming Visible*,[10] described as *disappearing ink*.

That exhibition traced the lives of five women whose work shaped industries, saved lives, and reshaped history—only to be nearly erased out of it. Their contributions remain. But their names and stories are easy to miss—unless someone is willing to look closer, and keep digging.

Hazel Fellows, a skilled seamstress, helped engineer one of the most iconic artifacts in modern history: the Apollo spacesuit. The suit she worked on was a pressure-controlled, multilayered, customized spacecraft built to keep a human body alive on another world. Fellows and other women like her, many of them longtime garment workers at ILC Dover, partnered with NASA engineers to prototype, test, and refine the suits by hand. Their contributions required ingenuity, precision, and deep material expertise. And yet when NASA filmed a documentary in the 1970s highlighting this engineering feat, Fellows and her colleagues appeared only as silent hands. No names. No voices. The only person identified on-screen was astronaut Charlie Duke. As curator Emily Margolis put it, "We're seeing their work made visible, but they're also erased at the same time." They appear in the frame but are absent from the story. Their silence was not chosen—it was editorial.

Hisako Hibi, a Japanese American painter, lived and worked in the San Francisco Bay Area before World War II. In 1942, after the signing of Executive Order 9066, she and her family—along with more than 120,000 Japanese Americans on the West Coast—were forcibly removed from their homes and incarcerated in government-run camps, despite their having committed no crimes. They were given less than a week's notice. Hibi spent three and a half years at Topaz, an internment camp in the remote Utah desert. And yet, amid this traumatic displacement, she painted prolifically. Her works from that period—soft, luminous oils of camp life and desert skies—offered testimony, resistance, and grace. One painting, *Flooding Clouds*, carried an inscription on the back: "Free, free. I want to be free, free as the clouds I see up above Topaz." But when the war ended, and she returned to California, many of the paintings she had left with a friend for safekeeping were gone. The friend had died. Her work had vanished. As curator Melissa Ho reflected, "This metaphor of disappearing ink . . . I've seen it so often." It doesn't take fire or violence to erase a legacy. Sometimes all it takes is time, silence, and no one looking.

Elizabeth Keckly wrote her own memoir—reclaiming her story after surviving enslavement and building a thriving dressmaking business in Washington, DC. She became a trusted confidante to Mary Todd Lincoln, designing many of the First Lady's custom gowns. Yet despite reclaiming her voice on the page, her narrative rarely rose to the surface of public memory. As curator Dorothy Berry reflects, "Keckly and many other women of her time wrote their own memoirs in disappearing ink." Even today, when we admire portraits of Mary Todd Lincoln, we notice the fabric but not the hands that made it. The buyer is remembered. The maker remains anonymous.

Margaret Knight, one of the most prolific inventors of the nineteenth century, held over two dozen patents, including the machine that revolutionized paper bag manufacturing. Her invention reshaped retail packaging—yet for years, her contribution was dismissed or attributed to others. During a legal battle to defend her patent, she was forced to prove that a woman could even *conceive* of such a mechanical design. Knight's legacy offers a cautionary tale about how we define genius—and who we allow to embody it. As Ashleigh Coren, a Smithsonian curator, puts it: "Knight's story reminds us to look beyond just those who shattered ceilings. There are thousands whose stories never even made it into the building."

Isabel Morgan, a virologist working at a time when women in science were often backgrounded or dismissed, made three foundational contributions that directly shaped Jonas Salk's development of the polio vaccine. She proved that an inactivated virus could produce immunity, helped identify the three major strains of the poliovirus, and quantified the antibodies needed for protection. Her work formed the scaffolding of Salk's breakthrough—yet Morgan herself is barely mentioned in the public history of the disease. As curator Katherine Ott notes, "She's a shadowy figure because she didn't leave many papers. But she was like two degrees from being Jonas Salk." Her absence from the spotlight wasn't due to lack of impact. It was due to a system that rarely spotlighted women like her to begin with.

Again and again, the pattern repeats. The contributions remain, but the credit is redirected. The names are left out or footnoted or quietly revised. The labor is absorbed into collective memory—without ever becoming individually acknowledged. The stories are spoken, sometimes even written down, but they pass by unheard. Unnoticed. Unclaimed.

And this is not simply about women.

It is about anyone whose identity doesn't fit the dominant narrative: people of color, LGBTQ+ individuals, immigrants, disabled voices, the historically marginalized. Even when these individuals tell their stories, even when they document them, structural forces conspire to dim their visibility. Archives neglect them. Institutions devalue them. And slowly, generation by generation, their existence recedes from the official memory.

Worse, the erasure becomes internalized.

And this erasure leaves a mark—not only on history but on the people still trying to find their place within it.

Liz Harmon, a curator at the Smithsonian who spoke to me during an interview for a special *Forbes* article[11] I wrote for 2025 International Women's Day, described interviewing women researchers who, despite full careers and public accolades, still said they wouldn't donate their papers to a university library or research center because they felt themselves "not important enough." It wasn't because their achievements were small but because invisibility had taught them that they ought to stay out of the spotlight.

And this isn't merely a historical problem—it echoes forward into boardrooms, hospitals, law firms, and classrooms.

Legal scholar Kenji Yoshino calls it *covering*: the act of softening or downplaying your identity so you can blend in—not to deceive, but to belong. According to Yoshino, covering isn't about hiding who you are; it's about shrinking it. It's about showing up, but toned down, wearing your culture in grayscale. It's like reaching for authenticity with one hand while pulling it back with the other. This is a survival response to structural norms that reward sameness and punish difference. It thrives not just in overtly exclusive spaces but even in those that claim to be inclusive—because policies may invite difference, yet the system still prizes comfort. Comfort often means conformity.

A study he coauthored with Deloitte[12] found that 61 percent of professionals reported covering at work. Sometimes covering has to do with appearance—removing natural hairstyles, lowering voices, or dressing in a way that feels inauthentic. Sometimes covering is about affiliation—avoiding culturally significant events or not disclosing group memberships. Other times, covering is related to advocacy—staying silent rather than defending one's own group. And, most invisibly, it's association—distancing oneself from others in the same marginalized group to avoid "being grouped."

According to Yoshino, covering is exhausting, isolating, and comes with consequences. It saps creativity and dampens engagement, sending the message: You can be here—but not all of you. In many ways, covering is today's continuation of historical erasure—just in a suit and with a badge swipe. And just like those women who hesitated to donate their papers, many professionals hesitate to bring their full selves into the room—their boldest ideas, divergent points of view, lived experiences, and the body of knowledge that comes not just from expertise but from identity because a system of unspoken rules has taught them those stories might be liabilities.

At the 2024 Emmy Awards, actor and activist John Leguizamo delivered a fierce, funny, and unflinching speech about representation in Hollywood. He spoke of growing up in Queens, rarely seeing anyone who looked like him on-screen, except through "brownfacing": Marlon Brando playing a Mexican in *Viva Zapata!*; Al Pacino playing a Cuban gangster in *Scarface*; Natalie Wood playing a Puerto Rican beauty in *West Side Story*. "Everyone played us, except us!" He spoke the hard truth.

When Latinx characters did appear, it was often through cartoon characters like Speedy Gonzales, the "fastest mouse in all Mexico," or his lethargic sidekick, Slowpoke Rodriguez—stereotypes that mocked rather than mirrored real lives. As Leguizamo plainly stated, "That's how we saw ourselves because that's all we saw of ourselves."

If all we see are distorted reflections, we learn to expect distortion. If all we hear are partial histories, we imagine only partial futures. If all we witness are caricatures, we begin to believe them.

In a world crowded with noise and partial reality, the rarest skill is attunement—the ability to notice the voices most people have learned to ignore. Leaders who act not only as sages on the stage but as guides on the side, who recognize that excavating hidden stories that unlock the pieces that help us all widen the field of vision—before the rest of the world catches on—are the ones who make the greatest impact.

Rediscovery isn't just a gift to the past. It's a responsibility to the future.

For leaders, the challenge is clear: Important stories often don't surface on their own. They need conditions—an environment where voices long muffled feel safe to rise. When we overlook this, we miss more than individual insights; we lose the wisdom that could guide us through volatility and change. Rediscovering these hidden truths is a strategy for widening perspective, shrinking blind spots, sharpening empathy, and strengthening decisions in an ever more uncertain and ambiguous business environment.

Even when stories are rediscovered, their power can still slip through our hands. Treat them like trumpets and all we get is noise. Listen to them differently, and they sustain culture and memory, spark imagination and possibility. The next chapter will show you why.

chapter 4

BEYOND THE TRUMPET

Why Leaders Can't Afford to Miss the Richest Possibilities of Story

Long ago, I had a yoga teacher who told us a story about how the Americans found their trumpet in yoga.

Years earlier, she had studied yoga in India. One of her teachers there asked the class to imagine yoga as a vast palace filled with treasures beyond imagination. When Americans stumbled upon this palace, her teacher said, they were dazzled—but instead of exploring its breadth, they found a trumpet that enchanted them. They carried it home, paraded it proudly, showcased to everyone the magical quality of its sound. Over time, the trumpet represented all of yoga in the American imagination: beautiful, striking, easy to market. It became another instrument of fitness. But the rest of the palace went unnoticed.

The same dynamic, how many Americans tend to narrowly view yoga, has also unfolded around storytelling in the United States.

When traditional storytelling began reviving in tents and festivals in the 1970s, the business world took notice. The scope of it—the history, the communal purpose, the artistry—was vast. But what caught on was the piece most immediately useful: its power to persuade. From that point forward, storytelling in business became shorthand for making ourselves more memorable, more influential, better positioned to reach goals and advance careers.

I helped reinforce this belief myself with my debut book, *Let the Story Do the Work* (2017). It was praised for its practicality and encouragement—even Stephen Dubner of *Freakonomics* called it out by name.

But storytelling has always been more expansive than usefulness alone.

This chapter widens the lens with glimpses into traditions from different corners of the world. It also gives you hints on why so many people, beyond culture or psychological or professional hurdles, still hold back when asked to tell stories—especially when framed as self-promotion. I used to be puzzled. Why, I wondered, even with coaching, even under the banner of "for their own good," do so many still resist? Now I know. The self-serving orientation makes it feel less like deep, human-centered connection and more like products on display. I didn't realize what I appreciate now. From humanity's earliest days, stories served many purposes across millennia, and almost all of them were larger than the self.

WHY MY DAD IS THE BEST STORYTELLER I KNOW

I lay in bed with tears streaming into my pillow. My knees throbbed so badly that even the smallest movement sent shock waves through my body.

Yes, I'd been warned. Teachers, classmates, even the student monitors had told me not to run at recess. The new playground wasn't finished yet, and sharp gravel covered the ground. But I was in third grade—restless from hours of sitting still, always getting scolded for not paying attention or for distracting others. So, when the bell rang, I bolted. It felt like an escape, all that pent-up energy breaking loose at once.

And, of course, I fell.

A jagged patch of gravel caught me, and I went down hard. My knees and palms took the brunt of the fall. The skin on my knees was scraped raw, bloodied in patches.

That night my mother dabbed on an ointment meant to heal, but it burned so fiercely I was sure she had set my knees on fire. Secretly, I wondered if this was her way of teaching me a lesson that might finally stick. Back in bed, the pain refused to subside. That's when my dad came in and asked if I wanted to hear the story of the Monkey King. He knew it was hardly a question. By third grade I had heard the story dozens of times, maybe more. And still, I never got tired of it.

The Monkey King, Sun Wukong, was my hero. According to legend, he was born from a stone. Endowed with the gift to fly, transform into multiple shapes, and fight with a golden staff that expanded or shrank at will, he crashed the gates of heaven, battled celestial armies, and even claimed the title Great Sage Equal to Heaven. Mischief, defiance, wit—he was all of that.

But his story didn't end with rebellion. After being trapped under a mountain by the Buddha himself, Sun Wukong was given a task in exchange for his freedom: to protect the monk Xuanzang on a pilgrimage to India in search of sacred scriptures. Along the way, he battled demons, outsmarted evil spirits, and stood guard against every threat on the road. His strength was unmatched, but it was his cunning—his gift for seeing through illusions—that kept the band of eclectic characters alive in *Journey to the West*, the grand epic first compiled in sixteenth-century China.

Looking back, I can see why this story gripped me. Sun Wukong was a figure of raw power transformed into service. A trickster who matured into a protector. A rebel who used his gifts to safeguard wisdom that would guide and serve ordinary people. At the time, though, I couldn't have explained any of that. I just knew he was my hero. And late that night, while my knees still burned, I drifted to sleep in the sound of my dad's voice, carrying me into yet another of the Monkey King's adventures.

Grammatically, the title of this subsection should've been "Why My Dad *Was* the Best Storyteller I Know." He passed away unexpectedly soon after I finished graduate school. I had just started my first full-time job and never had the chance to learn from him as an adult.

I would give anything to hear his voice again. Yet whenever I think about the saga of the Monkey King, I hear it—his gentle tenor narrating each scene. Sometimes I even smell the ghost of cigarette smoke that clung to his dress shirts. He is not here to guide me through the dilemmas of adulthood. But his compassion for my mistakes, and his love for me, still live inside every story he told. That is the inheritance of storytelling—a voice that outlasts a life. But this is only a glimpse of its full power.

STORIES ACROSS THE WORLD: THE POWERFUL THREAD OF CONNECTION

My father's voice gave me more than comfort on those nights. It gave me an early understanding of what stories were meant to do. More than trade tools to polish résumés or close deals, those stories bound me to something larger—culture, shared memory, imagination, possibility, connection across generations.

And that is only one thread in a vast fabric. Across the world, for as long as people have gathered for thousands of years, stories have carried a force of connection. That force has never been confined to the self; they extend outward—to land, to heritage, to knowledge, to survival, to fellow humans. What follows is a sampler, a few glimpses from different corners of the world that hint at just how wide and varied are the ways that story has always helped us connect.

SAMOA: STORIES ROOTED IN THE LAND

I first encountered Samoan students in the late 1990s, when I was a staff counselor at the Asian American and Pacific Islander student center at Washington State University. I'll admit I knew little about their histories then. To make up for it, I spent long evenings in the library, paging through books on Pacific cultures, trying to catch up.

It was my first real job. I had moved to Pullman, Washington, a college town where most people were students or families tied to the university. My boyfriend was working in Brussels. I was single, new to the community, and lonely in a way that even constant busyness couldn't fill.

That was when I came across the Samoan word *fanua*.[1] It means "land" but also "placenta." One word holding both meanings—people and place, bound together as tightly as a child to their mother. Birth, labor, even ancestral bones buried in the soil: all folded into the definition.

I carried that metaphor with me. Even though I was a stranger to Pullman, far from family or home, the idea of *fanua* reminded me that the land itself still nourished me. I was not cut off. I was tied, in some elemental way, to the place that supported me.

In Samoa, stories keep this tie alive. Oral traditions—*tala le vavau* (ancient stories), proverbs, fables, chants—pass on how to live with land and with one another. Among the most cited is the tale of Metotagivale and Alo, invoked by orators and preserved in proverbs that still guide decisions about rivers, crops, and relations between villages.

Here, story is not a trumpet. It is an umbilical cord, carrying sustenance that supports life and responsibility across generations.

INDIA: THE HERB WHERE MYTH AND MEDICINE MEET

A few years ago, I lost my father-in-law. He was the youngest of three brothers and the first to go. His oldest brother, Uwe Krieg, was still practicing as an obstetrician-gynecologist well into his eighties. He lives in a small town in northern Germany where every doctor matters.

One summer, my husband (that same boyfriend who once worked in Brussels), our girls, and I went to visit Granuncle Uwe—short for grand-uncle. We asked him for stories, any stories. There were dramatic ones from his childhood in the chaos of World War II. But the ones that stayed with me were the everyday ones. He told us about his house calls. How, often, the patients weren't in acute danger; if they had been, they would have gone straight to the hospital. But still, when he walked into the room, something shifted. People sat up a little straighter and looked a little more hopeful, optimistic. They felt relief. Dr. Krieg was here, and it seemed all would be okay.

It reminded me how much healing is held not only in medicine but in presence, in story, in what people believe about the person or the ritual that arrives at their bedside.

That's why the tulsi plant—holy basil—carries such weight in India. Its leaves do have proven medicinal powers: They soothe fevers, calm inflammation, steady blood sugar, strengthen immunity.[2] But tulsi is also myth.[3] Its story tells of Vrinda's devotion, of betrayal and transformation, of a plant born from ashes and sanctified by the gods. And for centuries, families have circled tulsi plants in their courtyards, offering prayers, water, reverence—knowing it is medicine, yes, but also loyalty, sacrifice, and protection.[4] Like Granuncle Uwe's house calls, tulsi teaches that healing is never just about the body. It is also about the story we carry with us.

Here, story is no trumpet. It is a leaf—binding together myth and medicine, spirit and science, family and faith.

ITALY: THE VOICE THAT CARRIED A CITY

For centuries, Palermo's streets rang with the sound of the *cunto*.[5] Rooted in Sicily, this tradition of improvisational storytelling is believed to trace back to the Greek dithyramb—choral performances that laid the groundwork for tragedy and, eventually, modern theater. By the Middle Ages, it had taken root in Palermo's piazzas. The *cuntisti* stood on wooden platforms, armed only with a booming voice and a prop—a sword, a cane—and spun epics that could last for hours. Crowds wept, heckled, demanded. The storyteller had to bend the tale in real time, improvising to hold the room. It was, in essence, one of the world's oldest forms of improv theater (take note, Chicago).

That thrill of improvisation is something I know. In 2018, I stood before nearly a hundred executives and family-business owners, asking for someone to share a draft of their story aloud. My "trick" usually worked: Peers would point out the strongest draft in their group, and the author, buoyed by their encouragement, would agree. Not Jason. He shook his head, looked down, refused. His resistance was clear, and for a moment the room froze. Trying to avoid escalating the situation, I pivoted and began moving toward someone else. And then—just as suddenly—Jason changed his mind. What followed was a story about childhood poverty, about his meteoric ascent in business, about his wife's and daughter's near-fatal illnesses, about loss and perspective and love. His voice cracked. When he finished, the entire room stood to applaud.

It was a moment of improvisation—the crowd urging, the storyteller resisting, the eventual breakthrough—that felt akin to what those Sicilian *cuntisti* had been doing for centuries.

Today, only a few voices remain. Salvatore Piparo performs in strict Sicilian dialect, keeping the cadence and the climax, but his tales are no longer of knights. They are of young Palermitans facing the Mafia, corruption, a city in decline. Like Jason's story, like the ancient street performances, the *cunto* still adapts. It listens for what the people need and reshapes itself in response.

The *cunto* has never been a trumpet for one performer's brilliance. It's a mirror, reflecting Palermo's struggles and hopes in the cadence of its streets.

TRINIDAD AND TOBAGO'S CALYPSO: THE PEOPLE'S NEWSPAPER

One summer in Portugal, an hour outside of Lisbon, my family and I were facing a small crisis. Both phones had died, our eldest was carsick, and we had no way to play her usual music, the only proven way to soothe her motion sickness. Then came the idea: Why don't we sing ourselves? Off-key, windows down, we took turns choosing songs we all knew. The peak was our wild chorus of "Into the Unknown!" from the celebrated animated movie *Frozen 2*. Lots of cars whizzed by us on the road carrying strangers staring at us, one even making the sign of the cross, as if our chorus needed divine intervention. We laughed our way through the last stretch.

That car ride didn't carry the weight of history, but it reminded me of something just as important: how song binds people together, even in moments of discomfort, even when nothing else works.

In Trinidad and Tobago, that binding force is calypso.[6] Born from the West African *jeli* tradition—singers who carried history and genealogy in verse—calypso became what locals called "the people's newspaper." In French Creole and later in English, it reported what was too urgent or too raw for print: politics, crime, migration, pride, longing.

Its lyrics became proverbs. Sparrow teased that "saltfish" was sweeter than anything else. Winston "Gypsy" Peters urged, "Little Black Boy, go to school and learn!" Denyse Plummer's "Nah Leavin'" became a collective vow to stay, to love a flawed homeland. Parents repeated these lines to children; elders passed them on as warnings or encouragement.

And always, calypso folded hardship into humor, critique into rhythm. Its choruses traveled faster than newspapers, carrying both sting and solace. For those abroad, a single line—"Trini to de bone"—could summon Carnival, family, beaches, belonging. Like my family's singing in that rental car, calypso was about voices joining together—wit and resilience set to rhythm, carrying communities forward in song.

Here, story is definitely not a trumpet. Rather, it has been a vessel traveling a journey that's sometimes ragged, sometimes joyous, but always necessary.

AFRICAN AMERICAN PREACHING: A VOICE OF HOPE[7]

In African American churches, preaching stands at the center of worship. It carries history and hope in one voice, with roots stretching back to the West African griot—the storyteller who bound communities through memory, rhythm, and song. A sermon unfolds as narrative, poetry, lament, and joy braided together. It is call and response, the congregation talking back, turning words into dialogue and dialogue into healing. And it is musical: cadence rising and falling, the preacher's chant drawing the people into a shared epiphany.

At its heart is hope. Hope in the God who hears the cry of the oppressed. Hope for freedom beyond this life and, just as urgently, for dignity and justice in this one. The preacher begins with hardship but does not end there. Through rhythm and response, sorrow is named, then carried upward, until the whole room rises together.

I thought of this when working with KJ, a leader at Google who came to me for coaching. He began our sessions surrounded by what he described as "a jumble of memories, some of them painful, some pleasant, but few I thought had much value to my current situation." He led with data analysis and precision—the tools that had carried him far. But they had also left him, in his words, "hitting a brick wall" in persuading others.

As I helped him work through his stories, a transformation took place. He called it "a liberating experience . . . like barriers falling all around me." He began to tell the messy, difficult "origin story" of his team—not just the successes, but the struggles. In his words: "This level of vulnerability helped me deepen my relationship and commitment from the team. Some of them told me they had no idea how many challenges I had to overcome to get us to where we are today."

In those moments, I wasn't a teacher applying a framework; I was more like a partner in rhythm, sensing the rise and fall until his voice carried its own momentum. His story was no longer a chart of results; it became, in his words, a way "to articulate my team's accomplishments and values and paint a picture for what's next." That movement from wall to release, from tight argument to liberating story, carries something of the same arc I've seen in Black preaching: hardship named, then liberated, until what seemed like burden becomes strength.

The sermon, the story, has never been a trumpet, polished and attention seeking. It is a chorus, with rhythm, dialogue, memory of hardship, and a voice that rises until the whole room joins.

STORIES AS MANDATES FOR POWER

Stories have always built more than bonds; they have built empires. In America, Manifest Destiny[8] cast conquest as divine right, smoothing over the violence of displacement with the language of inevitability. In China, the first emperor, Qin Shi Huang,[9] inscribed his rule as the Mandate of Heaven, sealing it into the Imperial Seal so that each successor would inherit not just land but cosmic legitimacy. In Saudi Arabia,[10] the covenant between Mohammed Ibn Saud and Muhammad ibn Abdul-Wahhab was elevated into myth—a story of continuity and divine favor that shielded the state from dissent.

These were not stories of belonging or devotion. They were architecture for power, hammered into place to silence contradiction. Unlike the trumpet in the yoga parable—a fragment mistaken for the whole—these trumpets were meant to be loud: boasting, self-serving, and deafening enough to drown out every other sound.

THE TRUMPET AND THE PALACE: WHEN THE FRAGMENT IS MISTAKEN FOR THE WHOLE

These empire-building stories are architecture for power. They reduce complexity, erase interruptions, and recast conquest as destiny. They remind us that stories are used as vessels to expand and dominate.

These storylines—Manifest Destiny, the Mandate of Heaven, the covenant of Wahhabism—show how stories can be used to sanctify power. They de-emphasize fractures, smooth over defeats, and present rule as inevitable. And it is this strain of storytelling—story as mandate, story as persuasion—that modern-day business has caught most eagerly.

I was not immune. Long before I knew what my professional calling would be, I was steeped in story as tradition: my father's voice, myths from my childhood, parables passed down. But when I entered the professional world, I found myself swept into another current. As an admissions officer at the University of Chicago Booth School of Business, I saw firsthand how storytelling tipped the scales—who was admitted, who was turned away. Often the tipping point was the story: the framing, the through line, the sense of direction in an applicant's arc. It was the trumpet all over again—the fragment lifted from a palace and mistaken for the whole. And I, too, learned to play it well. I was mesmerized by the single fragment's beauty, its sound, its power—and I didn't stop to wonder what other treasures might lie within the grand palace of storytelling.

For years I carried that lesson forward. Story as advantage and leverage. In the twenty-plus years since Booth, I've taught and coached leaders across industries, sharpening their narratives for impact. By most measures, I became good at it.

But something kept tugging at me. Alongside the clients eager to hone their stories, I met just as many who hesitated. Despite talents and expertise, they recoiled from the very premise. To them, storytelling framed as self-promotion felt wrong—like stepping into a spotlight meant for something else entirely. That resistance stayed with me. Eventually, I realized something. This resistance echoed something older, something I had once known but forgotten: Stories were never built only to sell more products or advance careers. From the first tale whispered to a child, they were meant to hold more—connections, relationships, legacy, reverence, hope, survival. Stories, for as long as human society has existed, are meant to be vessels for the greater good of humanity, not just trumpets for individuals' gain.

KATHAK: THE STORY LARGER THAN THE SPOTLIGHT

Thirteen-year-old Reena Shah was rushing. She had just finished her piano lesson across town and was now standing in the foyer of her friend Priya's house. "I made it!" she exhaled, dropping her backpack before hugging her friend. Within minutes, the two longtime dance partners, along with two other girls, were changed into tunics and leggings, ready for practice. As they headed down to the basement, Reena asked with a spark of anticipation, "Do you think today we'll finally get our song?"

Reena was first-generation Indian American, her days filled with school, friends, tennis, volunteering, piano—and kathak. To many outsiders it was "just dance." But in kathak, dance and story are inseparable. The word itself comes from *katha*—story. And for centuries, *kathakars*, or storytellers, carried epics like the *Mahabharata* and *Ramayana* into village squares and temple courtyards, their gestures and rhythms animating religious devotion, intrinsic joy, and elaborate celebration.

Over time, the form absorbed new influences. During the Bhakti movement, kathak flourished as devotional performance, telling stories of Krishna and divine love. Later, under Mughal patronage, Persian and Islamic elements reshaped its music and movement: whirling spins, intricate footwork, expressive facial communication. Today, kathak carries all those layers—temple and court, Hindu and Muslim, from ancient to Bollywood to Western-influenced mash-up. Each *gharana*, or lineage, teaches a distinct style, but the essence remains: Kathak is story in motion.

Reena and her classmates began each lesson the same way: shoes left at the door, cotton tunics tied, bells fastened at their ankles. Bells were earned in sets of twenty-five, a measure of progress that jingled with each step. Before the first beat of practice, the girls bent low, hands sweeping toward the floor, offering thanks to the ground, to their teacher, to their parents, to the chance to dance at all. Only then did the rhythm begin.

For Reena, kathak was never about the spotlight. It was about the fun of moving, the community of practice, the connection it gave her to her parents' world. Her father, a trustee of the Jain temple in Bartlett, Illinois, had helped plan and fundraise for years until the temple finally opened—on her thirteenth birthday. That day, she performed kathak in the new sanctuary, bells ringing in step with a celebration of community and continuity.

She could not have known then that two years later her father would pass away unexpectedly. At fifteen, in the hollow left by his passing, kathak became something more. It was her tether—keeping her connected to him, to the values he embodied, and to the heritage that had shaped them both.

Reena grew up to be an engineer, a litigation consultant, a digital strategist, and, to me, a colleague and dear friend for nearly two decades. Reena Shah is Reena Kansal now. In talking about kathak, what permeates is not striving for achievements or shining in the spotlight. Instead, it is the way she described joy: dancing in the summer rain, bells ringing brightly, the rhythm carrying her somewhere larger than herself.

Kathak also kept her rooted in Jain practice. She has been vegetarian all her life, and her father, who helped build the Jain temple in Bartlett, Illinois, wove community into her sense of self from the start. Dance carried those same values: reverence for the ground, gratitude to teachers and elders, gestures of respect folded into every practice.

Now she has shifted from a performer—a sage onstage—to a guide on the side. For more than a decade she has taught kathak to children—including her own—passing along the stories she grew up with, adapting them for modern, young ears. Through her, another generation of Indian American kids finds a sense of place, connection, and legacy.

That is what story has always been meant to do—not to parade the self but to anchor us to gratitude, to a sense of belonging, to our people and the traditions that came before and will outlast us. For centuries, stories have carried more than self-advancement: They have bound communities, marked celebrations, carried worship, and passed down knowledge. They have built empires, yes, but that is only one strand in a much larger weave. At their core, stories have been vessels—for continuity, for values, for the ties that endure long after a single life has passed.

Back in chapter 3, I wrote that story isn't just a gift to the past. It's a responsibility to the future. This chapter has tried to widen that lens even further. To show that stories are not just trumpets to polish résumés or proclaim power but vessels to hold values, preserve community, and carry meaning across generations. That is why we have spent these opening chapters on the *why.* Why story, curiosity, and story discovery matter. Why we should strive to be elite but not elitists. Why, in this moment, it matters more than ever.

With that foundation in place, we can now turn to the *what.* What, exactly, are leaders listening for? What kinds of stories are hidden in organizations? What do facilitators help people uncover?

It is from this foundation that my distinct approach to business storytelling has grown. I make time for discovery. I help others uncover what is often hidden in plain sight. Storytelling, practiced this way, becomes less about performance and more about curiosity and discovering—where culture, values, community, insights, and subtle influences gradually come into view. The trumpet still plays its part, but now as one note among many, resonating within the fullness of the orchestra.

the *what* section

chapter 5

OPPORTUNITIES ABOUND

What Hidden Skills Separate Good Leaders from Great Ones

"This can't happen!"

On October 23, 2023, Gayla Braziel received an email from the United States–Japan Foundation. Her grant application had been rejected. Without this funding, one of her programs would die—along with a piece of President Carter's legacy.

But the grantor had little awareness of what was truly at stake. And, ironically, Gayla hadn't realized that they didn't know. Wasn't everything written thoroughly and clearly in the application? she wondered. What played out in the weeks after October 23 illustrated something more complex than a simple yes and no answer: how easily opportunities are missed when we didn't realize that we fail to communicate what really matters. Not just for those whose stories could tip decisions in their favor—but for the people who need to hear those stories in the first place. This chapter is about recognition—the ability to notice story moments before they slip by. Too often, we think of storytelling as a performance: a leader delivering a polished narrative from a podium. But the real leverage comes elsewhere. It comes in the unguarded times when a story is wanting to surface but hasn't yet found its way out. Leaders who can spot those opportunities—and invite stories forward—change the trajectory of decisions, relationships, even organizations. In the pages ahead, we'll explore how to cultivate that kind of vision: how to see the moments that matter and how to help others bring their stories into the light.

THE STORY THAT CHANGED A DECISION

Gayla wasn't one to take no for an answer. She sat down immediately to write a follow-up message, typing as fast as her thoughts could form. "This can't happen," she kept repeating to herself, a mantra driving her forward. As the director of Federal Programs for Sumter County Schools in Georgia, Gayla is used to writing grant applications, used to stretching federal dollars to bring opportunities to students in her high-poverty, rural district. Her job is to make sure students in this underresourced corner of the state have access to transformative learning experiences they might not otherwise encounter—programs that widen their sense of the world and their place within it.

Jake Schlesinger remembers what he thought when he first read her proposal. "Unimaginative and overly expensive," he told me one morning, sitting across a white café table in Washington, DC. With a flick of his wrist, as if brushing away a pastry crumb, his body echoed his thought. Jake was new to his role as CEO of the US-Japan Foundation. A former economic reporter for the *Wall Street Journal*, he'd spent more than thirty years covering policy, business, and markets, including a stint as bureau chief in Japan. He was used to evaluating numbers—and fluent in the language of cultural exchange. With more than eighty applications to consider during his first grant-making cycle, however, he and his colleagues thought Gayla's program was "an easy no."

Then, on October 24—just one day after the decisions had gone out—Jake received an email from Gayla. Most applicants accept the verdict. Some apply again the next year. They don't appeal. Gayla asked to speak. Jake said yes.

THE ZOOM THAT REFRAMED THE QUESTION

When Jake joined the Zoom call, he wondered whether the conversation was going to change anything. The rejection had been sent. Gayla's exchange program didn't align. Her proposal—thorough though it was—felt tethered to the past. A legacy program with honorable roots, yes, but not enough momentum to meet his foundation's evolving priorities. This call was a courtesy, a chance to show transparency to the public, maybe an opportunity for him to learn a thing or two. The call would be a professional grace note at the end of a polite and repeated no. Or so Jake thought.

And then Gayla appeared. Not to plead. Not to question. But to tell the story.

She didn't cite page numbers. She didn't restate the logic. She wasn't even defensive. She spoke, as leaders often do when stakes are high and time is short, from memory. And from something deeper than memory: conviction.

Gayla spoke of Jimmy Carter and the Peace Bell in a small Buddhist temple in Japan that refused to melt during World War II, which still rings with hope because of his urging. Of a tiny town in Georgia that had endured floods, business closures, and the slow ache of economic loss—and still held fast to its friendship with a similar Japanese city across the Pacific. A connection not of convenience but of commitment. She described students who had never owned a suitcase, whose families had never applied for passports, and whose first airplane ride took them to places like Hiroshima. Those students returned with the same Southern drawl but with eyes that had seen how World War II was experienced from the then enemy.

Jake listened. Then he pontificated. Then—though he wouldn't have named it at the time—he began to see differently. He stopped thinking like a CEO of a storied foundation. Instead, he started thinking more like a steward, a witness, a participant in a story much larger than a line item.

And then the question appeared in his heart: "Do I want to be the person who ends the Carter peace exchange?"

The answer came quickly. No, of course not. The rejection his staff sent weeks earlier wasn't wrong. But it was incomplete. Gayla hadn't changed the facts. But she brought forth the soul and essence of the exchange program—what is truly at stake if it were to lose its sole funding source. Later, in an interview fifteen months afterward, Jake would say, "The conversation turned a hard no into a hard yes." But perhaps it wasn't the conversation at all. It was the story—finally given space to breathe.

Had it not been for Gayla's persistence and for Jake's open mind and heart, that high school exchange program carrying President Carter's legacy would've been in jeopardy. This much is clear. So one obvious takeaway from Gayla's triumph is the importance of telling stories with conviction and clarity. But a deeper, more urgent insight reveals itself when we step back, way back. This chapter shows you what might be possible if more leaders—not just those with stories to tell—recognized the hidden, pivotal moments when a story needs to be told. What if leaders didn't wait for someone to step into the spotlight and instead were on active lookout and helped bring these important stories out in the open?

Indeed, these types of opportunities abound. But leaders need to know how to spot them.

THE STORIES WE DON'T TELL, BUT SHOULD

Over the past sixteen years coaching executives to be more persuasive through classical story elements, I've heard reflections like these from clients again and again:

I was roped into doing a demo call with a potential customer. Our biggest competitor was also my former employer from a while back. The sales lead put me on the spot expecting me to dump all the reasons our product was better. I was a tech guy and ready to talk features and functions. That prospect's eyes just glazed over. I was less experienced back then. Someone should've asked me to share a story on the strengths of our products from an end user's perspective as compared to our competitor's product.

Whenever I tried to convince customers why they should configure our platform a certain way, they would push back and tell me how I don't understand. Maybe I would be more persuasive if I knew to show them what'd happen when they configured the platform the wrong way.

My team and I tried our best to reassure our client counterparts that we're their resource, not a threat. But it seemed like the more we explained, the tenser everyone became. So I gave up and instead made the introduction as brief as possible, assuming the sooner we got to work and demonstrate our values, the sooner the clients would relax and trust us. While it's true, thinking back, had we told them simple stories of how our expertise transformed other clients' operations in the past, the chasm in the beginning could've disappeared much quicker.

My ex-spouse and I see the world very differently. We got into it, debating and then arguing and then fighting. Now, I wonder what would've happened if we were to share stories of why we see things a certain way and getting away from you-versus-I language and feeling like we're constantly attacking each other.

The annual review at my company is all about highlighting what we have accomplished that year in a fact-based yet compelling and impactful fashion. One year earlier in my career, I was very upset by my review. I felt I "exceeded" expectations, but my manager felt I "met" them. For years, I felt the problem was with the manager. Now that I am in her position, I realize this was a problem with how I told—or, in this case, did not tell—my story.

The beginning of any panel discussion at conferences is really boring. People read introductions from scripts and sound robotic. And it's usually about a long list of how accomplished and amazing the speakers are. Would anybody less than accomplished get to speak in the first place? And besides, I can read their conference profiles. Why doesn't anyone tell us why we should care to know those résumés in the first place?

I could fill an entire book with scenarios like these. The contexts and people vary widely, but the core challenge remains the same. When attention is fickle, complexity is high, resistance is strong, and time is tight—but the stakes are high—we tend to resort to a familiar approach: spray and pray. We spray our audience with a high-powered hose of facts and data. We pray something will stick and that everyone will walk away with something useful. But winning without persuading just doesn't work that way.

WE DON'T USE WHAT'S EFFECTIVE

Imagine walking into a kitchen stocked with every tool modern chefs or cooking enthusiasts could want—wood-fired pizza oven, Japanese-style mandolins, sous vide circulators. And imagine you have access to this kitchen and yet, night after night, you microwave leftovers in a plastic bowl.

That's essentially what a 2018 study by the Economist Intelligence Unit[1] found when they looked at communication in the workplace. They surveyed hundreds of employees across roles, seniorities, and industries to uncover what gets in the way of effective collaboration.

Yes, they found the usual suspects: time pressure, unclear roles, clashing communication styles. But one insight was especially damning: The tools that people said worked best were hardly used. Video calls, collaborative whiteboards, structured visuals—tools with real impact—were left untouched. Meanwhile, email reigned supreme, even though most agreed it wasn't that effective.

It's not that we don't have the tools; we do. We just keep reaching for what's familiar, even if it doesn't help us the way we really need.

When I began teaching storytelling in 2010, it wasn't exactly seen as a core leadership competency. In fact, people often assumed I wore a funny hat and played the banjo to entertain corporate retreat crowds. Back then, storytelling in business was still a novelty—quaint, charming, and often misunderstood. But things have changed.

Today, the baseline understanding of storytelling's power has risen. At every coaching session, every training event, clients can easily recall the stories that have moved them in the workplace, stories that helped them trust a colleague, change a mind, or find a sense of belonging in an unfamiliar room.

"Show me how to tell *that* kind of story," they say. That's the heart of almost every request. And it makes sense. The desire to shine in the spotlight, to deliver a compelling narrative from the front of the room, is both natural and admirable. But here's what's often overlooked: In focusing solely on becoming a sage on the stage, we risk missing a far more transformative opportunity—the chance to lead by becoming a guide on the side. Because the most powerful leaders don't just tell great stories. They help *other people* tell theirs.

Why would a leader choose to step out of the spotlight? Especially in a world of fractured attention and limited time?

Quite simply, one person, no matter how important and powerful, can't be and shouldn't be the only person talking. Leaders need other voices if they want to achieve important, sometimes impossible, feats. And if they want to succeed in today's volatile, uncertain, complex, ambiguous, and highly competitive world, they need to rely on other voices to build teams of teams. Here are a few critical examples.

1. Lead highly productive teams with divergent values.
2. Transform conflicting viewpoints into informed decisions.
3. Nudge people to speak up more.
4. Access the character of their teams beyond competence and credential.
5. And ultimately—get to the heart of the story.

1. LEAD HIGHLY PRODUCTIVE TEAMS WITH DIVERGENT VALUES

When Karla Trotman became the second-generation CEO of her family's manufacturing business, she quickly noticed the management team wasn't exactly functioning as a cohesive whole. Departments worked in silos. Communication was minimal. And one senior team member, in particular, stood apart.

Ngọc Lan was a production supervisor who had worked her way up from an entry-level assembler. She consistently delivered strong results. Yet her colleagues kept their distance, describing her as someone who "worked them too hard."

Karla knew something had to shift. Why, she wondered, were other leaders keeping Ngọc Lan at arm's length instead of learning from her? To change the dynamic, Karla began holding regular management meetings—not to log face time but to build understanding. At the start of each meeting, she introduced a small ritual: a prompt to open the conversation. Something simple, personal but innocuous. Something human. One day, she asked, "Tell us about the first job you ever held. What did you learn from it? And how did it impact the way you work today?"

When it was Ngọc Lan's turn, the room fell still.

She told her colleagues that she was one of the original Vietnamese boat people in the late 1970s. She arrived in the United States at nineteen—too old for high school, too unprepared for college. So she worked, first as a seamstress and then in electronics assembly.

She learned English, raised a family, put both her daughters through graduate schools. She bought rental properties and could even retire early to help care for her grandchildren.

And through it all, she credited one thing: her work ethic, the kind born from survival, from fleeing persecution, from watching her country burn and refusing to let a tragic war define her life. Work, to Ngọc Lan, was never something to "balance." Work is her North Star that has guided her to prosperity. Work is a duty, a privilege, something sacred. So when she saw others striving for this thing called "work-life balance," it confused her, as if there were a map everyone else had been handed—one she'd never seen.

When she finished speaking, a silence swept across the room. Not awkward. Not tense. Just . . . quiet.

Karla remembers it as a moment of enlightenment. For the first time, the team saw Ngọc Lan not just as a hard-charging workaholic—but as a person with a story. A story that explained her intensity, her expectations, her pride in her work. The walls cracked open, and the air lightened up. People responded with kindness because now they understood what had once felt off-putting. And it wasn't a formal speech that changed the way they saw her. And it definitely wasn't a town hall presentation or a top-down memo.

It was a story. A story that had a chance to be told.

And more importantly, it was a leader—*a guide on the side*—who created the space for that story to be told.

2. TRANSFORM CONFLICTING VIEWPOINTS INTO INFORMED DECISIONS

When two people find themselves in conflict, what usually happens?

If they've had positive parental modeling or exceptional professional training, they might collaborate—choose the path of resolution, mutual respect, and clear communication. But that's the ideal. More often than not, people avoid conflict altogether (yours truly included). Others go head-to-head, turning disagreements into an Olympic event, where victory isn't just about winning medals but also about preserving honor. Some accommodate. Some compromise. And context matters—always. But at the heart of it, most people caught in conflict don't know what they're fighting about. Not really.

They're reading different maps, standing at different coordinates, and yet they both believe they're navigating the same terrain. Misunderstanding doesn't happen just when people disagree—it happens when people believe they *already* agree on what the disagreement is about.

Take the workplace debate over "remote work." For some, remote means never setting foot in the office again. For others—often executives—it means hybrid: three days in, two days out. Stanford economist Nick Bloom calls out the muddle directly: Leaders and employees use "remote" and "hybrid" interchangeably.[2] No wonder constant collisions happen—because expectations don't match. Gallup finds the same pattern. Six in ten employees say they want hybrid work, but when you press further—how many days, which days, what counts as presence—the answers scatter.[3] And SHRM adds another layer: generational divides. Baby boomers, Gen X, millennials, Gen Z—each carries a different map of what "flexibility" means.[4] No wonder frustration brews. It's not just a conflict of interests; it's a conflict of definitions.

This is why disputes often aren't about the substance at all. Instead, it is about the illusion that we're talking about the same thing. Let's begin with a humbling truth, wrapped in a psychological concept.

THE ILLUSION OF EXPLANATORY DEPTH

Coined by cognitive scientists Leonid Rozenblit and Frank Keil in 2002,[5] the term *illusion of explanatory depth* describes our tendency to believe we understand things far better than we actually do—until we try to explain them. We think we understand how zippers work, how inflation is measured, or why stars shine . . . until we have to articulate it. Then, suddenly, we find ourselves fumbling.

Rozenblit and Keil asked people to rate how well they understood common objects and systems—things like toilets, helicopters, and thermostats. Participants gave themselves high scores. But when asked to explain them step-by-step? Their confidence plummeted. Conflict is no different. We think we understand our own stance. We think we understand the other person's. We think we understand the conflict at hand. But when we slow down, we often find gaps: assumptions, shortcuts, vague definitions we've never thought to question. This is where story facilitation can help.

One of the simplest and most effective tools I use is something I call This Versus That. It's a guided exercise designed to surface subtle and yet critical distinctions we rarely examine. It helps people move from certainty to curiosity, and from assumption to shared understanding.

Let me explain.

Over the past fifteen years, I've noticed something: Most people aim to *persuade* when all they really do is *prove*. They present facts, quote sources, and offer charts. (Endless charts, in fact.) But persuasion is not about being right—it's about making your audience feel seen, heard, and understood so that they become pursuable. It's about resonance, relevance, and emotional logic. It's about making the case of change.

So I'll often ask clients a deceptively simple question: "What's the difference between proving and persuading?"

A pregnant pause always follows. Then the stumbles slowly begin. "Well . . . proving is when you . . . um . . ." "Persuading is more like . . . uh . . ." The struggle is the tip of the iceberg. As people try to articulate the difference, they bump into the edges of their own presumed understandings that are mere assumptions. But more often than not, people mistake assumptions as facts. And if we're in a group setting, those assumptions diverge in surprising and often unproductive ways. What one person considers obvious, another has never considered at all. And suddenly, the map starts to clarify.

Here are more examples I often pose to clients:

- In health care: What's the difference between curing and healing?
- In education: Information versus knowledge?
- In real estate: Price versus value?
- In collaboration: Alignment versus agreement?
- In leadership: Managing versus leading?
- In storytelling: Suspense versus surprise?
- And in life: Being smart versus being wise?

None of these pairs are opposites. They're siblings—close, familiar, but distinct. And when we take the time to tease them apart, we give people a chance to *understand what they really mean*, not just what they've assumed. We shift from fighting over vague concepts to clarifying shared definitions.

That's what a guide on the side does. They don't dictate the map. They help others realize they're holding different ones. And then, together, they chart the path forward.

3. NUDGE PEOPLE TO SPEAK UP MORE

Think of a time when you had something to say—but didn't. Maybe it was during a meeting, a project debrief, a quick hallway huddle. A key detail was being overlooked. You had a hunch the group was heading in the wrong direction. You opened your mouth. Then closed it. Later, when the consequences began to unfold, you said to yourself: *I knew it. I should've said something.*

Now think of someone else—someone who *did* speak up. Who pointed out a flaw others missed, flagged a blind spot. And instead of being thanked, they were met with resistance. Or worse.

One client told me about a woman at her company who raised a concern during a pre–product launch meeting. Her insight—though initially dismissed—ultimately saved the company millions. But in the moment, her tone was labeled "abrasive." She was called difficult. Defensive. She became *that* person in the meeting—the one people began to avoid. She had been right. Her timing, impeccable. Her reward? Isolation.

This is the paradox of speaking up: Sometimes we regret what we didn't say. Other times, we regret the cost of having said it. So people stay quiet because, over time, the cost of expression starts to feel heavier than the cost of silence.

And silence, it turns out, is expensive.

Across industries, across continents, the research tells a stark story: When employees hold back, companies bleed—in ways both visible and hidden.

Research across fields underscores the same pattern: When people withhold their voice, organizations pay the price. In health care,[6] studies show silence is linked to reduced safety, concealed errors, and even systemic failures that surface only when crises erupt. In broader organizational research,[7] silence erodes creativity, fuels burnout, and drains job satisfaction. Employees fall quiet for different reasons—fear, resignation, or even to protect others—but the effect is the same: Potential is stifled. Other studies tie silence and its close cousins, cynicism and isolation, to frustration,[8] absenteeism, and a loss of trust. What emerges is clear. The quieter an organization becomes, the less resilient and effective it grows.

What the research makes clear is this: Silence isn't neutral. It's a tax—a heavy one. It siphons away talent, innovation, resilience, and it erodes trust. When people don't speak, organizations don't just lose ideas. They lose their future.

How does silence begin?

Not all at once. As chapter 3 showed you, we are already facing the overwhelming obstacles generated by many stubborn, entrenched reasons. Additionally, silence could start with one meeting. One misstep. One sharp look across a conference table that says: *be smaller next time.* The story that follows is just one story. But if you listen closely, you might hear echoes of many others.

For years, she carried it like a scar under her blazer.

By the time I coached her, she was a managing director at a large publicly traded company. She was respected, seasoned, in command. But when she spoke about presenting to senior leadership, her voice thinned. Her eyes flicked sideways, as if searching for exits no one else could see. It hadn't always been like this. The fear had a beginning. A before and after.

It started with a former CEO. A sharp, loud, addicted-to-dominance type. In meetings, if he spotted a flaw or something he didn't like in her presentation, he wouldn't wait. He'd cut her down in front of her peers. No yelling. Just small, precise incisions. Humiliation by a thousand paper cuts.

More than a decade had passed. That CEO was long gone. She had survived him, outlasted his two successors, grown in title and scope and influence. But the fear lingered.

"I don't mean to compare myself to people who've been through war," she told me, her hands open in that fragile pose of confession, "but sometimes I still feel like I have PTSD from those meetings. I still have nightmares."

What struck me wasn't just her fear. It was how invisible it was to everyone else. In meetings, she looked composed. She contributed. But there were moments when she shrank, held back, looked down. She let an incorrect data point slide without pushing back. And then came the well-meaning feedback: You should speak up more. Own the room. Show more executive presence. Despite being offered with good intention, this advice skips a beat.

If she could've done it, she would have already.

• • •

When people don't speak up, it's not because they're lazy. Or disengaged. Or incapable. It's because the climb out of silence is steep—and they haven't yet found a foothold. As leaders, mentors, facilitators, we can't just encourage people to speak. We need to show them *how*. We need to offer a ladder. A safe one. A sturdy one.

I call it the Three Levels of Speaking Up.

Not a checklist but a practice framework. A way to build the courage muscle gradually, intentionally—especially for those who are carrying impostor syndrome, cultural deference, or old wounds from the past. Let's take this climb slowly, together.

THREE LEVELS OF SPEAKING UP—HOW WE BUILD THE COURAGE MUSCLE

We often treat speaking up as a single act—a bold leap into the unknown. But in reality, it's a progression. A series of steps we take to find our footing again, especially after a stumble or silence that once cost us something. And like any muscle, the courage to speak up grows stronger not through sudden strain but through steady use. Think of it less like a switch and more like a ladder. Each rung offers a way forward and upward—anchored, incremental, possible. Here's how the climb begins.

Level One: Clarify and Summarize. This is the lowest, least risky rung up. You don't have to declare an opinion or challenge the status quo. You're simply lighting a lantern in the dark, naming what's unclear or reflecting what's been said so others can follow the thread with you.

You might say, "Wait. What do we mean by 'engagement' here?" Or "It sounds like we're prioritizing conversions over awareness—am I hearing that right?"

There's risk here, to be sure. You're admitting you don't fully understand. At the same time, you're also inviting others to slow down, to examine the assumptions baked into thoughtlessly declared statements. What you're really doing is service. You're creating common ground. You're making it safer for someone else—other silent ones—to join the conversation.

Level Two: Add and Subtract. Once you've grown comfortable clarifying and summarizing, you begin to shape the conversation. You add what's missing—an overlooked perspective, an underestimated risk that hasn't yet been considered. You subtract what's misaligned—gently asking whether a pet idea or favored project still belongs at the top of the list.

You're no longer just listening. You're building and sculpting. Helping the team see more clearly, think more broadly, decide more wisely.

Level Three: Challenge and Change. This is the highest and riskiest rung. Here, you disrupt the current. You challenge assumptions, question direction, name dynamics that may have gone unspoken.

You say, "I'm worried we're prioritizing speed over quality." Or "We've done it this way for years, but does it still serve our purpose?" Or more bravely still, "I noticed Anne was interrupted several times, and I think we're missing something valuable."

At this level, the risks are commensurate with the reward. As you grow comfortable with clarifying and summarizing and adding and subtracting, you gain the confidence needed to take this level of risks.

Three Levels of Speaking isn't about jockeying for attention. It's about adding values. It's not about getting it perfect. It's about giving others a pathway—one they can step onto gently, without fanfare, without fear of free fall. It works because it honors the climb.

As leaders, we can use this framework to guide others whom we sense have something important to say but often don't. Like Karla who nudged Ngọc Lan's story forward, let's become leaders who are acting as guides on the side.

To say: "I haven't heard from you yet, and I'd love to."

To ask: "What feels missing to you right now?"

To affirm: "That question guided us to the answer we've been looking for—thank you for asking it."

We don't need more sound bites; we need more invitations. Often, the stories that matter most arrive on tiptoe. And the courage it takes to tell those stories is sparked by one welcoming signal. Sometimes, the insight that changes everything is the one that took the longest to show up.

4. ACCESS THE CHARACTER OF THEIR TEAMS BEYOND COMPETENCE AND CREDENTIAL

"Tell me about yourself."

It's one of the most common—and most poorly answered—questions in professional life. We've all heard it. We've all answered it. And more often than not, we default to a tidy résumé summary: where we went to school, what titles we've held, how many years we've been doing the thing we do.

But rarely—if ever—does that kind of answer actually *tell* someone who we are.

Rissa Redden saw this all the time. Over a career spanning agency, consulting, and global in-house leadership roles—including years at PwC—she worked closely with senior executives navigating high-stakes communication moments. And time after time, they tripped over introductions.

"They'd introduce themselves with a list of facts," Rissa recalled. "'I'm a CPA in this state. I've been doing this for twenty-five years. I work with a variety of clients.' It was so boring."

She didn't mean it disrespectfully. The facts were impressive. The work was important. But in moments that called for trust, connection, or persuasion, people weren't listening for facts. They were listening for *meaning*.

"Why not tell me what you love about the problems you solve?" Rissa would ask. "Or a moment when you helped a client through something similar to what we're pitching now?" When people do share like that, she's noticed, the energy in the room elevates. Instead of nods and polite smiles, you get curiosity. Questions, and then connections. A human moment. Still, many professionals hesitate. They worry it'll sound too soft. Too personal. Too . . . story-like.

But that's exactly the point.

Rissa and I first crossed paths over a decade ago when she came to one of my presentations. Since then, we've collaborated in several ways, including working with her teams and the CEO at one of her former companies. More recently, she completed my story facilitation training, bringing her signature mix of curiosity, precision, and deep listening to the work. She could fill her LinkedIn's "About" section with a timeline of impressive titles and accomplishments (and, like most of us, she has). But the part that reveals *who she is*? That lives in the About section she wrote using one of our storytelling exercises:

> I am a cinephile. I love movies in the park. Movies on the plane. Classic movies. Screwball comedies. When I watched *The Royal Tenenbaums* for the first time, I felt like I had found my people. For me, the movie is about creativity and quirky characters.
>
> My upbringing was also about creativity and quirky characters. At my home, growing up, coloring books were not allowed. My artist mother believes in the importance of drawing your own lines and coloring within them—or outside the lines. She is a big believer in the power of creativity.
>
> My father, on the other hand, holds a PhD in inorganic chemistry. He's a big believer in data-based decision-making.
>
> The field of marketing is often described as one part art and one part science. Marketing is a perfect fit for me as I am also one part art and one part science. Literally.

It's delightful. It's vivid. And it reveals something far more important than a résumé can offer: a glimpse into how she sees the world.

In our training sessions, Rissa arrived at that version of her story through one of the first exercises I teach, "Paired Introductions." Instead of asking people to explain their leadership style or list accomplishments, I ask something deceptively simple: How do you usually spend your Saturday mornings?

The answers, predictably, are unpredictable.

Some people use the time to slow down from a hectic week. Others devote it to family, to solitude, to faith, to errands, to unfinished art projects, to long-neglected dreams. Whatever they say, it almost always reveals what matters to them—*not just what they do, but why they do it.*

If you ask someone to describe their character directly, most will give you a blank stare—or worse, a string of corporate clichés: "I'm a servant leader." "I'm a strategist." "I'm results-driven." "I'm passionate about innovation." And that tells you almost nothing. But give them the right prompt, and a story starts to emerge. A story that shows—not tells—who they are. This is where many well-meaning professionals get stuck: They think listing events in order—where they've worked, what they've done—is storytelling. It's not.

Recounting events is not telling stories.

Data, information, and facts don't carry meaning on their own. We—the humans—assign meaning. And if we don't tell our audience what those facts mean, they'll fill in the gaps themselves. We may not like the version they come up with.

This insight echoes Simon Sinek's concept of the "Golden Circle."

In his widely shared TED Talk and book *Start with Why*, Sinek explains that when most people communicate, they begin with *what* they do, then explain *how* they do it—and maybe, if there's time, mention *why* it matters. But the most inspiring and trustworthy leaders do the opposite: They start with *why*, then *how*, and finally *what*.

This order matters—not just rhetorically, but neurologically. The why speaks directly to the limbic brain, which governs emotion, trust, and decision-making. The how and what live in the neocortex, which processes logic and data. Here's the parallel in story work:

- *Why* = Character
- *How* = Competence
- *What* = Credential

We live in a world where credentials are publicly available, and competence is assumed. But character? That has to be revealed. And story is how we do that. Of course, once a story surfaces, it still needs shaping. That's where my IRS storytelling structure comes in: *Intriguing beginning, Riveting middle, Satisfying end.* (We'll go deeper into this in chapters 9 and 10.)

But the first step—the *real* step—is to stop listing and start revealing. Because if we want to know what someone is truly made of, we don't just need a CV. We need a story. As we've seen, character doesn't just emerge on its own. It needs space. It needs prompting. It needs strategic intention.

5. GET TO THE HEART OF THE STORY.

Every December, I gather the leaders I've worked with over the past year into one room. There's coffee, a scattering of notebooks and computers, a hum of anticipation. And in December 2018, I offered one exercise that reminds everyone, "You don't need a lifetime to know someone's character. Sometimes, you just need twenty-five minutes, and then the right story emerges."

That exercise was called the Paired Introduction—the same one that helped Rissa build her vivid, inviting LinkedIn bio. One client, Jenny, brought a new hire with her, a woman named Christina. During the exercise, Christina was paired with a client from a completely different organization. They spent about twenty-five minutes together, asking and answering a list of simple but revealing prompts I had designed. And when it came time for each participant to introduce their partner to the group, something extraordinary happened.

When Christina's partner stood up and shared the story he had crafted about her, Jenny—the hiring manager—drew her shoulders backward as if she needed more space. But more space for what?

"That's it!" she exclaimed, her voice cutting through the room. "That's so Christina. That's why we hired her!"

Everyone smiled, with an instinctive recognition. What had taken Jenny's team months and dozens of interviews and meetings to fully appreciate about Christina, a perfect stranger had captured in less than half an hour.

How is that possible?

It's possible because they had been guided—methodically—to notice and seize the small moments that most people blow past. The tiny stories that reveal character when facts cannot. It's possible because Christina and her partner worked under a time constraint. There was no room for overthinking, no time to retreat into polished but hollow words. And it's possible because they had a structure: simple enough to follow, flexible enough to honor any story's shape, sharp enough to draw out meaning rather than merely facts.

The real magic lay in the technique and process. It was also the attention. The willingness to listen for what matters—not just what is said, but what is shown.

If you look back across the stories in this chapter—Gayla standing for her program's legacy, Ngọc Lan sharing her North Star of work, Rissa's informative and yet delightful self-introduction, Christina's essence captured by a stranger—you'll see a common thread. It's not just storytelling. It's story discovery.

The noticing.

The wondering.

The inviting.

Leading others requires leaders to become emotional cartographers. What is that? An emotional cartographer is that sage on stages—and a guide on the side. Someone who "sees" the emotional terrain, senses when something important—a viewpoint, tension, an insight, experience—is missing, helps others articulate what matters even when they can't do it themselves. In every room, there is a story that could change everything. The most effective leaders of the twenty-first century know how to make space for it.

Would you like to know what this entails? Let's go to chapter 6.

Chapter 6

LEADING THROUGH CURIOSITY AND STORY DISCOVERY

What Mindset Leaders Possess Shapes What They Find

I could tell by the way their jaws tightened and their eyes narrowed that this was going to be a tough sell.

Spring break in Hawaii is sacred. For a brief and rare period, four urban dwellers vow to unplug. No phones, no meetings, no distractions. We eat every meal together, not just when schedules allow. We're with each other 24/7 for more than ten days, not just when work and school release us. My two adolescent daughters actually enjoy spending time with their parents. They're even protective of family time. So when I proposed that a complete stranger would be joining us for part of our much-anticipated getaway, I wasn't surprised by their skepticism.

I have been hoping to collaborate with the Canadian filmmaker Anthony K. Do for quite some time. His creative instinct made him the ideal partner, and I had hoped to procure his talents for my company's videos. His price tag, unfortunately, was out of my reach. But after a series of negotiations, we made it work. There was just one hitch: The only time he was free was during our spring break in

2025. One way we made the numbers work was for him to stay with us. For five full days.

I pitched it to the kids as a way to support Mom's entrepreneurial adventures. They reluctantly agreed.

At our first dinner, the signs were unmistakable. The girls sat up straight. Overly polite, they kept asking Anthony if he needed anything, which was a sure sign of distance masked as courtesy. The Hawaiian air was warm that evening, but around the dining table, the mood was cool. Then, seemingly out of nowhere, the energy began to transform.

The change started small: A few giggles sprinkled in between a few sudden bursts of chuckles. Then came waves of deep belly laughter that echoed into the garden as areca palms swayed. Alina and Melia learned about Anthony's abandoned journey in computer programming and investment. By the time the barbecue chicken and pineapple salsa were gone, we had moved on to his six-month stint in Iceland, filming Hafþór Júlíus Björnsson—best known for playing the "Mountain" in the series *Game of Thrones*—to document his grueling workout routine. The girls were transfixed.

And then came the Ed Sheeran story.

"Have you seen the photo[1] of the world's strongest man, log-lifting Ed?" Anthony asked, grinning. Four sets of eyebrows shot up. We're all fans of the English singer-songwriter with a massive global following. Anthony pulled out his phone to show us the image: Hafþór and Ed, forming the shape of a capital T—Hafþór as the vertical line, Ed as the horizontal. The photo had gone viral, featured everywhere from *Entertainment Weekly* to *People* magazine.

What unfolded afterward was even more captivating. Very few people in the world realized that this moment—the iconic photo, the VIP reception, the improbable pairing—happened only because of Anthony. He was the one who pulled the strings. He made the creative connection. It was his instinct and diplomacy that brought the worlds of a strongman and a pop star together, not just for a photo op but for a shared moment of joy for Ed's world touring team and for Hafþór's adoring family.

No one had to say a word. I could see it in my family's faces: Anthony, this former stranger, was now a figure of wonder. The spell had been cast.

Even Anthony was surprised. Understated, humble, and reserved, he's not one to talk about himself, volunteer stories—certainly not his most thrilling and accomplished ones, and definitely not on the first night with a family he hardly knew. At one point he paused and wondered out loud, "How did I end up telling all these stories?"

The answer was simple.

A facilitator was in the room.

That facilitator knew just enough of Anthony's backstory—but not everything. She was attuned to what her family might be curious about. And this facilitator was guiding gently, like a leader charting new territory with her team, an explorer who didn't know every path but had a shared destination in mind.

That evening, that facilitator was me.

I was physically present, but my influence was nearly invisible. And yet the outcome was unmistakable. Because I knew my family and because I knew enough of Anthony's past, I could drop questions—casually but deliberately—at the right moments. By the end of the evening, when those important stories had surfaced, ice melted, and affinity blossomed.

WHERE COMMUNICATION STALLS, DESIGN THINKING BEGINS

"Between what is said but not meant, and what is meant but not said, most love is lost."

The quote is widely attributed to Khalil Gibran, the Lebanese American writer whose 1923 book, *The Prophet,* remains one of the most translated literary works in the United States.

The quote has always resonated with me for how plainly it captures the fragile calculus of communication. But lately I've been drawn to something deeper inside it. If you replace just one word, you see a whole new layer of meaning:

"Between what is said but not meant, and what is meant but not said, most *opportunity* is lost."

Opportunity to connect. Discover. Partner. Collaborate. Innovate. Resolve. Transform. All of it—within reach, yet often missed. Why? Because we say things we don't mean. We mean things we don't say. Until someone—often unnoticed—is in the room, helping things get said and heard more fully and leading people to discover what was already waiting inside them.

This is the enduring impact of facilitation.

Facilitation helps you discover stories that you didn't realize you need to hear so that you and your team can embark on a path you couldn't see possible. Facilitation enables story discovery that opens new opportunities previously deemed nonexistent. Modern leaders can no longer afford to be a sage onstage *only*. They must also learn to be a guide on the side. That's why facilitation is an indispensable twenty-first-century leadership skill. That's what this chapter is all about.

WHAT FACILITATION IS AND ISN'T

Facilitation isn't confined to timekeeping or agenda management. And it certainly isn't commanding the room with predetermined answers. So what is it, really? To understand how I came to see facilitation as a leadership discipline, I need to tell you about a door. More specifically, a Norman Door.

You've likely encountered one. A door with a handle that invites you to pull when, in fact, you need to push. These doors, whose design betrays their intended function, are everywhere. They're annoying, misleading, frustrating, and sometimes even dangerous.

Why are they called Norman Doors? Because Don Norman, in his classic book *The Design of Everyday Things*, was the first to call attention to them as evidence of a larger failure: the failure to design with humans in mind.

Don was a pioneer of what is now widely known as human-centered design. He coined the term "user experience" and changed the way industries worldwide think about design—not as decoration but as an empathetic response to how people live, think, behave, and feel. He championed concepts like affordances, signifiers, and—critically—*discoverability*: the ability for something's function to reveal itself through human-centeredness and thoughtful design, and hence, human-centered design.

He taught one of my last courses at the Kellogg School of Management. We kept talking after I graduated. Over time, Don became more than a professor; he became a mentor. Back then, storytelling wasn't a "thing" yet. So I was circling around it, trying to define what I sensed was there but remained elusive. What could it possibly mean in business? For leadership? For change? How do you build a practice—and a thriving business—around something so abstract, omnipresent, and deeply human?

Don helped me think through all those questions, and more, over my starting years. He coached me through building my company and writing my first book, *Let the Story Do the Work*. My approach to storytelling was shaped by his way of thinking: When something didn't work, it's not a failure of the users—it's a cue to examine the design and the larger system in which the design is meant to serve.

This is where the intellectual lineage of my facilitation work comes from.

Don could look at a door and see everything that was broken about how it was designed. I listen to a conversation and sense where it snagged—what was meant and not said, and what was said and not meant. Missed connections, stalled momentum, ideas that die a wrongful death in the corner. Those are my cues. Like Don, I believe in human-centered design. Too often, we blame people, typically the audience, when communication fails. But what if the real problem is how the conversation is set up? Furthermore, I ask: Is it the structure?

The timing? The relationship? The process? The trust level in the room? What's blocking what wants to reveal itself?

For me, facilitation is anything but a soft skill. It's a design intervention. A strategic intent. It's how we excavate what people didn't even know they needed to say. I teach clients how to build conditions that allow a hidden insight to emerge, a vulnerable truth to rise, a stuck group to move forward. Don was after usability; I'm after possibility. He watched how people fumbled with objects; I sense how people stumble with each other as their words tumble randomly every which way, stalling even the most well-intended groups of people. And where he championed *discoverability* in physical design, I apply it to the narrative space.

This brings us back to Gayla and Jake.

In chapter 5, I told the story of how Gayla, against the odds, changed Jake's mind. She turned a flat rejection into support for her grant application. But what if it wasn't Gayla's writing that failed to earn the grant initially? What if it wasn't Jake's inattentiveness or his committee's lack of care?

What if it was the grant application process itself?

What if the problem was in the design—the way *and* the sequence in which the questions were asked, the assumptions built into the process, the signals that buried the true potential of Gayla's high school exchange program?

Don handed me a lens. A way of seeing, a mindset, and a discipline of attention. I don't do this work because I've been at it officially for fifteen years and counting, and now want to declare its importance. I do it because I inherited a way of seeing—through Don's influence—and I've spent a decade and a half applying, testing, and adapting that vision across industries, cultures, and ranks.

At its best, facilitation doesn't stop at clearing up miscommunications. It reshapes how we engage. It invites immersion—a way to put ourselves in someone else's shoes. It is designed for emergence. At its most powerful, facilitation opens a process of story discovery, shared meaning, and unchartered possibilities others completely miss.

THE INVISIBLE ARCHITECTURE OF LEADERSHIP: WHAT MAKES A FACILITATOR, AND WHY IT MATTERS

If facilitation enables story discovery, sense making, and the opening of new possibilities, then who exactly is a facilitator?

Is it a job title? A formal role reserved for someone trained, certified, credentialed? Sometimes, yes, but not necessarily. A facilitator isn't defined by a degree or designation. A facilitator is defined by what they make possible through the intentional and skillful guiding of thoughts, conversations, and explorations. Every leader should be a facilitator. And a leader of leaders? Especially so. Because in the work of leading—of coaching teams through uncertainty, conflict, complexity—it's not enough to direct. Leaders must help others discover what they don't yet realize they know. They must build the kind of environment where shared meaning can be created, not just where messages are delivered.

At a very fundamental level, facilitators may not stand under the spotlight, but they guide the room and mold the discussions. They draw people out. They help the unsaid come to light. And while their impact may be subtle, it is consequential. So what distinguishes a true facilitator? Three core qualities arise again and again:

1. They are *Other Centric*: grounded in service, not spotlight.
2. They are *curious*: not just seeking what's new but drawn to uncertainty—willing to embrace incomprehension as both the starting point, the journey, and the destination.
3. They're *pragmatic—not dogmatic*: ones that are unattached to any particular worldview, or way of knowing or doing.

These facilitative qualities are not soft traits. They are leadership disciplines. And they affect the very climate in every room, the people in the room, and elevate the collective and cumulative outcomes.

1. OTHER CENTRIC: WHEN A MIND SHIFT WAS REQUIRED

Sometimes the answers are right in front of us. But we're not paying attention.

In 2004, three months into a new role as an admissions officer at the University of Chicago Booth School of Business, I began to itch. At first, I wrote it off—suppression was a skill I had long mastered. But one night, before stepping into the shower, I caught a glimpse in the mirror: red, angry rashes spread across my abdomen like a mob of tiny rioters.

Not until my doctor diagnosed it as stress-induced eczema had I realized that I hadn't slept much in weeks. I was preparing to travel through Asia—seven cities in three weeks—representing our MBA program to thousands of prospective applicants. It was a high-stakes trip because the brand-new deputy dean decided to join me, very green to admissions at the time, in Tokyo and Seoul. Japan was our first stop, a country she deemed as our most important market.

I tried everything: medication, meditation, deep breathing, and nonstop knitting. Nothing worked. Until I had a conversation that elevated my point of view.

A current Japanese student, Toshihiko Irisumi, was helping me prepare. He was generous with his time, experience, and expertise. As we talked, our conversation drifted from logistics to culture. Toshi (what he went by) shared a story about working late one night with his team in Tokyo. They went to a nearby fast-food restaurant and stuffed themselves so they could push through. But back in the office as they were settling down in their cubicles, their managing director walked in—smiling, gracious—and he surprised them with a dinner reservation at a fancy steak house to thank the team for their hard work.

No one said they'd already eaten. Instead, they deferred to the senior-most person in the group to respond. To everyone's private dismay, this person waited maybe two seconds, demurred for a few culturally appropriate hesitations, and declared, "*Domo arigato gozaimasu!*" Off they went for their second dinner. Work had to wait.

Expectations—over personal comfort—were honored. That story changed how I saw everything.

Toshi and his team's involuntary double dinner during a stressful project might be a bit unusual, but the kind of deference to authority and long hours of work are definitely common. Japanese employees' total dedication to their employers is well known in the world. To them that's just life, but to those who decided to apply to top-tier US business schools, the additional workload required to put together a competitive application is like signing up for another part-time job. There I was, preparing for a tour meant to support applicants. And yet I'd been obsessing over myself: my delivery, my performance, my ability to impress. I had positional authority—deciding who got into business school—but I'd missed the moment to *facilitate*. To help others think clearly. To see themselves more fully.

Our events were speaker centric: filled with data, rankings, glossy stats. But what prospective students really needed was guidance and understanding.

That realization lifted the pressure. I went from "How can I impress?" to "What does this audience need from me?" I listened more. I adjusted more. I gave what was truly useful. And that's when the inflammation on my skin began to ease. Because I'd stopped centering on myself. I had begun, at last, to facilitate. Not by leading from the front but by tuning in from the side. That's where every true facilitator begins: with others.

2. CURIOSITY: THE DISCIPLINE OF EMBRACING INCOMPREHENSION

What is curiosity—not in theory but in practice?

It's not about being captivated by shiny objects or quirky facts. It's not about the thrill of being the first to figure something out. It's definitely not, as Mrs. Lee, my third-grade teacher, would attest, about getting up mid lecture without permission to peer at what my best friends were working on.

True curiosity is a discipline. A learned capacity to remain present inside the ache of not-knowing—and to allow that ache to guide you somewhere worthwhile.

I was reminded of this in the fall of 2024, staring at a one-page handout for Ann Morgan's online workshop: Incomprehension Exercise. A single page—dense, disorienting, defiant—made my left temple throb. The words were in English. I recognized the alphabet. But the meaning remained elusive.

The excerpt read:

644 Moussa, son of Zara, said that he is iron.
645 Everything that is attached with iron must be undone with iron.
646 (undecipherable)
647 (undecipherable)
648 He said that he, among his rival half-brothers, is the horn of the great ram.
649 (undecipherable)
650 It is Our Lord who twisted it, nobody can straighten it out except Our Lord.
651 Moussa . . . (undecipherable)
652 (undecipherable)
653 (undecipherable)
654 He said he is iron.

I read it once. Then again. And again. The repetition only deepened the fog. My mind reached for patterns: Is this code? A manifesto? I could feel the intensifying ache of not understanding and not even knowing *how* to begin to understand. My fingers itched to google it. But I resisted because I knew this was the terrain of the workshop. This disorientation *was* the assignment.

Ann Morgan's Incomprehension Workshop is built on a radical proposition: that the experience of not understanding a vast body of literature, even when it's been professionally translated into English and—especially for English-language readers—is not a gap to close but a space to explore.

Ann first made waves in 2012 with her blog *A Year of Reading the World*, where she read a book from every UN-recognized country (plus two more) in one year. It was an extraordinary act of literary exploration. But what followed was even more transformative. In reading widely across borders, languages, and literary norms, Ann confronted her own limitations as a reader. She encountered books that eluded easy comprehension: narratives that sidestepped Western arcs and sentences that never settled into clarity.

Rather than retreating, she dove deeper.

She noticed her discomfort. She watched her reactions. And she began to ask: What does my confusion reveal about me? What am I assuming? Whose stories do I expect to "get"—and why?

This became the seed of her Incomprehension Workshop. Participants read text excerpts with no author, origin, or context provided. They are encouraged to voice what they don't comprehend, to notice when they feel the need to explain or decode and, importantly, pause at this point. Instead, Ann asks them to interrogate what seems to be unsettling them. She asks them to ask questions even if, and maybe especially when, they have no idea where to begin. She models living in ambiguity. Ann's mantra: Ask, don't answer. It's an exquisite exercise in curiosity. And it mirrors what great facilitators do.

During one of her many workshops, she gave her participants the same cryptic excerpt I had read. Their imaginations went straight to overdrive: Some speculated it was a covert recording of an assassination plot; others envisioned a crime thriller. The fragments "said that he is iron . . . among his rival half-brothers" felt to them like a clue in a mystery.

In truth, the lines were a translated performance record of *The Epic of Askia Mohammed*, an ancient North African saga recited by a griot in the Songhay language. The revelation was disorienting—and illuminating. As Ann put it, the guesses weren't mistakes; they were mirrors. They revealed "the fears and resonances that lay close to the surface" and the tropes people default to when meaning is scarce.[2] The workshop helped each person uncover their interpretive habits—the assumptions shaped by their cultural background, the "frequencies to which their ears were attuned."

This is the kind of curiosity I mean. The kind that holds still inside confusion and notices its own reflexive tendencies. That doesn't reach too quickly for certainty and instead listens to what dissonance might reveal.

Curiosity, as I've defined it, has three core elements:

- **Humility**—Owning the fact that even with expertise and experience, we never see the full picture. Others hold pieces we don't have. These pieces help us see the fuller picture.
- **Tolerance for discomfort**—Not just noticing but staying with the feelings that incomprehension provokes: frustration, embarrassment, irritation, even shame. And transmuting those feelings into fuel to discover what's missing.
- **Navigational skill**—The ability to work through uncertainty—resisting premature resolution, patiently walking, crawling if you must, toward collective clarity.

Curiosity in Practice: When the Plan Falls Away. I didn't know it then, but I'd been practicing this form of curiosity long before I had language for it.

It was six years before I attended Ann Morgan's Incomprehension Workshop, but looking back, the spirit was already there—especially in moments like this one.

I was leading a training with a group of sales executives. The day's agenda included a mock pitch. Participants had been preparing for hours. One presenting team had just finished, and we were about to debrief. Normally, this is where I'd ask questions and coach the group toward sharper messaging. But that day, something nudged me to change course.

Instead of guiding the conversation myself, I invited two volunteers for an impromptu role-play. That open request alone raised the stakes and energy in the room. Seeking volunteers always creates a ripple effect because it converts the dynamic from "being taught" to "cocreating." And by this point, we had built trust. They were ready.

I explained the setup: "This mock pitch that the presenting team just delivered was part of a high-stakes sales presentation. Now, let's imagine that the exec team on the client's side has to brief their board (this is the impromptu part). So here's the scene my two volunteers are role-playing in. One of them is a client executive who listened to the pitch. The other is a client board member who didn't. These two run into each other at a coffee shop. They have only a minute. The board member asks, 'How did the pitch go?' That's it. Just start walking toward each other and go."

Brian and Sue volunteered. I had them start from opposite ends of the room. As they met each other, they laughed awkwardly about how to greet—"Handshake? Fist bump?"—a little unscripted levity. Then Brian, who role-played the board member, asked Sue, "Hey, I heard the presentation was yesterday. How did that go? What's the takeaway?"

And Sue froze.

She is a seasoned leader. But in that moment, she hesitated, mumbled a bit, and eventually admitted, "Sorry, I wasn't paying attention. I was trying to get my own mock pitch ready."

The training included the group CEO; she was present the entire time. What Sue admitted to was bold, unscripted honesty. The room was charged with awkwardness and stillness. I felt embarrassed on behalf of Sue and my own frustration with how this role-play exercise was heading. I could've smoothed it over, pivoted, thanked them, and moved on. But by staying with this moment of not-knowing, I also saw a door opening. Something raw and real had now arrived.

And because I kept myself in the ache of incomprehension, everyone in the room remained too.

"I couldn't have dreamed of a better volunteer." I turned to Sue and offered this heartfelt observation: "You just gave us a glimpse of reality most of us are too polite to point out: We don't always pay attention. Even when we're supposed to. Even when it's in our own interest, we're distracted. We're preoccupied with other priorities. And that's who our audiences are."

Then I turned to the room: "This is what you're up against. You work for days, perfecting your story, your visuals, your delivery. And then you present to people whose minds are elsewhere because they are, well, humans." The mood intensified and relaxed at the same time. My executives felt seen. Yes, they had done many presentations to rooms full of distracted people. They had in fact been wondering what all those hours of hard work were for. At this point of their training, they were all in, 100 percent. They all wanted to know what to do about it.

I had planned to steer the training one way—but the real learning had just presented itself. As a facilitator, you prepare. But you also let go. You have to be nimble enough to abandon your script when something better emerges. You must pay attention enough to notice a gift has just been dropped in your lap even if it doesn't look like a gift initially. That's what curiosity demands: the flexibility to follow the incomprehensible, especially when it arrives unannounced.

Afterward, I asked a few closing questions. "How many of you have presented to a group you *knew* wasn't paying attention—even though it was in their best interest to listen?" Hands shot up. What followed was an impromptu storytelling session about painful, embarrassing experiences that were also funny at times. It was cathartic. A breeze of fresh air rushed in. The room belonged to them.

Then I asked, "Knowing that this is your reality, that people are often distracted and preoccupied, how should you prepare your pitch differently?" Now they answered with insight stemming from their lived (painful) experience. Their ideas were smart, grounded, actionable. And more importantly—they believed their own ideas because those are actionable items unearthed through story discovery. And this whole process, curiosity in action and the resulting transformation, was made possible through facilitation.

Curiosity is not a soft personality trait. It's a leadership discipline. It's the engine of every great question. And the gateway to the final—and most defining—quality of a facilitator.

3. HOW DO WE REALLY "KNOW"? ONLY BY BEING PRAGMATIC, NOT DOGMATIC

Tucked among the noise of YouTube shorts is a strange little parable—easy to scroll past, harder to forget. It imagines a conversation between two unborn twins. It's circulated in many versions, but the heart of it is this:

> In a mother's womb, two babies talk.
>
> One asks, "Do you believe in life after delivery?"
>
> The other says, "Of course. Maybe we're here to prepare for something more."
>
> The first scoffs. "There's no life after delivery. What would that even be?"
>
> The second wonders aloud. "Maybe we'll walk with our legs, eat with our mouths, discover new senses."
>
> The first dismisses this as absurd. "The umbilical cord provides everything. It's a scientific fact!"
>
> "Maybe we won't need it anymore," the second offers.
>
> The first counters, "If there's something more, why hasn't anyone come back to tell us?"
>
> Then comes the crescendo.
>
> "But surely we'll meet Mother," says the second baby.
>
> "Mother? You believe in Mother? Where is she now?" The first baby is incredulous.
>
> The reply comes gently. "She's all around us. We are of her. Without her, this world wouldn't exist."

The first baby, firm in logic, concludes: "I don't see her. So she must not exist."

The second baby finishes: "But sometimes, in silence, if you listen carefully, you can feel her presence."

It reads like a thought experiment, but what it reveals is deeply human: We differ not just in what we believe but in the ways we come to believe at all. One baby leans on logic; the other, on intuition. Together, they expose a fundamental tension in how we come to know.

Cognitive scientist John Vervaeke of the University of Toronto offers one of the most nuanced but integrated frameworks for this inquiry. Drawing from psychology, neuroscience, philosophy, and anthropology, Vervaeke names four ways humans come to know: procedural, perspectival, propositional, and participatory.[3] Together, they form what he calls "an ecology of knowing"—a pluralistic, interconnected view of human intelligence and wisdom.

THE FOUR P'S OF KNOWING

- **Procedural Knowing**: Knowing *how* to do something—like riding a bike or baking a cake. It lives in the body, formed through practice and repetition.
- **Perspectival Knowing**: Knowing *what it feels like* to be in a situation—like sensing danger before data confirms it. It's embodied awareness shaped by context, emotion, and time.
- **Propositional Knowing**: Knowing *that* something is true—like facts, principles, or statistics. This is where most academic and professional training tends to live.
- **Participatory Knowing**: Knowing *with and through* the world—like when a jazz ensemble improvises or a team falls into collective flow. It's cocreated and relational, not just cerebral.

Vervaeke's central insight is that wisdom—true, adaptive wisdom—requires us to integrate all four. And most modern conflicts, he argues, stem not from what we know, but *how* we know. When people approach a challenge armed only with one form of knowing—especially propositional—and dismiss the rest, discovery stalls. Worse, power imbalances emerge. And from there, collaboration fractures.

THE REAL-WORLD CONSEQUENCES

How do we know one group of people's way of knowing is "better" or more reliable than another group's?

In business and academia alike, epistemological clashes—conflicts between different ways of knowing—are often misdiagnosed as personality, credential, sophistication, or culture issues. In truth, they are knowledge collisions. Consider two real-world examples.

CONSERVATION: WHEN DISCIPLINES COLLIDE

In the 1990s, in Central Africa's rainforests, the sharpest divide wasn't between national borders but between academic ones. Biologists and anthropologists arrived to tackle conservation with radically different ways of knowing.

Biologists, grounded in procedural and propositional knowing, mapped species, tracked habitats, and drew a straight line from human encroachment to biodiversity loss. Their solution was fortress conservation: create protected zones, even if it meant displacing people.

Anthropologists, guided by perspectival and participatory knowing, listened to Pygmy communities in Cameroon who, after being relocated, lost not just food sources but entire ways of life. Where biologists saw data, anthropologists heard silence: erased rituals, land stories, cultural ties.

The clash was bitter. Biologists dismissed the social accounts as "anecdotes." Anthropologists called the biological evidence incomplete, blind to lived reality. The result was neither effective conservation nor justice. Projects stalled. "Paper parks" existed only on maps—underfunded, poorly patrolled, with poaching on the rise. Local communities, excluded and impoverished, had little incentive to protect land they no longer inhabited.

Philosopher Evelyn Brister, who documented these disputes,[4] noted that conservation biology didn't just dominate the policy space—it captured it. One way of knowing drowned out the rest. And in doing so, it sacrificed both trust and outcomes. When one way of knowing monopolizes the frame, collaboration fractures. The forest example makes visible what's easy to miss in boardrooms: Without integrating multiple forms of knowing, even data-rich strategies unravel.

THE ECONOMY: TWO STORIES, ONE SPLIT REALITY

Consider the US economy in 2023 and 2024. By the standard measures economists prize—GDP growth, historically low unemployment, record-setting corporate profits—the story was clear: The economy was strong, resilient, even booming. Those indicators represent *propositional knowing* at its peak: abstract, data driven, objective.

But ask ordinary Americans how the economy was doing, and the answers painted a very different picture. Many households felt squeezed. Prices for groceries and rent had climbed faster than wages. Even as inflation cooled, the memory of six-dollar eggs or skyrocketing gasoline bills remained. Everyday life carried the residue of scarcity and strain. This was *perspectival knowing*—what it *feels like* to live inside those numbers. And it was *participatory knowing* too—how neighbors compared notes in checkout lines, how families adjusted spending, how communities shaped their sense of reality through shared experience.

The clash was stark. Economists insisted people were "misperceiving" reality; consumers insisted economists were out of touch. Headlines[5] like this one blared: "America Won the War on Inflation. You Still Think the Economy Stinks." But the deeper truth was that both sides were telling stories filtered through different ways of knowing. The data didn't capture how rising costs rewired daily routines, eroded trust, and weighed on optimism. And lived experience couldn't always account for the broader structural dynamics shaping the market.

The consequence? A gulf of distrust. Policies touted as successes landed flat. Many political leaders seemed unmoored from the people they claimed to serve until they were sent the official notice with election results. And a rare window of economic resilience was overshadowed by cynicism—because one way of knowing drowned out the others.

SO, HOW DO WE BRIDGE THE DIVIDE?

It's tempting to start with frameworks, KPIs, or mediated protocols—and yes, they have their place. But the most durable bridge between ways of knowing is built first and foremost on mindset, not on tools. It begins with *other centricity*—the willingness to consider that someone else's perspective, even if foreign to your own, carries key pieces of the fuller picture you are trying to see. It deepens with *curiosity*—the humility to admit you don't have the full picture yet and the courage to stay in that unknowing. And it culminates in the mindset of being pragmatic—not dogmatic—with how people know.

Leaders—those with a facilitator's orientation—don't enter the room to close it down with conclusions. They walk in to open it up because they always wonder. They resist the comfort of certainty, the performance of knowing. Instead, they ask—not because they lack answers but because they believe others hold part of what's needed. They believe others can arrive at insights they don't yet know they possess—if given the right design.

THE STRATEGIC EDGE OF FACILITATION

And yet, being pragmatic—not dogmatic—is just the beginning.

To move discovery into alignment and insight into action takes more than curiosity. It requires a deeper kind of leadership—one that influences the room without overtaking it. A way of guiding that quietly rearranges the mental furniture, shifts what others notice, and opens a different kind of path forward.

This is the strategic edge of facilitation.

David Brooks, in an April 2025 *New York Times* column, described what he believes to be the Trump administration's one stroke of brilliance: relentless initiative. He writes: "You learn from these [military] strategists that a leader who takes the initiative forces his opponents into a reactive mode. He forces his opponents to respond when they are not yet prepared. He destroys the enemy's planning by presenting them with situations they did not anticipate. The purpose of permanent offense is to produce in the minds of your opponents a sense of disorientation, defensiveness, disruption, and mental overload."

It's an unsettling paragraph. And yet—it calls our attention to something essential: Initiative changes the landscape.

Brooks draws on military strategists—Clausewitz, Sun Tzu, John Boyd—to make a point about power and the changes it causes. But what struck me most was how his framing reveals our cultural blind spot. We see initiative as dramatic. We associate it with domination. We measure it by visible disruption when in fact initiative could also come in another form that is much subtler and nearly undetectable. The most powerful shift wasn't offense—but reorientation. Not blitzing through assumptions—but "merely" slipping underneath them.

That is the work of facilitation.

Facilitation is not the use of force; rather, it's through attunement. Not by overruling plans but by expanding what's possible within them. Not aimed at opponents but in service of teams, clients, and collaborators.

A leader who facilitates well can still produce mental overload—but of a much more delightful kind: the kind that stills the room, mid-thought. That reorients a conversation and makes someone pause and say, "I've never thought about it that way before."

This is why facilitation is a hard skill in disguise.

It takes discipline to listen this well, courage to interrupt with care, and patience to follow the thread until the real insight emerges.

The goal isn't to command and demand. Instead, it's to change the conditions—so others can see what possibilities were always there, just out of view.

Once leaders are equipped with these facilitative mindsets, mastering the most critical facilitation tools—in the next chapter—will feel like fitting their hands in gloves specifically designed for them.

Chapter 7

WINNING WITHOUT PERSUADING (YES, AGAIN)

What Great Facilitators Know That Most Leaders Miss

How does someone you've never met in person make you feel so seen that not only do you grow but you grow to know yourself in a way that was once elusive?

Gregory Warner is that someone.

There's something about him that feels uncannily familiar, like a close friend I didn't realize I was missing. Other times, he reminds me of a favorite cousin. We have a familial affinity, as if we'd grown up around the same kitchen table—even though we met only in late 2023, and all our conversations since have been over Zoom, text, and voice memos.

There are moments he feels like a coach. Other times, like a therapist. (To be clear, he is neither.) He listens in a way that loosens what's knotted, and he seldom gives advice. Instead, interacting with him often allows clarity bubbling up to the surface. And then there's what I can only describe as x-ray vision. He sees past my posture. He hears what sits behind my words. He notices what's tugging at me before I've even registered a pull. It's not magic, I don't think, but it might as well be.

This is his superpower.

And if you understand what Gregory does for a living, it starts to make more sense.

Gregory Warner is an award-winning journalist, international correspondent, and podcast host. He spent years reporting from conflict zones in Afghanistan, Rwanda, and Ukraine. He's covered terrorism, civil unrest, and postwar trauma. He's also composed poems about health care job growth, jogged alongside homeless running club members in Philadelphia, and unpacked what empathy means inside a Kentucky call center.

He's best known for creating and hosting *Rough Translation*, the NPR podcast that follows the cracks in cultural understanding—the places where an idea that feels obvious in one country turns strange in another. His stories carry humor, depth, musicality, and clarity. They're rarely about what you expect, and they rarely leave you unchanged.

Still, if you're not Gregory—if you're not an acclaimed journalist with more than two decades of experience—you might assume this ability to perceive so sharply is something you either have or you don't. But I don't think that's true. I think it's something we can learn. And I think—after having been a story facilitator myself (unofficially) since 1996—I've gathered a few strong clues as to how. In this chapter, I will show you how facilitation lets the story do the work—and how three core skills—listening, reflecting, and synthesizing with reframing—form the heart of a facilitator's superpower.

OMG . . . YOU READ MY MIND

Before I talk about the facilitative tools, let me give you a glimpse of Gregory's superpower in action.

One crisp October morning in Park City, Utah, I was deep into preparing for my keynote when I saw a notification on my phone.

That little rectangular box popped up and distracted me. It's Gregory. It's a voice memo, barely three minutes long, which prompted a reply beginning with, "OMG . . . you read my mind. How did you do that?!"[1]

For a few weeks, we've been trying to hash out a plan for him to help me with my book manuscript, this one you're reading. We're both strapped for time, but we want to collaborate. Eventually, we decide on him serving as a developmental editor. My book has three main sections, each with three to four chapters. I send one section to him at a time for his feedback. While he reviews, I keep writing.

A reasonable plan, it seemed, but I was very uncomfortable with it. My editor at HarperCollins, Tim Burgard (*Hi, Tim!*), and I had already agreed that I would send him one chapter at a time for his review. Couldn't Greg read my chapters first so I can incorporate his comments before sending it to Tim?

No, my almost-cousin insisted.

Gregory didn't have the time to do reviews chapter by chapter. More importantly, he elaborated on the ideal writing process, one where I had the space to write uninterruptedly, free from having to knit a cohesive whole as each idea, sentence, anecdote, argument, research insight is finding their way to the page. I couldn't argue with his logic. Still, I couldn't accept the plan—even though it came wrapped in excellent advice, from a far more experienced writer. We'd circled the same ground for days. Then a voice memo arrived that crisp October morning. In this memo, Gregory stopped proposing—and started naming. Gently, clearly, he reflected back what I hadn't yet dared to admit.

The voice memo began with:

> "What I'm hearing is that you're somewhat concerned about Tim seeing your first draft . . ."
>
> *Did I say that? I didn't. I don't think so. But . . . He's so right.*
>
> ". . . because what you're thinking is that your first draft is really going to be very skeletal and full of questions, and you

want somebody to be able to read that and help you think about that . . ."

Uh . . . yes. Duh! . . . So why couldn't I articulate it myself?

". . . before you send it to Tim."

Of course. That's Tim. My editor at HarperCollins!

"If that's the case, let's name that and think about that."

Name what? Think about what?

"I think you should think rather than what Tim wants, or about impressing Tim, or maybe, you know, helping him feel like he's really gotten something professional and polished. I think you should think about what's helpful to you . . ."

What?! I should think about what's helpful to me . . . ME?!

Gregory named it.

I was very uncomfortable with his proposed plan because deep down I wanted—no, I needed—to impress Tim. But not just Tim. Really, anyone I come across. As an immigrant of immigrant parents and grandparents, impressing others is my way to survive. I carry a lifelong burden to prove myself—so deeply wired, it's become my way of earning my place. If I impress you, I survive.

Even in the context of manuscript writing, Tim was supposed to help me. But I flipped the script quietly and all alone, until Gregory named it. Then, and only then, I started opening up to the possibilities of creating a setup—for me—that would be more beneficial to me, and ultimately more beneficial to everyone else. Greg, of course. He and I wanted to collaborate but with plenty of constraints. Tim and my publisher, definitely. They want nothing but the highest quality book out of me. And me, as only a second-time published author, with still plenty to learn.

So how do the rest of us—those without journalism awards or voice-memo clairvoyance—learn to do what Gregory just did? Let's start there.

FACILITATING VERSUS TEACHING VERSUS PRESENTING

In chapter 6, I outlined the three core mindsets and qualities of an effective facilitator: being Other Centric, Curious, and Pragmatic —not dogmatic. But what exactly does a facilitator do? And how is facilitating different from teaching—or from simply presenting?[2]

Gregory wouldn't call himself a facilitator. Most people wouldn't. The word can feel oddly corporate or even clinical, like a term buried in a retreat schedule or tucked away somewhere on a whiteboard under "team offsite." And yet, what Gregory did with me—his disposition and attention, his skillful reframing, his invisible guide ropes—*was* facilitation. Pure and powerful.

It's the same work I've been doing since 1996, long before I had the vocabulary for it. Back then, I didn't have a title. I just knew what it felt like to help a group reach something bigger than any one of them could've done alone. Over the years, I've tried on other labels: teacher, trainer, presenter. And while each role can support learning and spark change, facilitation remains distinct—more collective, more fluid, more improvised, more concerned with the wisdom in the room than the expertise at the front of it, and consequently far more powerful.

So what's the difference?

Let's start with what these three roles have in common.

Whether you're presenting, teaching, or facilitating, your job is to convey something meaningful. All three involve shaping a shared experience. You need clarity, presence, a clear sense of purpose. You need to be "on," tuned to your audience, responsive to group tempo. And at their best, all three can change minds and elevate abilities, not just share information.

But the similarities stop there.

The deeper differences lie in where the spotlight falls, who owns the knowledge, and what kind of space gets created. Presenting is often about control—about cleanly delivering a story, a pitch, a message. It's a one-way arrow. Teaching is a bit more porous; it welcomes questions, checks for understanding, but still assumes that one person holds the answers. Facilitation flips the whole architecture. The facilitator doesn't fill the room with certainty. They open the space for exploration.

If teaching is driving the bus, facilitation is directing traffic. If presenting is a solo performance, facilitation is jazz—improvisational, cocreated, responsive to the beat of the group.

A facilitator isn't always the subject matter expert, but they *are* experts in the process—of learning, of navigating group energy, of making meaning. They listen differently. They don't just designate whose turn it is to talk; they tune into what's not being said. They sense hesitations. They frame questions that unlock what was stuck.

Where teachers aim to transmit knowledge, facilitators aim to discover wisdom and insights. Where presenters intend to persuade, facilitators invite participation. Where traditional leadership rewards certainty, facilitation honors the art of not-knowing—of letting the group arrive at something original together.

Facilitators are not lecturers or puppeteers. They're guides and shepherds. They don't dictate outcomes—but they steward the process. They keep their hands light on the reins but their attention sharp. The path may be unpredictable, but they hold a sense of the shared destination.

And this is what makes facilitation a critical leadership capacity. It's not about being the main character. It's about helping others *become* the protagonist—guiding them not to your prescribed outcome but to a collective destination. A leader who facilitates steps off the stage and creates a field. They read the chemistry, feel the rhythm, and, in turn, they adapt in real time. And through this process, something more lasting takes root: shared ownership, psychological safety, camaraderie, and the confidence of a group that discovers it can solve problems and achieve new heights together.

Facilitators do not teach you what to think. They help you listen to what you already know. And that's where we begin—with the first of three core actions in this chapter: listening. True listening recognizes what's unspoken. It creates room for discomfort, curiosity, and surprises. It reshapes the conversation—and sometimes, the people in it.

A facilitator is a sage on the stage becoming a guide on the side—in its purest form.

1. ON LISTENING

Some of the best moments to listen are when no one realizes you're listening.

Back in 2004, I was working as an admissions officer at the University of Chicago Booth School of Business. Part of my job was overseeing a group of forty-four graduate assistants—MBA students who helped read applications and interview candidates. They had their own open workspace within our office. They came and went freely, often using the space to socialize. And since I was their direct manager, my presence quickly faded into the background. I was just . . . there. Available, just in case. Which meant they often forgot I was around. And that's when I caught glimpses of MBA student life that were not meant for my ears. One particular kind of comment always piqued my interest:

"That class module is the world's most useless!"

They were talking about the required experiential leadership course that all first-year students had to take. Most students appreciated its value—except for one specific module: listening. The complaints varied in tone and words, but the core sentiment was always the same: "Why are they teaching something so basic? Haven't we been listening our whole lives? What is there to learn?"

Listening isn't like public speaking. It's not like negotiation or pitching, where action is visible, energy is measurable, and outcomes are easy to judge. Listening—when it's done well—can feel like nothing is happening at all.

And that's exactly why it's so easy to dismiss, overlook, and get wrong. But what if listening isn't what we think it is? What if it's not a passive state but a practiced leadership skill? What if it's not the absence of action but the beginning of transformation?

A growing body of research suggests that listening, done well, can be far more powerful than persuasion. In a comprehensive study titled "I Am Aware of My Inconsistencies," researchers Guy Itzchakov, Avraham N. Kluger, and Dotan R. Castro[3] found that high-quality listening doesn't just make people feel heard—it actually prompts deeper introspection, reduces defensiveness, and increases people's willingness to consider alternative views.

How?

Because high-quality listening creates psychological safety. It allows someone to reflect on their own views without fear of judgment or rebuttal. In contrast to persuasion—where counterarguments often trigger resistance—listening invites a person to explore their own thinking more fully. And in that space, something subtle but profound happens: Ambivalence becomes tolerable. Contradictions no longer feel threatening. People begin to loosen their grip on overly rigid stances—not because they've been convinced but because they feel accepted.

The researchers found that this kind of listening—marked by attention, empathy, and nonjudgment—can reduce the chance of holding extreme views and increase internal openness. In other words, listening makes mind opening possible.

This research has major implications for leadership, especially in the way leaders create space for nuance, complexity, and mutual exploration for teams, adversaries, partners, and competitors alike. The study reinforces what many experienced facilitators know instinctively: that people are more likely to revise their thinking when they don't feel like they're being pushed to.

And that brings us to silence.

WHAT JUST HAPPENED?

If you paused, flipped back, squinted, wondered if your copy of my book was defective—you're not alone. Most people do. In fact, I predict some might even email my publisher to ask if something went wrong in production. (But shhh, don't tell anyone I did this on purpose!)

Nothing was wrong. The pages were blank on purpose. But the questions they engendered? Those are the real point. Because silence—like blank space—is rarely neutral. We rush to fill it, with answers, questions, ideas, and the nearest available noise. A gap in sound or content feels, to many of us, like a problem to solve.

But what if it's not? What if that flicker of discomfort, when you weren't sure what came next, is exactly what silence is meant to do?

SILENCE IS GOLD

In the West and North American culture especially, silence can feel suspect. We interpret it as awkward, empty, or even hostile. In meetings, it often cues someone—anyone—to step in and fill the void. In conversation, it can signal disconnection.

But a comprehensive, interdisciplinary research study invites us to rethink that reflex.

One of the most complete explorations comes from a 2022 study titled "An Exploration of Silence in Communication," authored by Ángel López Gutiérrez and Juan José Arroyo Paniagua of ESIC University in Spain. Published in the *European Public & Social Innovation Review*,[4] the paper challenges the idea that silence is the absence of communication. Instead, it argues that "people who communicate perfectly control silence"—that mastering silence is as crucial to communication as words are.

The study draws from linguistics, behavioral science, cultural studies, even cinema and music, to make one point very clear: Silence is not passive. It is active. Strategic. Sometimes more honest than words. Across cultures and contexts, silence expresses fear, respect, tension, empathy, resistance. It creates space for meaning to emerge. It allows for complexity to take form without being glossed over.

This is especially true in leadership.

In brainstorming sessions, for example, silence is oxygen. When used intentionally, it creates just enough pause for a buried insight to burst into the open. In cross-cultural teams, silence may convey humility, reflection, or restraint—virtues that easily go unnoticed when measured by Western standards of assertiveness. And in facilitation, silence acts as white space: the breathing room between inputs. It's how we show we're listening, not just to respond but to allow something deeper to arrive.

As the authors point out, silence also shapes power. "Nothing strengthens authority so much as silence" is a quote, as the study's authors pointed out, attributed to Leonardo da Vinci. But they're quick to add: Silence must be used with intention, not avoidance. Because while some silences deepen trust, others—like evasive or deceptive silence—can erode it.

Silence communicates. The question is whether we're paying attention.

So what would happen if we trained ourselves to recognize it as part of the message and to master it? Speaking clearly and confidently matters, always. But just as often, it's the well-timed pause that gives people the space to process their own thoughts and thereby earns their trust.

THE BEST WAY TO GET SOMEONE'S ATTENTION IS TO GIVE THEM YOURS

Ironically, the better you are at listening, the more willing others become to listen to you. This virtuous back-and-forth—attention given, attention returned—is one of the most undervalued forms of influence. And few people embody it better than Philip Galanes.

An American writer, lawyer, novelist, and longtime advice columnist, Galanes is best known for his "Social Q's" column in the *New*

York Times Sunday Styles section, where, since 2008, he's responded to awkward social dilemmas with wit, warmth, and striking clarity. In a podcast interview,[5] Galanes was asked what makes for truly great advice—the kind that people actually hear and take to heart. His answer was simple and unforgettable: "The mark of really great advice is listening so closely that you're almost the same person with the person who's asking for the advice."

What profound advice, but also a nearly impossible stance to assume. Most advice, however well intended, is given from the point of view of the givers, not from that of the receivers. It's easy to see through the fog when we're not in it. Before we're able to "listen so closely" that we're almost the same person with the person who is in need of advice, we need to cross over a bridge.

2. REFLECTING

"All experience is preceded by mind, led by mind, made by mind." So begins the *Dhammapada*, a collection of teachings that has shaped human thought for more than two thousand years. Far from a religious tract, the *Dhammapada* offers practical, sharply observed insights into how our perceptions shape our reality. And Gil Fronsdal's contemporary translation—praised for its clarity, precision, and poetic restraint—makes these teachings newly accessible, even to readers with no particular interest in Buddhism.

The opening line alone gives us pause: If all experience begins in the mind, how do we ever come to understand our experience clearly when everything is being "filtered" by our mind?

It turns out, most of us aren't even aware that our mind is doing all the filtering work.

The late writer David Foster Wallace offered a metaphor in his 2005 commencement address at Kenyon College: Two young fish are swimming along when an older fish passes by and says, "Morning, boys. How's the water?" The young fish swim on for a bit before one turns to the other and says, "What the hell is water?" The metaphor,

Wallace explains, is that the most important realities are often the hardest to see. We are immersed in our assumptions, our perspectives, our mental models—so fully, we don't even notice them.

That's why reflection—as a relational act—matters so deeply. To reflect is not just to see; it is to help others see themselves. A well-timed paraphrase, a distillation of what someone just said, an honest mirror held with care—these are examples of gestures that can illuminate what was previously hidden, even to the speaker.

SEEING WHAT IS ALREADY THERE

One cold February afternoon, when the Chicago sky had already gone dark by 4:30 p.m., I opened the monthly professional development call for my Certified Story Facilitators. What happened next was a quiet burst of warmth: a eureka moment that sparks bright light in a dark tunnel.

It was still early in the year, but by then, most people had already abandoned their New Year's resolutions. So I wanted to offer an alternative. What if, I proposed, we used our own storytelling power to tilt the odds of success in our favor?

Before the call, I'd asked each facilitator to reflect on a personal goal they had set for 2025. Then, inspired by the book *Atomic Habits*, I introduced three frames for habit formation: goal driven, system driven, and identity driven. Most people set goals—run a marathon, write a book—without thinking much about the systems that support them. Fewer still begin with identity. But identity, I reminded them, is where real transformation begins.

Then I asked them to do something harder: tell a story—not about the goal but about what pursuing it reveals about who they are. In breakout groups of two people, each facilitator would listen carefully, reflect back what they heard, and help their partner uncover an identity that might otherwise remain hidden.

In one of those breakouts, Bernhard Krieg and Alessandra Rolffs were paired. She spoke freely, thinking out loud about her resolution to exercise more. But something kept snagging. She couldn't quite connect the desired behavior to the deeper thread beneath it. She circled around it, uncertain.

"I'm just . . . happier when I exercise," she had said, basically in passing as she described the hectic nature of her life.

Fortunately, before she went further into the details of her life, Bernhard caught it and reflected it back.

"Isn't that it?" he asked. "You're happier when you move your body. That's not a goal. That's who you are."

Alessandra blinked. Silence. Then, eventually, she marveled. "How did I not see that?"

Not only did the beginning thread of identity behind the goal begin to emerge, but the very spotting of it also made her feel seen. And in that reflection, she recognized something that had always been there but hadn't yet come into focus. Reflecting together is how we catch the currents of thought and feeling as they flow through our lives. It's how we notice the water.

THE MIRROR, NOT THE ECHO

So what *is* reflecting?

Very simply, reflection is the act of holding something up—an idea, a feeling, a situation—so it can be seen more clearly. We often think of mirrors when we think of reflection: surfaces that show us what's there, whether we're ready to see it or not. But mirrors don't exist only in glass. They exist in people too.

As facilitators, we become that reflective surface. Not polished to perfection but clear enough to help others glimpse what's already present, living beneath our awareness. This is not the same as echoing. Echoing is necessary. We need to hear our own beliefs and feelings in another's voice. Sometimes, even a word-for-word repetition of what we just said can be affirming and validating. It tells us, "You were heard." That alone is powerful.

But reflection goes further.

If echoing says, "I heard you," then reflecting says, "Here's what I see in what you said." It catches not just the words but the meaning inside them. It holds up a mirror to reveal—with nuance, care, human intelligence, and just enough distance to allow the speaker to view themselves anew. I've come to think of it like this. A good mirror doesn't change your face. It shows it back to you—faithfully, gently, sometimes for the first time. A facilitator becomes that mirror. Not flawless or flattened. But honest and compassionate. Clear enough to reflect what's already there, waiting to be seen.

To be listened to like that—to be reflected like that—is rare.

Most of us are used to being corrected, advised, redirected. In fact, I'm rather certain that most of us have been listened to and reflected back only then to have something being pitched to us, leaving us feeling a little used and maybe even "dirty." But to be truly reflected is different. Reflection doesn't tell us who we should be, what we should buy, which path to take. True reflection reveals who we already are, through illumination. And that's what makes reflecting such a vital part of leadership. When people feel seen—truly seen—they step more fully into themselves because someone reflected something real about themselves back to them.

At this point, you might be wondering: *Is all this reflection really necessary?* Wouldn't it be faster to just tell people what to do—or persuade them with a clear argument?

Absolutely. In some ways, it is faster. But speed isn't the same as impact.

If reflecting feels unfamiliar—or even inefficient—pause to ask why. It may feel effortful because it's rare. But that rarity is exactly what makes it powerful. When you reflect someone's truest essence, you're helping them see themselves, sometimes for the first time. And that act—simple as it seems—can change the trajectory of your team, your relationships, and your leadership.

REFLECTION AS A SOCIAL SURVIVAL TOOL

Here's the deeper reason reflection matters so much: Self-identity is profoundly social. Research in psychology and sociology shows that we become who we are through our interactions with others.

From the earliest moments of life, we learn to understand ourselves by watching for cues—how someone responds to our voice, how they smile, how they look away. Over time, those signals shape our self-concept.

This is a core idea in human development.

A pioneering American sociologist, Charles Cooley, called this the "looking glass self"[6]—the idea that we come to see ourselves through the imagined gaze of others. George Herbert Mead, influenced by Cooley's work, and also a pioneering sociologist in his own right, built on this, arguing that our identity is formed through "role-taking"[7]—the ability to view ourselves from another's point of view.

And here's the kicker: We don't grow out of this. We carry this wiring into adulthood. We remain porous to social feedback[8]—consciously or not.

Reflection, then, is not some optional leadership skill. It's a relational act with long-term consequences. When you reflect someone clearly, honestly, and with compassion, you help them assemble the building blocks of their self-identity. You shape how they understand themselves—even if they can't always trace that influence back to you. And yet, this is not about control or manipulation. People still choose what feedback to internalize.[9] That's what makes reflection powerful—but also ethical. Unlike persuasion, it doesn't twist the facts, spin the angle, or steer someone to a conclusion. It simply says: Here's what I see. That clarity—offered without judgment—can be a beginning point of transformation.

LEADERS OF LEADERS AND THE POWER OF REFLECTION

To become a leader skilled in reflecting *for* and *with* others, we ought to begin with ourselves through self-reflection. Unfortunately, self-reflection doesn't typically show up in leadership competency frameworks—especially not for CEOs or other leaders such as surgeons. But the evidence is clear: In roles where outcomes have high stakes and time is tight, reflection becomes a lever for clarity, trust, and lasting influence.

Yet reflection is often the first thing leaders drop when time is short. And the last thing they want to practice when discomfort is high. "The hardest leaders to coach are those who won't reflect—particularly on themselves," writes executive coach Jennifer Porter in her 2019 *Harvard Business Review* article "Why You Should Make Time for Self-Reflection (Even If You Hate Doing It)."[10]

Porter explains why so many leaders resist it. They feel a bias toward action, a hunger for measurable ROI, and avoid a mindset of curiosity and not-knowing.[11] Reflection, by contrast, feels slow and imprecise. It's like standing still in the middle of the goal while the ball comes flying in—when every instinct says to lunge.

But that stillness is exactly the point.

As Porter puts it, "Reflection gives the brain an opportunity to pause amid the chaos, untangle and sort through observations and experiences, consider multiple possible interpretations, and create meaning. This meaning becomes learning, which can then inform future mindsets and actions."

For leaders, this "meaning making" is crucial to their ongoing growth and development. Research backs this up. From the same article, Porter shows that call center employees who reflected for fifteen minutes at the end of each day performed 23 percent better after ten days than those who didn't. UK commuters who used travel time to reflect felt happier, more productive, and less burned out.

Yet many senior leaders still don't know how to start.

Some think reflection means journaling (it doesn't have to). Others assume it's indulgent. But Porter offers simple, pragmatic alternatives: walk, talk, sit, think. Start with small questions:

- What are you avoiding?
- How might you be contributing to a difficult relationship?
- How could you have been more effective?

Even ten minutes of this—scheduled, intentional—can create the cognitive space leaders need to stop reacting and start learning. As most of us can attest: Growth doesn't come from moving faster. Instead, it comes from making meaning.

But self-reflection is only the beginning. The real test of reflection—its reach and resonance—comes when it moves beyond the individual, especially in environments where decisions are swift, stakes are high, and speaking up doesn't come easy. In fact, some of the most compelling lessons on reflection don't come from boardrooms at all— they come from operating rooms.

In 2023, an article in *Annals of Laparoscopic and Endoscopic Surgery* outlined a structured framework for surgical reflection, where each team member shared observations in a protected environment.[12] This process—individual reflection followed by group discussion—helped uncover cognitive biases and align the team's understanding, enhancing decision-making and patient safety. Another study, drawing on direct observations of cardiac surgical teams, showed that surgeons who used *tone-setting* and *engagement-facilitating* behaviors—rather than criticism—were rated significantly higher by their teams.[13] This reflective style correlated with fewer negative interactions and better psychological safety. And finally, in a pilot within a plastic surgery training program in Australia, critical reflection was introduced to help trainees surface their thought processes.[14] This approach led to sharper clinical reasoning and professionalism—evidence that structured reflection supports both technical and relational growth.

These studies consistently point to the same insight: When surgeons institutionalize reflection—shifting from individual telling to collective noticing—they create environments where teams learn, adapt, and operate more safely.

Whether in surgical rooms or boardrooms, these leaders use reflection to make space for others to see more clearly. They share what they notice, without rushing to interpret. They don't hand down conclusions. They offer perspective.

And in that offering, a real-time transformation is taking place: People feel seen. Patterns come into view. Responsibility becomes shared. Reflection, in their hands, becomes less about direction—and more about discovery. And that discovery becomes the ground where initiative takes root. They win, and they win together.

But reflection alone isn't enough. I like to think of listening and reflecting as forms of divergent thinking because they open up whole new worlds of possibility. Once leaders unlock those worlds, they face a new task: to synthesize and reframe. This is where convergent thinking comes in. It's how leaders begin to pull the pieces together into new meaning, new possibilities.

3. SYNTHESIZING AND REFRAMING

I'm procrastinating.

With only eight more weeks before my manuscript deadline, I've completed just 50 percent of this book. Instead of writing, I'm reading. Instead of reading research papers relevant to my topic, I'm hooked on a novel. Not even a work of fiction about human dynamics, communication, or anything remotely applicable. I'm mesmerized by Jamie Ford's 2019 novel, *The Hotel on the Corner of Bitter and Sweet*, which spent two and a half years on the *New York Times* bestseller list. It's a historical fiction set in Seattle, alternating between the 1940s and the 1980s. The story follows Henry Lee, a Chinese American man, as he reflects on his childhood during World War II and his present-day life as a widower.

Alina sat in front of me, scarfing down her breakfast egg sandwich, trying to peel me away from the novel so I'd help her prepare for her impending workshop. We're in Olympic Valley, California, together. She's the only sixteen-year-old at the prestigious Community of Writers conference in 2025, younger than most of the other 119 participants by decades. She and I huddle every morning, to do check-ins and to center her for daylong interactions with professional adults. I relented and put my book down—but not without asking her first, "You don't know much about Asian American history yet, do you?"

"Nope!" Only half the "nope" comes out of her mouth as she takes another bite.

"You don't really care about history, do you?" I ask, already knowing the answer. Her head has been squarely in the young adult fantasy genre since fourth grade.

"No, I don't. But I *know* it's important," she says, spearing the last of the side salad she's made herself to even out the egg sandwich.

"So why don't you read more history? Even historical fiction?" You can't blame a mother for trying.

"History is about people screwing things up." She actually uses more colorful language. "And. Here we are." My rising high school senior sums up her position.

Normally, I'd let her many free-flowing observations pass. But not this time. This time, I noticed something. With a few words, she educated me on why thousands of years of human stories have taken such low priority in her quest for reading and knowledge.

You could say that my teenager synthesized history—albeit very crudely—a mountain of information into eleven words. But that's not all. More critically, she framed history as an important-but-not-urgent topic. And if I have any chance of persuading her to spend more time immersing in the nonfictional world, I'd better begin by understanding how she's already making sense of it. How she synthesizes, how she frames—even if just to herself.

It would've been easy to dismiss Alina's comment as flippant. But something about it stayed with me. "History is about people screwing things up." Crude, sure. But also remarkably efficient. So efficient that it's helped her organize her world around it. She was telling me, in her own shorthand, how she makes sense of the past. What matters, what doesn't. What feels useful, what sounds like blah blah blah to her adolescent ears.

Beyond offering an opinion, she was also performing a function I've seen leaders struggle with for years: synthesizing information into meaning and then framing that meaning for others. Even if the audience was just me, across a breakfast table.

This is where linguist Nick Enfield's work becomes especially useful. In a conversation on the *Brain Inspired* podcast,[15] he describes language not as a mirror of reality but as a tool for moving through life with other people. Its purpose, he says, isn't to capture every contour of the physical world. Instead, humans use it to set direction, mark beginnings, narrow focus. A word doesn't have to be precise to be effective. It just has to help someone else know where you are and what you're trying to do.

For example, a flat surface with four vertical supports in the place where food is prepared in most modern homes is commonly referred to as a kitchen table. But I've heard many people describe their kitchen tables as the "gathering place," where busy members of the family meet daily, eat, and catch up with each other's lives. It is a place where many conversations and arguments take place and many memories are formed. Humans use language to point, anchor, define, and align. That's what language does best. In addition to allowing us to describe and disseminate, language helps us establish social coordinates.

Enfield's book title sums up the idea best, *Language vs. Reality: Why Language Is Good for Lawyers and Bad for Scientists.* The idea that language is meant to coordinate instead of convey a single truth can unsettle traditional ideas of communication around clarity and rightness. But it rings true. Even children, Enfield notes, figure this out early. They learn how to ask in ways that get results. They experiment with tone. They frame things to get a response. It's how social beings learn to move in sync. None of us come to language neutrally. We frame because we have to. We simplify, not because we're lazy but because we're wired for connection. And in complex environments—teams, communities, families—that kind of framing becomes essential. It tells others what we see. It gives them a way in.

That's what Alina did. Not perfectly, not elegantly, but efficiently. She took a broad, abstract concept—centuries of human conflict—and put it into a sentence that felt true to her. That's what reframing often looks like. It's a way to make meaning that someone else might pick up and carry with them. And while Alina's reframing was instinctive, others—like executive coach Ron Carucci—do this deliberately, spotting patterns across organizations and reshaping how leaders see problems. Here's a good example:

To say Melissa's life was hectic is an understatement. Her calendar, like those of many CEOs, had become an endless loop of one-on-one meetings—each one justified, each one feeling important, and yet collectively draining the time she needed for strategic thinking. Her team felt aligned, in theory. But decisions were slow, coordination was uneven, and most context was shared behind closed doors.

Ron Carucci has seen this pattern play out across organizations. Melissa's story was an example in his July 2025 *Harvard Business Review* article, "Why Senior Leaders Should Stop Having So Many One-on-Ones."[16] He synthesizes what's happening behind the facades of a very full calendar. One-on-one meetings, long considered a cornerstone of effective leadership, become counterproductive at the senior level. They isolate information, reinforce silos, and absorb an extraordinary amount of leadership capacity—all while giving the illusion of staying connected.

Carucci then reframes the problem. The issue isn't that leaders are meeting too often—it's that they're meeting *alone*. His recommendation is specific: replace many one-on-one updates with capability meetings—small, cross-functional conversations that bring two or three people together around a shared outcome or value stream. He recasts these meetings as being more than for producing and receiving status reports. Instead, in his new frame, capability meetings are sense-making sessions. The goal is integration.

In a capability meeting, the CEO isn't running down a checklist with each functional lead. Instead, marketing, engineering, and customer success might meet together with the CEO to address a shared customer issue. Product, data, and operations might convene to solve a friction point in onboarding. Everyone sees the same picture. Everyone hears the same priorities. The loop closes faster.

This is synthesis in action: noticing a pattern across companies that feels normal, then stepping back far enough to name the cost. And it's reframing in practice: shifting the goal of senior leadership time from "stay informed" to "build shared context." As Carucci writes, "When meetings are built around capabilities instead of reporting lines, they sharpen alignment while freeing time."

To synthesize, here's a simple visual I call 3 Tenets of Persuasive Perfection, to keep in mind: **Information → Concept → Emotion**

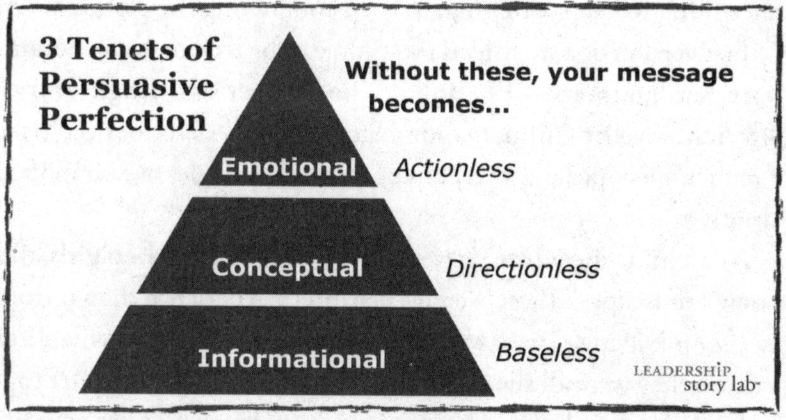

This is not a hierarchy of importance but a progression of resonance. Most of us start with *information*—it's everywhere, easy to access, and often where communicators default. But information alone is rarely what moves people. It overwhelms, fragments, or dissipates unless it's shaped with a unifying theme.

That's where the *conceptual* core comes in. When a leader or facilitator can synthesize the pieces—choose what to leave out, what to emphasize, how to pace and sequence—they make the information digestible, and meaningful. The concept acts as a scaffold, helping others locate themselves in the message.

And if the communicator has truly been listening—observing what's said and unsaid—they may also be able to speak to the *emotional* current running beneath it all. Not by performing emotion but by naming what's already present. The hesitation. The urgency. The hope. When synthesized with care, that's the part that lands deepest.

So the move isn't to lead with emotion or to drown in data. It's to start where people are already flooded—with information—and guide them, through concept, to what actually sticks: a message that *feels* true.

COMPLETE THE PICTURE

Even the most skillful synthesis can take us only so far—unless we stay willing to keep searching, to keep completing the picture when the first version of a story feels too simple to be true or even relevant.

In her landmark TED Talk, "The Danger of a Single Story," Nigerian novelist Chimamanda Ngozi Adichie describes the risks of reducing people, cultures, or countries to a single, oversimplified narrative.[17]

As a child, she wrote stories filled with British schoolgirls and snowy landscapes. These weren't her direct experience drawn from her life in Nigeria. These were scenes in the only books available to her, and they were all she ever had access to. It wasn't until later that she began to see what had been missing: a reflection of her own life in Nigeria, a story shaped by her own context, her own voice. Later, she realized just how much power stories hold—not just to reflect reality but to define it. "The problem with stereotypes," she said, "is not that they are untrue but that they are incomplete." One story becomes *the* story. Complexity collapses. Imagination narrows. And in that vacuum, dignity is often the first thing to go.

The story of my client Tina Peters could have followed that path.

WHAT SHE FOUND WHEN SHE KEPT LOOKING

Tina Peters grew up with one story about her father. He'd left when she was very young—divorced her mother, disappeared from her life, and didn't fulfill his part in child support. Her mother's stories about him were few but sharp edged. Over time, they calcified into a single truth: He was irresponsible and, therefore, not worth looking for.

And for decades, Tina didn't look. Until she became a parent herself. Something had evolved in her heart. The gaps in her origin story grew wider. She wondered who her father really was—if the story she'd inherited was the whole story. And so, she began to search.

It took time, perseverance, awkward phone calls, financial investment, and many moments of doubt. But eventually, she found him. And slowly, they began to talk. She heard his version of what happened—his regrets, his missed chances, his inability to repair what had been broken. The conversations didn't rewrite the past. But they opened something new. And then, one day, her mother called.

She'd received a check in the mail—an enormous check. Her father had sent her every dollar of unpaid child support, dating back decades.

That moment stunned Tina. But it wasn't the money; it was the lesson. "I'm not someone who rushes into one story so quickly that I stop searching for another," she told me. "It's dangerous to become so wedded to one story that you stop looking for others." Her father came into Tina's adult life late, but it wasn't too late. He had a chance to be a wonderful grandfather to her children before a terminal illness took him away.

That's what makes her story so powerful. Despite being used to seeing what seemed to be the "full picture," she remained open-minded to discover that there's in fact more to know and to understand.

FROM PERSONAL BLIND SPOTS TO PUBLIC CRISES

The willingness to keep searching beyond the first version of the truth goes beyond the personal realm. It also applies to the civic, cultural, and organizational arena. The same reflex that helps a daughter rediscover her father is the one that helps companies, communities, and countries avoid collapse.

When we stop at the first story, the most flattering one or the most viral one or the one that agrees with our views the most, we don't just misjudge people. We miss the signals of risk, fragility, even harm. We've seen it unfold on massive scales.

In 2023, Silicon Valley Bank collapsed with astonishing speed. For years, its leaders—and many of its investors—had been buoyed by a single, compelling story: that the tech sector was untouchable. (Haven't we heard this story once or twice before?) Growth was inevitable. The future was theirs. Few questioned what would happen if someday interest rates ever changed direction or the start-up bubble started to shrink. Fewer still asked what risks were quietly building beneath that smooth upward slope. The result? A panic-driven bank run that sent shock waves through the financial system.

Months earlier, a different kind of implosion hit FTX, the cryptocurrency exchange hailed as the future of finance. Its founder, Sam Bankman-Fried, was perceived as a visionary—a math genius, an altruist with messy hair and moral clarity. The media ate it up. So did regulators. So did investors. Almost no one looked closely at the company's opaque operations. The narrative was so shiny, no one thought to poke at it. Until it collapsed—and billions disappeared.

And now, we're doing it again. This time, it's artificial intelligence, except with one single story pitted against another single story.

One narrative goes something like this: AI will change everything. Automate everything. Know everything. Under this story, decision-makers across sectors are rushing to implement AI without fully understanding how it works, who it works for, and what it might break along the way. Biased hiring algorithms. Misdiagnosed patients. Chatbots hallucinating legal precedent. Another narrative runs counter to the first one. AI will end humanity as we know it. And if it doesn't, it will surely undermine the very core of what it means to be human. These narratives are seductive; they induce strong or weak morale. Worse, they inspire few questions, little curiosity, or the desire to embrace the discomfort of incomprehension.

In each case, the damage wasn't from poor decisions. No, decisions were triggered by those unquestioned stories. Stories that weren't examined.

THE POWER OF A DIFFERENT STORY

What pulls us out of the single-story trap?

Often, it's a facilitative leader, someone who can guide a team, a company, a community out of binary thinking and into deep discovery by creating space for new stories to surface, possibilities that weren't legible before and opportunities that are hidden from everyone in the room.

That's why this book is called *Winning Without Persuading.*

The title is a subtle tribute to my heritage. While brainstorming what to call this book, I found myself circling around a phrase I've heard since childhood: winning without fighting. It comes from *The Art of War* by Sun Tzu, a military treatise written in ancient China. The highest form of mastery, Sun Tzu wrote, is to win without engaging in combat. Victory without violence. Resolution without aggression.

Of course, I'm not trying to subdue anyone.

But I do want to disrupt a deeply embedded idea in Western leadership culture: that influence requires force, that winning requires argument, that to lead is to persuade others to see things *your* way.

That's just one story. And I'm offering another.

This book is about a different form of leadership. One that doesn't push people to follow—but draws them toward an opportunity they didn't know they shared. It's about the kind of leader who doesn't just "get buy-in" but builds the conditions for possibility to blossom collectively.

Winning without persuading is not passive. It's not soft. It's harder in many ways. Because it requires prioritizing others. It requires being at odds with your environment—seeking it out, in fact. It requires listening so deeply that something new can take root. It requires honoring stories belonging to someone else—but that you are brave enough to value.

HE LIKES BEING AT ODDS

You know who else likes being at odds with his environment?

Gregory Warner.

Yes, he has talents. But for most of his adult life, he's placed himself in situations where his assumptions get questioned. And instead of resisting, he gets curious. He doesn't defend. Instead, he inquires further and listens harder. He keeps circling back to the same animating questions:

What am I missing here?
How can I see what you see?[18]

This is not the kind of impulse that wins trophies. And yet, Gregory has earned more than his share: two Edward R. Murrow Awards, a Peabody, and others I'm probably forgetting. But when I asked what he's proudest of professionally, he didn't mention any of them. He told me instead about strangers who wrote to say his podcast helped them through a divorce. A pandemic. A painful transition. He told me about conversations where people said things they hadn't realized until they said them out loud. He told me about listening in a way that made people feel truly heard.

But what about the awards?

"I don't really have any pride in any professional accomplishments," he said. "Since I believe those are fleeting and in the past and not something I particularly remember or focus on."

Can a person get more Other Centric than that?

I know I'm not there—not yet. But I believe I can get better. I believe we all can.

Other Centric. Curious. Pragmatic. Listening, reflecting, synthesizing, and reframing. These may not be traits you're born with. But they can be skills you possess. I've seen it. I've trained facilitators since 2020, and the growth—the transformation—not just in them but in the people they serve is unmistakable. It's not easy. But it's real and powerful.

Facilitation isn't just something we do. It's something we become. So what does it take to lead like that? Let's open the toolbox in the next chapter.

the *how* section

chapter 8

WINNING WITH CRAZY GOOD QUESTIONS

How Curiosity Becomes the Most Powerful Voice in the Room

Some version of the following has probably happened in your life—maybe with a younger sibling, your own child, a niece or nephew.

When my youngest daughter, Melia, was five, she had a revelation that literally took her breath away. It was just before Christmas. She, her sister, Alina, my husband, and I were brainstorming what gift to get for their nanny, whom we all called Ah-Yee. The adults were marveling aloud at how energetic Ah-Yee was, even though she was around the same age as our parents. That's when Melia froze. "Ah-Yee is older than Dada?!" she gasped.

Only then did I realize Melia had been equating height with age. She was the shortest and youngest. Alina was older and therefore taller. My husband, the tallest, was the oldest. I came next. And how about Ah-Yee? She's taller than the kids but shorter than the parents—so clearly younger than us. But no. She was a grandparent's age. Melia's mental map collapsed. Her world was briefly, and wonderfully, blown open.

Here's another:

My dear friend Greg Kim, who lives on the West Coast, wanted his young children to remember our family between visits. One day, he held up a photo and asked his daughter Camille, age four, if she remembered our names. She pointed to Alina: "Alina!" Then to Melia: "Melia!" So far so good. Then her index finger hovered over me. Pause. It drifted to my husband. More silence. Then: a big smile. "Oh, that! That's *that* extra boy and extra girl!"

To Camille, the most important people in this other family were the ones her age. So naturally she remembered their names. As for the adults? Well, we're just extras.

Melia believed height meant age. Camille remembered the kids' names but not the adults'. Their thinking was clear, internally consistent, and—given their internal worlds—completely reasonable.

Adults don't outgrow that. We just trade up for more sophisticated assumptions, and expensive clothes. And often, those assumptions work—until they don't.

Consider Dave Whorton, founder of Tugboat Institute, a leadership network with hundreds of privately owned companies that are built around what he calls the "Evergreen" philosophy—businesses designed with humans, the environment, as well as profit in mind. Evergreen companies aim to last not quarters but generations, a goal diametrically opposed to the industry that had nurtured his career for over two decades and for which he has the highest qualifications to flourish in.

Whorton's résumé reads like a master class in Silicon Valley excellence: UC Berkeley undergrad, MBA from Stanford, consultant at Bain & Company, investor at TPG, partner at Kleiner Perkins, cofounder of drugstore.com and Good Technology.

And yet, despite that pedigree, he had never encountered a profitable and scalable model that embraced long-term thinking, environmental responsibility, and human-centered decision-making.

In his book *Another Way: Building Companies That Last . . . and Last . . . and Last,*[1] Whorton reflects on this blind spot with disarming honesty: "I had long been brainwashed to believe that most growth companies needed outside capital—equity and/or debt—to grow. . . . I had no familiarity with organic, self-funded growth rates. . . . In my entire experience at Stanford Business School, Kleiner Perkins, and TPG, nobody had ever mentioned anything like what Stack[2] was telling me."

Stack, in this case, was Jack Stack—founder, president, and CEO of SRC Holdings, one of the most successful 100 percent employee-owned companies in the United States. Based in Springfield, Missouri, SRC began in 1983 as a leveraged buyout of a failing manufacturing plant. Under Stack's leadership, it grew into a diversified business group with more than thirty units, more than two thousand employee-owners, and nearly $1 billion in annual sales as of 2025. Stack is best known for pioneering "open-book management"—a refreshingly new approach that teaches every employee how to understand financials, track performance, and participate in the company's growth.

In 2015, Stack gave Whorton a multiday tour of SRC's operations. One particular discussion stopped Whorton cold. Stack was explaining how SRC had grown—organically and without outside capital—for decades.

"There's a natural growth rate in business," Stack told him. "It depends on your business model and how well you manage your cash flow. If you look at your margins, if you look at your inventory, if you look at your payables and your receivables, you see there is literally a cash cycle, and that cash cycle determines how much cash you can generate in a period, which tells you how much you can reinvest in the business for growth without outstripping your financial resources."

Whorton stared at him, blinking. "What are you talking about?" he remembered asking.

Stack's growth methodology didn't compute. His strategy was such a departure from the ethos of Silicon Valley that he might as well be working from a different planet altogether. Stack's growth map sounded implausible to Whorton. It is built around financial transparency, employee ownership, and with a pace of growth tied to internal strength rather than external infusions.

Whorton was, by his own admission, dumbfounded.

But it has also transformed the way he viewed growth at scale. Old assumptions that had guided his career began to loosen. Instead of arguing him into a new belief, Stack had simply shown him a company philosophy that worked in a way Whorton hadn't known possible. That exchange with Stack planted the many seeds needed for Whorton to fully realize his own vision: another way to found, build, and lead businesses that last and last and last.

Although neither Stack nor Whorton had story facilitation in mind as this big lesson in entrepreneurial finance unfolded, the process in which Whorton's worldview expanded (much like Melia's and Camille's) very much runs parallel to the power facilitative leadership can bring about. Whorton was very successful in his previous career in Silicon Valley, but he was also deeply unhappy. He was searching for something he believed to be more humane, more sustainable, and actually far better for business long term. He didn't—couldn't—find it until his former assumptions, however sophisticated under the guise of the world's most elite institutions, were blown apart. In similar ways, leaders who are skilled in story facilitation can uplift a team's entire trajectory and, potentially, its destination. Its power lies in helping people notice there's more to what they previously assumed to be the whole truth while inviting them to reconsider their options in real time.

In this chapter and the next two, I'll step into the hows: how to lead in a way that invites discovery (chapter 8), how to tell stories that guide rather than impress (chapter 9), how curiosity and story discovery create the conditions for transformation (chapter 10). We begin here, with a powerful and yet gentle force that opens every room with possibilities: a Crazy Good Question.

So, let me ask you one. What is the difference between suspense and surprise?

IS IT SURPRISE OR SUSPENSE? AND WHO CARES?

Not long ago, I was introduced to a group of women from different walks of life. Though we came from different industries, eight of us shared a common aspiration: living well in a postpandemic world.

Over dinner one evening, the conversation bounced from work to travel to exercise regimens. Then someone mentioned Botox. Suddenly, the table lit up. Everyone chimed in at once, comparing providers, trading advice, debating treatment frequency. I had nothing to contribute, so I asked, a little sheepishly, "Does it hurt?"

Seven heads turned in unison. They stared. Then, incredulous, "You've never had Botox?!" They were surprised. But why were they surprised?

Maybe because of our age group or that Botox has become so ubiquitous that it's practically a rite of passage for anyone past thirty, they assumed everyone had done it. From my vantage point, I had always chalked up my youthful appearance to genetics or clean living or both. But clearly, my new acquaintances had a different explanation in mind. They were surprised because their assumption—unspoken but shared—had just been upended. And I was surprised that they were surprised.

The world is full of facts, perspectives, and experiences; we can't possibly know them all until we collide with them. Most of the time, that gap in knowledge doesn't matter, until it does.

Here is where facilitators can amplify their invisible power by making space for discovery. And to do that well, we need to understand the two emotional levers that great facilitators can pull: surprise and suspense.

If surprise is about the reveal, then suspense is about the wait.

Surprise jolts us. Suspense holds us. Surprise disrupts assumptions—we thought we knew, but we didn't. Suspense stretches attention—we don't yet know, but we want to. A facilitator working with surprise might help a team see that their "obvious" strategy isn't obvious to everyone. A facilitator working with suspense might let a silence hang just long enough for someone to say the thing they've been hesitating to voice. Surprise gives people no warning; suspense gives people time to feel the stakes. In stories, surprise is an unmistakable wake-up call, while suspense is what makes you lean forward and forget the relevance of time because you're just on the edge of understanding. In dialogue, suspense and surprise open mental space where ideas don't land with a thud but unfurl with an unassuming entrance.

This brings us to the heart of this chapter: asking Crazy Good Questions.

Whenever we're asked questions, our instinct is to respond. But to great questions, Crazy Good Questions even, we're being guided to ponder, reflect, and contemplate. Great questions direct our attention (the most precious resource that modern-day companies are vying for), redirect our curiosity, and nudge us to look where we haven't looked, to name what we haven't named.

Questions are a facilitator's superpower because they create space for dilemma, confusion, new perspectives, and ideas to emerge. When teams get stuck in the same old routine, a good question can reframe the problem. When people assume they're aligned, a question can surface where they're not. When teams fall into premature solutions, questions can slow things down just enough to make new thinking possible.

But more often than not, people don't ask questions. What happens then? What keeps them quiet even when something doesn't feel right?

WHAT KEEPS US IN OUR ECHO CHAMBER

In many organizations, silence is driven by fear. It could be fear of retaliation, losing credibility, jeopardizing one's standing. People have to weigh the risks of speaking up. But fear isn't the only force at work. Leadership and organizational scholar Jim Detert calls attention to something harder to detect: deep rules[3]—the unwritten norms that shape what people do and don't say.

Deep rules vary by team, company, and industry. But they often protect the same things: power, reputation, entrenched incentive, or the appearance of harmony. A leader may praise transparency but flinch when challenged. A company might champion collaboration but reward solo wins. In Whorton's case, the belief that growth at scale requires outside capital wasn't written down in some sort of venture capital bible. It didn't need to be. It was simply how things worked—what everyone understood without needing to say aloud. Detert notes that these patterns usually persist without anyone consciously enforcing them. Instead, the rules survive because they've gone unnamed—and when we don't name things, we don't challenge them.

His antidote to deep rules is asking great questions. Why? How can asking great questions challenge stubbornly entrenched beliefs?

OPEN DOORS

"Answers are closed rooms; and questions are open doors that invite us in," explains Nancy Willard, author of *Telling Time: Angels, Ancestors, and Stories.*

Poet, novelist, and Newbery Medalist Nancy Willard wrote with a rare blend of imagination and precision. Her work often blurred the line between the everyday and the enchanted, inviting readers into spaces where mystery was something wonderful to inhabit. This quote captures the very essence of her work: "Questions are passageways to new discoveries."

What Whorton experienced prior to his conversation with Jack Stack was familiarity mistaken for truth.

We all do this. We navigate the world using internal maps, what's worked, what's rewarded, what's assumed and confirmed by people we surround ourselves with. But every map is a reduction. The trouble comes when we forget there's territory beneath it. Asking great questions helps us find new ways. They reorient us. They illuminate the edges of what we presume to be the full picture.

FROM PERSONAL MAPS TO TEAM NAVIGATION

Inside organizations, internal maps shape team dynamics. In any given moment and without clear and honest pronouncement, people could hesitate, resist, clash, protect, or go quiet. How do leaders skilled in facilitation help teams, clients, partners move past these communication impasses? First, they need to understand a simple chart.

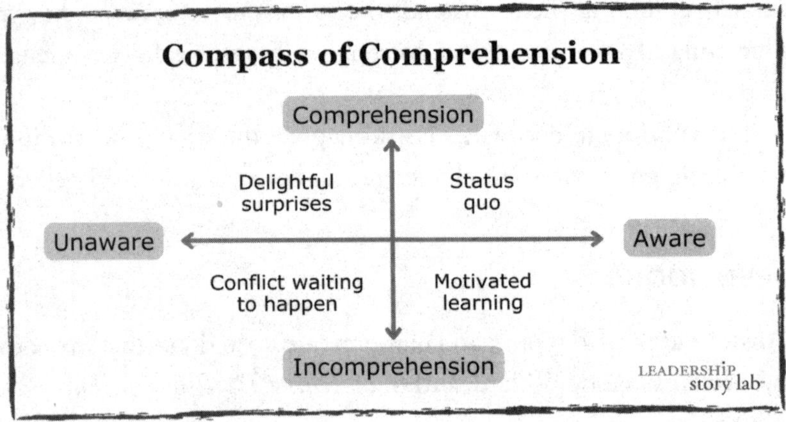

I call this the Compass of Comprehension.

It's a simple 2 x 2 that helps locate where people are relative to their distance to discovery—positive or negative. The horizontal axis represents *awareness*—how tuned in someone is to what's happening. The vertical axis represents *comprehension*—how much or little they grasp their comprehension pertaining to any particular topics.

In the upper right, where both awareness and comprehension are high, you get Status Quo—the zone where things run as expected, but these expectations rarely get questioned. We can easily imagine this: A senior leadership team debriefs a successful product launch. Everyone is clear on what went well, why it worked, and what to do next. No surprises, no questions, just momentum. They see what they assume to be the full picture and know exactly where they stand. They might even pass around kudos for a job well done. But because everything works out, they don't think to ask: What haven't we noticed to even ask questions about?

In the lower right, with high awareness and low comprehension, you find Motivated Learning—where heightened discomfort drives learning forward. Perhaps it could be when a midlevel manager hears that her direct report felt blindsided in a team meeting. She vaguely remembers when that direct report rolled his eyes at that meeting but hadn't understood what caused it. Now she's asking questions, following the thread. Her high awareness of her incomprehension is on alert. With curiosity kicked in, her understanding is catching up.

In the upper left, where comprehension is high, but awareness is low, people land in Delightful Surprises—a positive finding with delayed realization. They already "know" something essential but haven't yet noticed that they do. When it clicks, it can feel both elating and affirming. More than twenty years ago, I had a manager who was chronically unimpressed with my work. He rarely gave praise and seemed perpetually dissatisfied. So imagine my confusion when, one day, he asked out of the blue, "Esther, how are you so good at relationships?" I didn't know how to respond. Good at relationships? Did he mean being kind, proactive, helpful, staying in touch? That felt as simple to me as brushing my teeth. Why compliment someone for doing something that basic? But then I watched him struggle to maintain productive relationships with his boss, his peers, even his direct reports. That's when I realized: What came naturally to me was something he found difficult. His question helped me see a strength I hadn't owned. I was delightfully surprised.

Finally, in the lower left, where both awareness and comprehension are low, you get Conflict Waiting to Happen—misunderstandings and future clashes that remain buried until they boil over. Let's say there are two coworkers who keep misreading each other's emails. One thinks the other is passive-aggressive. The other thinks she's being micromanaged. Neither has named it because neither is entirely sure what's wrong. Both are operating with low awareness and low comprehension. Eventually, something small could ignite something big.

Great questions serve as a compass here. They don't tell people what to think. They help people notice where they are and where they could go next.

To break the deep rules, Detert offers three questions leaders can use to invite candor while keeping personal risk at arm's length. The first question, The Undiscussable—originally from organizational theorist Chris Argyris—is recursive, almost playful. What undiscussables would we discuss if we decided to discuss the undiscussables? It lowers the stakes just enough to let people name what usually stays hidden. The second, Fix the Follies, surfaces mismatches between declared values and actual incentives. For this, Detert suggests a direct prompt: What policies or habits seem to undercut the very things we claim to uphold? And finally, Explore the Veil Fails, which is to explore the experience gap between roles. Here Detert offers: What feels fair from some seats but not from others? And what might we see if we imagined switching places?

These questions, which are reflective in nature, don't magically solve anything. But when facilitated as a self-reflection exercise or group debrief, they gently pry open silences that are no longer productive.

This is what makes Detert's work so helpful when mapping with my Compass of Comprehension. In the Status Quo quadrant, for example, where awareness and comprehension are both high, deep rules often go unchallenged because everything *seems* to be working. And they usually are until they aren't. Success often breeds unexamined habits. It takes a certain kind of question to jostle people out of their comfortable hubris zone.

In the Conflicts Waiting to Happen quadrant, people often sense something is wrong, but they can't articulate it or feel it's not safe to try. Without intervention, the tension smolders. A well-posed question can move that tension into light, where it can be heard, examined, and eventually understood. When leaders pose these kinds of questions and act on what they hear, not only do they create psychological safety; they also create the conditions for transformation. They show that the culture isn't fixed. Rather, it's something everyone can help reauthor.

THE QUESTIONS THAT AWAKEN STORY

Detert's three questions can coax people to say what they couldn't say before. That's one kind of power. But there's another kind—more universal and subtle. These questions dislodge resistance and clear a path for the hidden story to emerge.

Let's think about it. What makes a story take shape? Is it surprise? Struggle? A turn you didn't see coming? Try answering one of these questions:

1. What's something in the first half of this year that you could use more or less of in the second half of the year? Why?
2. What was a mistake you made that turned out for the better?
3. What's one of the best things you've ever done just because you were told, "You can't"?

On the surface, they seem like a random assortment: a wish list, a lesson, a rebellion. But take a close read of the following sample responses to these three questions:

Question 1: What's something in the first half of this year that you could use more or less of in the second half of the year? Why?
"For some unexplainable cosmic reasons, three close friends got into serious car accidents the first months of this year. It pains me to see my loved ones getting hurt. I just wish that these random accidents would go away forever."

"I've been pitching this joint venture idea to senior leadership for months. I'd heard either nothing or excuses. Then all of a sudden something clicked, and they gave the green light and every support I asked for. I guess I should've asked for more. But I can definitely use more good news like this from now on."

Question 2: What was a mistake you made that turned out for the better?

"The early 2000s felt like an all-you-can-eat buffet for us in the housing market. There's so much money to be made, it seemed too good to be true. So I sold my investment properties in 2005. When the market kept going up well into 2006, I started kicking myself. Major FOMO. But then housing prices plateaued in the summer of 2006. Then came Bear Stearns, Lehman Brothers, and the global financial crisis, and housing markets didn't bottom until 2011. I didn't make as much return as I could've, but I also didn't lose my shirt!"

"High school and the first two years in college were awash with parties, drinking, and self-inflicted troubles. I was floundering. My parents intervened to no avail. But eventually, something clicked at the end of sophomore year. I worked and worked to bring my grades up, got extra advanced degrees to eventually be admitted to law school. I wasted a lot of precious time, but the experience really helped me empathize with why clients get in trouble with the law."

Question 3: What's one of the best things you've ever done just because you were told, "You can't"?

"I heard a story about Howard Schultz, the founder of Starbucks, who got more than two hundred rejections for funding when he was trying to bring Italy's coffee culture to America. So when I founded my first two ventures, I knew I had to brace for noes—lots and lots of them. I persisted. Had I withered I wouldn't have sold my first company, afforded the kind of lifestyle I have now, and (be stupid enough) to start another company."

"From the get-go, we knew a Muslim–Hindu relationship sounded like a train wreck destined to happen. And sure enough, we're both cut off by our families. Luckily for everyone, when the grandchildren came along, our families' minds and hearts were changed. If my spouse and I could tough this out, what else couldn't we weather together?"

These stories didn't come from prompts like "Tell us your leadership style," "What's your entrepreneurial journey?" or "What's the biggest business lesson you've learned?" The people sharing them were simply responding to well-crafted, story-inviting questions. In my experience, when someone's asked, "Tell us your story," the most common reaction is a wide-eyed look of panic, followed by something vague or overly polished. But when the right kind of question is asked, something softens. People temporarily forget to impress. They speak plainly and instinctively like they're talking to a close friend.

Last but not least, these three questions make it easy for people to step into their experience because they have something else in common. Over the years, I've come to see what underpins almost every genuine story. Three ingredients, again and again: conflict, contrast, and contradiction.

CONFLICT

It doesn't need to be epic. No car crash, no Chapter 11 bankruptcy filing. Conflict simply means that something gets in the way. One force moves in one direction, another pushes back. That's it. A desire meets an obstacle. A plan hits a snag. A smooth path turns bumpy.

Maybe you meant to get to your alma mater an hour early to appear as a guest lecturer—but summer traffic had other plans. Maybe you finally hired the right candidate, but HR dragged out the approval for three extra weeks. These aren't tragedies. But they're important building blocks of stories. Why? Because when conflict becomes obvious, tension enters the picture. The way forward isn't frictionless anymore, and what happens next suddenly matters.

CONTRAST

At its simplest, contrast is the clash of difference: light against dark, profitability against growth, long-term ownership against short-term exit. It's the juxtaposition of qualities that heighten each other by being set side by side. In story, contrast doesn't always drive the plot, but it shapes the setting. It reveals the stakes without ever needing to explain them. Old versus new. Ambition versus comfort. Divestment versus investment. In-person versus virtual. Consolidation versus diffusion. Contrast helps listeners see what might otherwise go unnoticed because it frames what is at stake. This, not that; then, not now. What once worked no longer does.

If conflict moves the story, contrast frames it. It gives the narrative dimension.

CONTRADICTION

Contradiction is the story's sharpest turn. It plays with what your audience thinks they know and then flips the script. While contrast puts two opposing ideas side by side, contradiction collapses them into a single instance. It's the unexpected yes inside a no. The leap of faith from someone known for caution. The celebrated leader who secretly doubts her own strength.

Contradiction often lives in tension between the inner and outer self: between what we believe and what we do, what we long for and what we fear, who we are and who we're expected to be. These are the messier collisions, the ones that rattle something within. When a story holds contradiction well, it doesn't aim to resolve the tension, at least not right away. Instead, it lets opposing truths breathe in the same sentence and paragraphs, showing us something we hadn't thought could coexist.

You don't need all three at once. But at least one of them is almost always there, animating the arc. They are the pulse of narrative tension—the heartbeat that lets a story come to life.

HOW DO WE DISCOVER WHAT WE DON'T KNOW, BUT SHOULD?

Nobel laureate and behavior economist Richard Thaler once said, "If you want to get somebody to do something, make it easy."[4] To that I'd add, if you want people to tell you their story, make it easy. How?

Start with a Crazy Good Question.

The questions I shared earlier weren't lucky guesses. They're examples of what I call Crazy Good Questions—queries designed to reveal rich, real, and story-based responses. What makes them powerful isn't just their emotional resonance but their underlying structure.

Each one contains at least one of the three narrative CCCs: conflict, contrast, or contradiction. But that's not all. Beneath the surface, these questions also excavate recognizable patterns, templates that can be learned, adapted, and applied. In fact, all Crazy Good Questions can be sorted into ten distinct types. These are not formulas. They're prompts that echo the patterns of how people make meaning—and how stories unfold.

Take the question "What's something from the first half of this year you could use more or less of in the second? And why?" On the surface, it sounds casual, almost like a conversation starter. But embedded in it are deeper narrative triggers. It nudges people to reflect on what they've lived through, to weigh the events in their year, and to consider a possible lesson or redirection. All in one breath, it invites memory, evaluation, and intention.

Or consider, "What was a mistake you made that turned out for the better?" That's a classic surprise question. It coaxes out stories with a twist—moments in time when a failure turned redemptive. Listeners perk up because it suggests a before and after, a turn they didn't see coming but now wouldn't trade.

And then there's this one: "What's one of the best things you've ever done just because you were told, 'You can't'?" On its face, it's about defiance. But dig deeper and you'll find more, much more. It draws from the self—a question about identity forged under opposition. It traces a different path, hinting at risk seeking or rule breaking. And it brushes against the superlative but in a high-stakes story that people tell not to brag but because it molded them.

How many different types are there exactly? And what are they good for?

THE TEN TYPES OF CRAZY GOOD QUESTIONS

What follows is a field guide, not rigid scripts with any particular order. These ten types can be adapted, sequenced in any number of ways, or combined. Use them to spark dialogue, to listen differently, and to mine stories that otherwise stay buried.

1. THE ORIGIN

Opens with a beginning

These questions bring us to thresholds: first venture, first love, first failure, first job. Any origin is a milestone on life's journey, and it marks a time when something started, even if we didn't realize it then.

Example: "When did you realize you were the one in charge?" or "How did we get here?"

2. THE WHY

Invites reflection and sense making

"Why" questions give people space to rewalk their path and search for meaning. They're not always answered directly—and that's okay. The story emerges in the circling.

Example: "Why did you choose to stay when new management made life so difficult for you?" or "What was the single best investment (could be financial, educational, personal, and so on) you have ever made? How has this investment paid off?"[5]

3. SURPRISE

Surfaces twists, turns, and unintended outcomes

These questions unlock reversals—mistakes that turned into wins and vice versa, plans that unraveled into better plans. They offer a backstage view into how life actually happens.

Example: "What is one thing that people seem to know about your job but in fact is not true?" or "What has surprised you most as you became your own boss?"

4. COMPARE AND CONTRAST

Reveals evolution

By inviting two snapshots in time or two competing values, this type creates a built-in arc. People naturally narrate what changed or what held steady.

Example: "What's one way your work feels different now than it did a year ago?" or recall in chapter 5 where I talk about the illusion of explanatory depth: "What is the difference between proving versus persuading?"

5. TELL ME MORE

Invites depth through curiosity

This type is about leaning in. You've just heard something that piques your interest—maybe it's surprising, maybe it's glossed over too quickly, maybe it doesn't quite add up. By asking to hear more, you're signaling that the person's experience is worth exploring.

Example: "You mentioned that your move changed everything—what do you mean by that?" or "Tell me more about why in this case leaving money at the table is a good idea."

6. SEEK THE MEANING

Gently probes for significance

Where type 5 is about depth, type 6 is about interpretation. These questions ask: What did that mean to you? What did you take from it? You're not asking for an epiphany—you're prompting a reflection that might never have been voiced.

Example: "All those awards—what did they mean to you?" or during a quarterly sales meeting, "What do you make of the latest numbers in the last two quarters?"

7. GREATEST

Elevates defining moments

A touch risky, this type asks for superlatives: biggest risk, proudest moment, hardest goodbye. People don't always answer definitively, but in reaching for their "greatest," they share something deeply revealing.

Example: "What's one of the toughest decisions you've ever made?" or "What's something you're very proud of in your career but haven't listed in your résumé or shared in your LinkedIn profile or company bio? Why not?"

8. A DIFFERENT PATH

Explores divergence and reinvention

These questions light up the roads not taken—or the ones people built themselves. You'll often hear stories of course correction, reinvention, or defiance.

Example: Simply ask, "What is one path you didn't take? Why not?" or "What's a decision you made that others resisted at the time?"

9. TAKEAWAY

Names the lesson

Sometimes the reflection comes last; sometimes it's baked in. These questions help people make sense of what an experience gave them—even if it came wrapped in failure.

Example: "What's something you learned the hard way?" or "During the period of leadership transition, what does the current generation of family business leaders want to pass on to the rising generation?"

10. THE SELF

Taps into identity

These are the mirror questions. They pull forward the stories that people use to make sense of who they are—often in moments of testing, contradiction, or becoming.

Example: "When did you realize you were no longer who you used to be?" or "What are the absolute favorite parts of your job? What do they tell us about who you are?"

This is the power of asking Crazy Good Questions: They keep us immersed, listening, discovering. They help leaders resist the lure of certainty and, instead, dwell in the fertile ground of not-knowing—a place where assumptions can loosen, hidden barriers can surface, and new possibilities can take root. Curiosity, after all, is a form of cognitive humility.

But questions alone won't carry the work forward. Eventually, someone has to speak and connect the dots. After making discoveries, leaders need to offer language that helps others make sense of what they've just unearthed. That's why, in the next two chapters, we'll pivot into the main craft of storytelling. While guiding others to speak is essential, so is learning when and how to speak yourself. After all, leaders are the sage on the stage. But not merely to perform. Instead, they lead the charge to cohere, model, and make sure that what's been discovered doesn't drift away.

Chapter 9

WINNING WITH STORY REFINING

How to Strategically Sequence Facts and Emotions, and Win

Since the beginning of my career teaching storytelling, I have had a secret sauce: Find a good room and fill it with bright, ambitious, interesting people. Once they arrive, I'd offer a structured creative process, pose a few questions, and—voilà—stories would bloom like wildflowers after a spring rain. And often, stories did emerge. When leaders opened up and searched hard enough, strategies transformed into scenes, former I-can't-tell-stories executives turned into spellbinding narrators.

But sometimes there are exceptions.

At one of my early trainings in the fall of 2011 with around twenty-five participants, I had what should have been a dream mix of volunteers to workshop their still-forming stories: two entrepreneurs, one board member, and one soon-to-be CFO. In the room, tall windows let in the setting sun. It felt like the kind of setting where the magic would just happen. If only.

After I explained the process, one of the entrepreneurs stood to speak. He launched into a detailed description of his product. He covered its features, the user interface, and the addressable market. He even remembered to cover the benefits of his product. His delivery was confident and clear. But something was missing.

Where was the story?

I kept waiting, for an unexpected tension, maybe a twist in plot, a shift in perspective. Nothing. Before I could find anything to hold on to, he was done with his "story." Twenty-four other participants offered polite clapping. He remained standing, looking at me for feedback. And I had nothing. I didn't even know where to begin because I wasn't sure what I had just heard. He had clearly worked hard on it. But it wasn't a story. That was the problem.

Back then, I hadn't yet realized that "story" meant different things to different people.

To some, it meant news—like "breaking story at six." To others, it was an investigation—"What's the story?" when someone's late or upset. In the start-up world, "Tell me your story" is really code for "Convince me to invest." But what I was looking for in that 2011 workshop—and what I have built an entire career on—was something else entirely. Not just information, logic, clarity, persuasion. Yes, those four qualities are important. But I was looking for one of the most important building blocks of story: transformation.

That moment—standing in front of a participant who had just delivered what he believed to be a story—forced me to confront something I hadn't fully thought through yet: We don't all mean the same thing when we say "story."

So what do *I* mean when I say "story"?

At its core, a story is a temporal chain of causally—not casually—related events. Something happens, and because that happens, something else happens. The people in the story aren't just narrators. They experience or provoke change even though they might not have intended to. And if there's no change, there's no story. Just a timeline. That's one of the most critical distinctions between storytelling and situation reporting. Stories don't just recount. They reveal. They carry meaning and reveal transformation.

This is why I often remind my clients: Recounting events is not telling a story.

You can list every analytical step in your investment modeling. You can highlight your performance records and still leave the audience wondering who you are at your core and whether you can be depended on when it counts the most. But when you describe what changed in you—how a challenge bent your thinking or what it cost you to stand behind your decision—then the room listens differently. Then you're telling a story.

In leadership storytelling, character matters more than credentials and competence combined because with a few clicks and a Wi-Fi connection, people can find your title and career track record. What's rare is access to your internal world—your values, personality, doubts, your moments of reckoning. The best leadership stories are not polished highlight reels. They are carefully chosen glimpses of character, anchored by credential and animated by competence. If character plays the lead role in a movie, credential and competence are the supporting cast. Unfortunately, most people flip it around. Often, they don't even have a lead role at all.

This is the craft: Leadership storytelling is the strategic sequencing of fact and emotion. It's an intentional arrangement—not just of events, data, facts but of emotional beats. There's a point of view, a framing, a breakthrough message, sometimes telegraphed and sometimes simply implied. But this is always the case: If *challenge* is the backbone of story, then *change* is the soul of it.

This chapter explores the architecture of story—how structure gives shape to meaning, and how the right framework can help leaders connect more deeply with their audiences. You've probably encountered many frameworks, but few that do as much with as little. With just three parts, the IRS model offers more than a storytelling scaffold. It provides a way to organize thought, sharpen message, and guide people through complexity. Simple enough to remember yet flexible enough to adapt, IRS gives leaders a practical method for crafting stories that spark curiosity and stay with people long after the meeting ends.

IRS

In 2010, I launched my company, Leadership Story Lab. I told anyone who'd listen that I teach classical storytelling elements to modern leaders. That line usually earned me a polite smile, a blank stare, and eventually, a hesitant question: *Wait—what do you do again?*

Fast-forward to 2025. These days, I say I coach executives to become more persuasive through the use of story. This time, I get nods of recognition. Sparkles of enthusiasm. "Oh, that's wonderful," someone will say. "Have you heard of the hero's journey?"

That enthusiasm—"Have you heard of the hero's journey?"—comes up a lot. It's often the first framework people reach for when they hear the word "story." And for good reason.

Joseph Campbell, the American scholar who popularized the hero's journey, spent his life studying myths across cultures. In his 1949 book, *The Hero with a Thousand Faces*, he proposed that underneath every great myth is the same basic arc: A protagonist leaves the familiar world, faces trials, gains wisdom or power, and returns home transformed. It's a sweeping narrative of departure, ordeal, and return—a universal storyline that Campbell called the *monomyth*.

The model has had enormous cultural reach. George Lucas used it to shape *Star Wars*. Many contemporary advertisers, writers, and therapists still lean on it as a template for understanding and communicating growth and transformation. It's elegant, epic, universal, and ubiquitous. But for most leaders, especially those trying to tell a three-minute story at the top of a meeting, the twelve-step journey of monomyth is also overwhelming.

My friend and collaborator Anthony Do knows this tension firsthand. You met him in chapter 6—he's the filmmaker who spent six months in Iceland capturing the daily workout routine of Hafþór Júlíus Björnsson, better known as the "Mountain" from *Game of Thrones*, for Hafþór's YouTube channel. Anthony has also trained with me on story facilitation. He's a deep, deliberate student of story and a longtime admirer of Campbell's work. He's studied the hero's journey in all its intricacy—twelve, sometimes seventeen distinct stages.

"I have a deep understanding of the hero's journey and the intricacies of that framework by Campbell. But for most people, storytelling is overwhelming," he once told me. "The genius here is how simple the IRS framework is. It condenses a whole universe of ideas and knowledge down to this three-letter acronym."

What is IRS? Cue the drumroll . . .

IRS—THE ONLY STORYTELLING MODEL YOU'LL EVER NEED

And no, it's not the Internal Revenue Service. Instead, it stands for:

- **I**—Intriguing Beginning
- **R**—Riveting Middle
- **S**—Satisfying End

Simple enough to remember. Powerful enough to build entire careers on.

I = INTRIGUING BEGINNING.

Why the beginning? Why not intriguing *middle* or intriguing *end*?

It's a fair question—and one that came up when I presented the IRS model to a group of more than sixty CEOs. The answer is attention. It peaks early. In those first few seconds—of a meeting, a Zoom call, a presentation, or a story—your audience decides: *Is this worth listening to?*

That's why the beginning matters most. Because if you don't hook people at the start, you might never get the chance to take them anywhere meaningful. Too often, we squander that opportunity. We open with greetings, logistics, a long-winded credential dump. It's not that any of those things are wrong, but they're just misplaced. When we lead with them, we unintentionally signal: You don't really have to pay attention yet.

But the beginning of any story is your best chance to earn the right to tell your stories. It's your chance to grab attention without shouting. To invite curiosity without forcing it. Pixar Animation Studio's Andrew Stanton—writer and director of *Finding Nemo*, *WALL-E*, and cowriter of the *Toy Story* series—put it this way in his 2012 TED Talk: "The audience actually wants to work for their meal; they just don't want to know that they're doing that." Stanton understood that people are natural problem solvers. They want to connect the dots. But only if it feels like part of the journey—not a trick or a test.

I saw this principle come to life in a course I taught for a group of executive MBA students from Thailand's Sasin School of Management. One of the scenarios I asked them to work with was this:

> *A recent major corporate change has been met with enthusiasm by your immediate team and cross-functional colleagues. But as the harsh reality of the change sets in, energy and motivation begin to wane. What story will you tell to reengage them?*

One student, Tian Srisuwan, stood up and began like this:

> When I was young, I grew up relatively poor. Not the poorest—we had food and a house—but still. We were all crammed in one room. Imagine that: four kids, two parents, one room. I didn't even have a bed—just a blanket. I remember doing my

homework by candlelight to save on electricity. Yet we had a car. A Jaguar. A 1994 Jaguar Xj8.

At that moment, every head in the room turned. You could feel the intrigue. We weren't sure where he was going—but we were going with him. That's the power of an Intriguing Beginning. It doesn't lay everything out. It pulls us in. Remember conflict, contrast, and contradiction from chapter 7? Back then, I talked about them as essential ingredients for helping others tell stories, how they can open a space for meaning to take forms. But in addition to an effective listening tool, it's also central to crafting your own stories, especially at the beginning. When used thoughtfully, conflict, contrast, and contradiction are powerful ways to turbocharge that pull when your audiences don't even know what has drawn them. They just feel that they have to find out more.

But there's another layer that helps: time and place.

When combined, you can set the scene effortlessly with time and place. "Time" isn't just clock time or calendar time. It can be a symbolic moment: storm season, sunset path, the crossroads. "Place" could be a physical location, a building, a region, but it doesn't have to be about geography. Like time, space can be symbolic. It can be about the stage (of career progression), at a crossroad (of a major decision), or a maze (of corporate politics). The point isn't to get poetic. On the contrary, it actually allows you to get grounded in a specific scene so that the listeners can picture it in their minds and feel it in their hearts.

You don't need to overexplain. A simple gesture can go a long way. Here's one of my favorite examples.

Ahmed Alfadhel, a corporate strategist, was a participant in one of my story facilitation programs. After I led his group through a signature exercise, I asked everyone to rework their own introduction. The following week, here's what Ahmed came up with.

> I stood in front of my wardrobe on my first day at the company, staring at two options: my traditional *thoob* or a sharp Western suit. But the real question wasn't about clothes. It was: How should I show up? As the tough outsider who commands respect—or as my real self, someone who believes in facilitation over authority?

He didn't start with his title, and he definitely didn't start with a summary. He began with a specific time in his life and at a specific location, where he was facing a choice, which symbolized something much deeper than what to wear to work. The tension, or the early glimpse of it, is transported through a visual: two sets of clothes. And we were all in.

R = RIVETING MIDDLE

"Why don't people just try a little harder and pay more attention?" I hear this complaint frequently from clients. I can empathize; attention is hard to come by. With so many distractions at our fingertips, even the most focused among us struggle to stay present. But part of the problem isn't just modern life. It's the way we were taught.

Our education system trained us to value clarity above all. Whether it was a term paper, a class presentation—even math homework—we were rewarded for being straightforward. In fact, we were often told to *show our work* in math exams. Even if we get the answer wrong, as long as our steps were clear enough, we'd still earn partial credit. And that training followed us into our careers.

At work, we're expected to communicate clearly. That expectation is rarely questioned. But maybe it should be. Because clarity doesn't always capture attention. Quite the opposite.

Think about the last time you sat through a presentation and felt like you already knew what was coming. Did you lean in? Probably not. When we think we know, we stop listening. And if everyone is relentlessly clear, all the time, what's left to discover?

This is where curiosity comes in.

As Andrew Stanton reminded us, the audience wants to *work* for their meal. They just don't want to *know* they're working. If you can create suspense and surprise, your audience will lean forward. They'll do the heavy lifting for you, and not because they have to—but because they *want* to. Isn't it wonderful?

Throughout this book, I've returned to the idea that curiosity is a leadership mindset. If you've made it this far, you probably already believe in it. But not everyone around you does. Your colleagues may not even want to be curious. So what can you do?

That's where *suspense* and *surprise* come in. As I described in chapter 8:

> If surprise is about the reveal, then suspense is about the wait. Surprise jolts us. Suspense holds us. Surprise disrupts assumptions—we thought we knew, but we didn't. Suspense stretches attention—we don't yet know, but we want to. In stories, surprise is an unmistakable wake-up call, while suspense is what makes you lean forward and forget the relevance of time because you're just on the edge of understanding.

A great story doesn't just keep the audience informed. It keeps them *engaged.* The most Riveting Middles offer just enough clarity to feel anchored—and just enough mystery to keep us guessing.

But curiosity alone isn't enough. It can't sustain itself forever. Suspense that never pays off becomes frustration. That's why I often tell leaders to imagine curiosity and clarity sitting on opposite ends of a seesaw. A good storyteller knows how to keep that seesaw in motion. If one side is too heavy, the seesaw stalls. Too much clarity? The story loses tension. Too much mystery? The story floats away. But when you alternate—just enough reveal, just enough wait—the story roars forward.

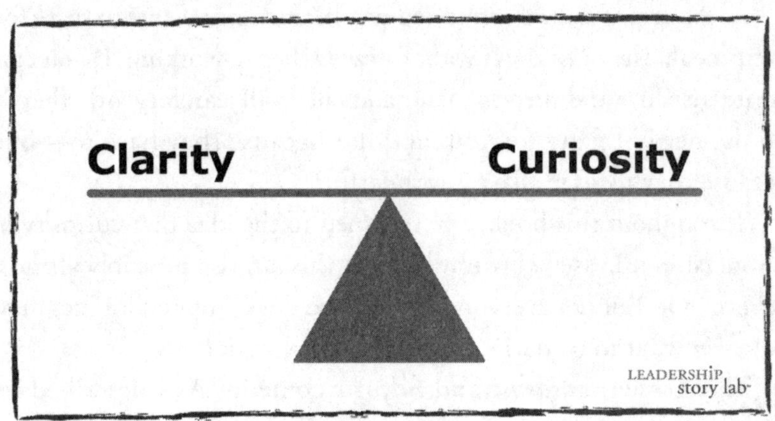

Let's return to two voices you met earlier: Tian and Ahmed.

Remember how Tian, an executive MBA student from Thailand, began his story by recalling his childhood: Four kids. Two parents. One room. No bed. Just a blanket. Candles for homework. But a Jaguar in the driveway.

That was a very Intriguing Beginning. Now here's his Riveting Middle. Remember the scenario Tian was building this story for? A major corporate campaign that garnered much excitement initially but petered out when obstacle after obstacle left teams feeling defeated. His story is meant to galvanize them again.

> Now, I know we just launched a new product. It had a good run! Last week, someone just entrusted $100,000 with us. It went amazing until three days ago. Our key partner collapsed—and our customers disappeared with them. I know it's hard.
>
> But do you know why we had a Jaguar?
>
> In 1998, during the Asian financial crisis, my father's logistics company was on the verge of collapse. In a last-ditch effort, he used the company's remaining cash to buy that Jaguar. Then he went door to door, showing up in that car to prove the business was alive and trustworthy.

It wasn't enough. He worked day and night. At one point, he got down on his knees to beg for a contract. I didn't see him for a year. But the company survived. And we thrived.

Then there's Ahmed.

You heard his opening earlier—standing in front of his wardrobe, choosing between a *thoob* and a Western suit, wondering not what to wear but how to show up. Here's what followed.

I chose to be myself. I greeted the team warmly, asked questions instead of giving orders, and tried to create space for their voices. I believed they'd appreciate being heard and involved.

But as weeks passed, the smiles faded. People stopped greeting me. My line manager pulled me aside: "You need to be more decisive. You're too soft." Then came the team feedback: "You always ask us what we think. We'd rather you just tell us what to do."

I was stunned. I felt betrayed. I had trusted them with respect and freedom, but they didn't seem to want it. I considered resigning. Clearly, I had failed. Maybe they were right. Maybe I wasn't leadership material.

Then something changed. A new boss came in, and slowly, the team began to change. Two left. I hired new people. Then the third left. I replaced her too. The new team? They didn't just accept my facilitative style—they *thrived* in it.

My new boss praised my leadership. My values, which once seemed like weaknesses, now aligned with the vision of the company.

That's what a Riveting Middle can do. It doesn't lecture. It reveals and builds, breaks and redeems. And most importantly—it carries tension because tension is what gets you attention. Behind it all, conflict, contrast, and contradiction drive your story forward and keep your audience engaged. We talked about how CCC applies in the Intriguing Beginning. It is just as important in the Riveting Middle too.

Look at Tian's Jaguar story again.

The *conflict* is personal and financial: a father on the brink of losing his business, making an illogical choice with the last of his funds. The *contrast* lives in the image: no bed but a luxury car. That tension—poverty wrapped in the appearance of prosperity—is what keeps us curious. And the *contradiction* is what makes the story feel human. His father's strategy seems desperate, almost foolish. But in the end, it works. And that uneasy logic—that strange, high-stakes bet—lands with emotional resonance.

Now think of Ahmed.

The *conflict* is subtle but sharp: his values versus the team's expectations. The *contrast* shows up in tone and outcome: A warm, collaborative leader perceived as too soft. A team that says it wants independence but craves command. And the *contradiction*? It's Ahmed himself. He doubts his leadership, nearly walks away—only to become the leader his company needs *without changing who he is.*

That's what CCC looks like in motion, not just a technique to create a hook at the start of a story but a core engine for holding attention throughout. And a Riveting Middle is more than the sum of suspense and surprise. It's about truths that rub against each other—and refuse to resolve too quickly.

S = SATISFYING END

Humans need closure.

Closure can take many forms. Sometimes it's clarity; sometimes it's a perspective-shifting question. We don't always need answers—but we do need *something* to hold on to. A signal that the journey has meant something. That we've arrived somewhere.

In leadership storytelling, the ending doesn't have to be tidy or triumphant. It just needs to feel *earned*. Take Tian's story. He was responding to a challenge posed in an executive education course I taught: What story will you tell your team when their initial excitement for a major corporate change begins to fade?

He began with tension: the surprising detail that his childhood home had no beds—but did have a Jaguar. That contrast piqued curiosity. In the middle, he revealed the contradiction at the heart of it: During the 1998 financial crisis, his father used the last of the company's money to buy that luxury car. It was a bold and risky move—a way to project confidence to clients when failure seemed imminent. And it worked. But not without pain and persistence.

Then came his close:

> And that's what I will do. I will fight. I will hustle. If need be, I will beg and get down on my knees. I will do everything I can in my power to overcome this challenge. I will buy the Jaguar. But I can't do this without you guys. So, please, walk with me.

Far from a summary or conclusion, his ending was a rallying cry that connected past and present, personal and collective. His was a story that moved from spectacle to solidarity.

That's what a Satisfying Ending does. It offers a pause that resonates, a sense of movement or realization. Sometimes that's a clear takeaway. Sometimes it's the reaffirmation of a shared belief. Often, what makes an ending satisfying is its emotional weight. We feel that something real has happened. That the story mattered. We are grateful to have listened to it. And maybe, because of that, we listen a little differently going forward.

Consider Ahmed's story as well.

He opened with a dilemma—two outfits on his first day of work, each representing a different leadership identity. In the middle, he chose authenticity and faced rejection for it. His team resisted his facilitative style. Feedback stung as doubts began to creep in. But instead of retreating or rebranding himself, he stayed the course. Slowly, the system around him shifted. And when it did, he was ready.

His story ended here:

What I learned is this: Being authentic is not always easy, but it's worth it. Just because your style doesn't fit right away doesn't mean it never will. Sometimes you're not in the wrong place—you're just ahead of the change. Even if you stand alone, don't lose heart. The tide can turn.

Satisfying? Yes. But how?

Because Ahmed honors the setback his authenticity had cost him. Instead of glossing over his disappointment and sense of betrayal, he leveraged that tension to earn our attention. And because the ending lands on something both true and transferable, we walk away feeling, well, satisfied.

THE LOGISTICS OF IRS

Knowing what the letters stand for—Intriguing Beginning, Riveting Middle, Satisfying End—is a good start. But structure alone doesn't guarantee impact. How you *build* each part matters just as much as knowing they exist. There are three key logistics to keep in mind when crafting stories using the IRS model:

1. **Proportion**—How much time or space each section should take
2. **Nested structure**—The concept of *mini-IRS* throughout I, R, and S
3. **Telling versus crafting**—Sequence matters.

1. LET'S START WITH PROPORTION.

There are three parts to a story: the I, the R, and the S. But that doesn't mean they each get a third of the space. In fact, their proportion looks more like this:

- I = 10 percent
- R = 70 percent

- S = 20 percent

Why so lopsided? If the beginning is so important, why only 10 percent?

Because attention is usually at its peak right at the start. That's your best chance to earn the right to tell the rest of the story. If you wait too long to hook your audience—if you stall in setup, credentials, background—your audience will drift. And once they've mentally checked out, it's hard to bring them back.

That's why the beginning, though crucial, should be brief. Sharp and intentional. You only need a few lines to earn their attention.

The middle, by contrast, is where the story breathes. It's the part that does the heavy lifting—where conflict, character, tension, and transformation unfold. Naturally, it takes up the biggest share: roughly 70 percent.

Then there's the ending—not a fade-out or wrap-up but a landing that makes the story mean something. Not as long as the middle, but not an afterthought either. That's your final 20 percent. This proportion isn't rigid, but it's a helpful guide.

Think about most talks, panels, or presentations you've sat through. What do they often have? A middle. And only a middle. There's no real beginning, no compelling end. Just content on content until time runs out and someone thanks the audience. That's when people walk out muttering, "Well, that was another hour I'm not getting back." But when you begin with intrigue—even briefly—you earn attention. When you build a middle that's riveting, you hold it. And when you close with purpose, you leave something memorable behind.

A story that respects proportion respects the listener's time—and deepens their trust.

2. MINI-IRS: NESTED STORIES WITHIN THE STORY

IRS gives you structure. But it's not a cage. Think of it more like scaffolding—or, better yet, like a set of Russian nesting dolls. Just when you think you've reached the center, you discover another shape inside. And another.

The same goes for story structure. Within a single presentation, anecdote, or leadership message, you can nest multiple mini-IRS arcs. Intrigue doesn't just belong at the top. Resolution doesn't only live at the end. Why is this important? Because real-world storytelling is rarely linear, especially in leadership settings. You're balancing expectations, formats, time limits, and sometimes, industry norms that feel allergic to storytelling altogether.

Take my clients in management consulting. Many are required to begin every client presentation with an executive summary. It's nonnegotiable. Clarity is the mandate.

So, should they toss IRS out the window? Of course not.

Instead, I encourage them to nest it. Plant a small spark of intrigue before, within, or just after the summary. Sometimes, that spark is a breadcrumb: "If you had asked me during our last update whether these developments were even possible, I'd have said no. And yet—here we are." Sometimes, it's a question that attaches to an intentional pause that lasts just long enough to earn the next slide: "What if the solution your competitor is chasing turns out to be your smallest risk?"

It's brief. But it creates forward motion. And that's what intrigue is really about: momentum.

You can also nest mini-IRS arcs inside the middle of your story—especially when it contains multiple scenes or episodes. Think of the middle not as a single chapter but a collection of turning points. Each one can have its own arc. And, ideally, each one builds toward the next.

Even the end can contain a flicker of beginning.

Think of a great TV show or streaming drama. Why do we end up watching yet another episode even when it's midnight and we swore we'd only watch one? Because just before the credits roll, a new question drops. Yet another twist, hint, and a reason to stay.

My negotiation professor at Kellogg, Vicki Medvec, understood this deeply. At the end of each class segment, just before break, she'd dangle an idea related to the topic coming up next. Something only the punctual would hear in full. Students would scatter toward coffee or bathrooms, but they'd return fast. Because they wanted to know what that next part was about. In addition to teaching negotiation, she was demonstrating the power of strategic sequencing of facts and emotion.

That's what mini-IRS lets you do. It gives you permission to be nimble, to be creative, and to play. IRS is a guide, not a handcuff. Use it to frame your story—but don't be afraid to flex it. Nest, layer, and sequence the elements to fit your context. Even when external rules constrain you, you can still follow protocol—and deepen your impact.

3. REVERSE ORDER: SKIP TO THE END

Once I've taught the IRS framework—Intriguing Beginning, Riveting Middle, Satisfying End—I don't just send participants off to try it on their own. I guide them through it, one piece at a time, to make sure each element gets the attention it deserves.

We start with the beginning, of course. After all, intrigue is the first hurdle. But then comes a moment I love. Once we've shaped and refined the I, I turn to the group and ask a simple, almost rhetorical question: "Now that we're done working on the Intriguing Beginning, the only logical next part for us to tackle would be . . . ?"

I let my voice trail off. And 100 percent of the time, the room chimes in confidently, "The Riveting Middle!" And then I say, "Satisfying End."

Cue the momentary confusion. A few furrowed brows. Wait—what?

Of course we start with the end. Because if we don't know where we're headed, how do we know what kind of story we're telling?

When I ask why we'd write the ending before the middle, someone inevitably offers the right insight: "We need to know where we want to land—what we want people to take away." Exactly. Imagine playing basketball without hoops or soccer without goals. What are we even playing? Not much—just a lot of running and shouting, throwing and kicking things around.

But once we have the beginning and the end—once we've framed our purpose and sketched our landing—we know what kind of journey the middle should take. How long it should be. What to include. What to let go. It doesn't just make the writing easier. It makes the story *work*.

So when you sit down to write your own IRS-based story, remember: The most efficient path might not be linear. Once your beginning is sharp and clear, leap ahead. Draft the end. Only then will the middle reveal itself.

So there it is. IRS.

Three simple letters that do a deceptively complex job: helping you craft stories that engage, hold, and land. Stories move people to care, to change, to act. You've seen how this works: an Intriguing Beginning earns attention. A Riveting Middle holds it. And a Satisfying End delivers meaning. You've learned that proportion matters, that stories nest, and that sometimes the best way to build the middle is to skip it—temporarily—and aim for the end.

But this isn't the end.

Because structure alone isn't enough. Even the best-structured story falls flat if it lacks resonance. What makes a story stick—what makes it feel true—is its emotional underpinning. The shape of the feeling that moves through it. That's where we go next.

In the final chapter, you'll see what happens when leaders put it all together—everything this book has explored: the facilitative mindset, the craft of questioning, the power of tension, and emotion. You'll meet leaders I had the privilege to coach as they stood before a crowd to tell a story that was personal, strategic, and unforgettable.

You'll also meet a Nobel Prize–winning economist, illuminating how stories have led to market crash as well as innovations. We will also take a closer look at one of the most misunderstood forces in storytelling: emotion.

Chapter 10

WINNING WITH LEADERSHIP STORYTELLING

How Curiosity and Story Discovery Create the Conditions for Transformation

The chef-recommended, three-course dinner had been served. The birthday song had been sung, and the Black Forest cake had been eaten. Eleven of us were gathering our belongings, ready to call it a night, when the twelfth guest finally arrived. She slipped in looking tentative and apologetic. Even with summer traffic on a Friday afternoon in downtown Chicago, it shouldn't take two hours to make it to dinner. Did something bad happen?

It was late May 2023, and the occasion was my birthday dinner when I got the news. My dear friend and longtime collaborator, consumer anthropologist Gina Fong, stepped into the private dining room just as my guests and I were saying our goodbyes.

"I'm so sorry I'm late," she said, "but I had a good reason."

Barely in her first year as a clinical assistant professor of marketing at the Kellogg School of Management, Gina had just been voted by its MBA students as Professor of the Year—beating out five other beloved faculty who had either won the honor multiple times or had been nominated year after year. She had been swept up in the surprise ceremony, and one thing led to another until she'd missed nearly my entire birthday party.

"Esther, I couldn't have done this without you," she said, wrapping me in a bear hug. "This award is ours."

Gina's career spans more than twenty-five years in direct consumer research, helping companies design and deliver exceptional product experiences. Like many who train with me, she was already a natural storyteller. But she wanted to articulate what she did intuitively so she could apply storytelling to her research, curriculum design, and teaching itself. For example, she designed her ten-week course around IRS: week one heavy on intrigue; the middle seven weeks filled with riveting learning experiences; the final two weeks trending toward a Satisfying End. Each week, her class is packed with story after story, each following the IRS structure. Her teaching evaluations glowed with comments about how her storytelling pulled students in, made theories concrete and accessible. This award felt entirely deserved.

With this honor, however, came an unexpected challenge. As the recipient of Kellogg's highest teaching award, she would have to deliver the faculty address at the upcoming convocation. Here are the parameters: no more than five minutes, an audience of six thousand, and less than three weeks to prepare. So we got to work.

Before going directly to Gina's speech, it's worth pausing and examining three elements that made her speech a master class in storytelling. These three elements run beneath the IRS framework: scene, summary, and reflection.

SCENE. SUMMARY. REFLECTION.

If the IRS framework is the structure of a great story—how it engages, holds, and lands—then scene, summary, and reflection are the narrative tools that bring it to life. Like color, light, and shadow in a painting, each serves a distinct purpose. Layered onto IRS, they elevate your storytelling from functional to unforgettable.

Scene is where storytelling starts to feel alive. A scene is not a concept—it's a picture. A moment you can see with your mind's eye. It's short on telling and long on showing. It invites your audience not to analyze but to experience. When you set up a good scene, you're pulling people into a specific time, at a specific place, with specific people. You're activating their imagination and emotions, not just their cognition.

Most strong scenes include some combination of the following elements. *Dialogue*, for starters, words exchanged in real time, like the moment in chapter 9 when I asked, "Does it hurt?" and my acquaintances asked in unison, "You've never had Botox?" Then there's *sensory detail*: what someone saw, heard, smelled, tasted, or touched. A whirring fan, lukewarm coffee, the arctic air blasting in a hotel meeting room during a summer conference. Next, *a distinct location*—not just "at work," but "by the whiteboard near the window overlooking the empty parking lot." Add to that a few *concrete objects*: a binder, a red pen, a computer screen with Post-it notes all around its edges. And finally, there's *emotion in motion*. Not "she was upset," but "she blinked fast, water pouring out as if an eyelash had lodged itself in her eye." You don't need much. But with the right kinds of details that make a moment specific, the picture sticks. You don't need every element in every scene. But with just the right amount, told at the right time in the sequence, your audience will be transported from their present self into the moment you want them to experience.

Summary is the narrative's logic. It's what most business professionals already know how to do, and often too well. From executive summaries and pitch decks to board memos and earnings reports, summary is everywhere in business communication. It highlights key data, strips away noise, and moves briskly through the details. It is logical, informative, efficient. But here's the catch: Summary is also where meaning and feeling often go to die. In the relentless pursuit of clarity, business communication becomes flat. It forgets that clarity alone doesn't move people. It may orient the audience, but rarely does it stir them. Still, summary has its place. It can zoom out when data is stuck in the weeds. It can connect dots across scenes. It can remind people of what matters most. When paired with scene and reflection, summary gives a story defining silhouette. Just don't let it run the whole show.

Reflection is what makes a story wise. It's what separates a report from a narrative, an update from a spark of insight. Reflection is meaning, drawn with the benefit of hindsight. It's what the storyteller has come to understand, not just what happened but what that happening meant. Memoir writing coach Marion Roach Smith calls it, "Not just what happened to you, but what you've done with what happened to you." And while it's the rarest of the three tools in business, it's often the most impactful. Reflection is where the storyteller frames the experience for the audience. It's where a personal experience becomes shared insight.

Unlike scene or summary, reflection doesn't require external action. Much like my friend Dado Slezak, whom you met in the introduction of this book, reflections can lead to inner epiphany. It's what allows a leader to say, "How did I play a role in this unexpected outcome?" or "I thought I had failed, but what I didn't realize until much later is that the team was waiting to see if I'd stand by them." Reflection is what invites listeners to pause and ask, "What would I have done?" or "What do I believe?"

That's the framework. But the best way to understand scene, summary, and reflection is to see them woven into a real story. Gina's 2023 Kellogg commencement address is a perfect case study. Here it is. You'll see all three tools at play, layered over the IRS structure.

> Recently, on a rideshare to work, a complete stranger gave me a gift. However, it was not a gift I could touch or see.
>
> Three Fridays ago, I was traveling to an unfamiliar neighborhood in the early morning for a special work project. Sometimes my rideshare drivers are chatty; sometimes we barely exchange a

word. That morning, I was greeted by a driver with a mile-wide smile who practically sang my name as I climbed into the back seat of her car. Little did I know that that complete stranger would give me a gift that morning.

My students know I am obsessed with the art of gift giving. As a consumer anthropologist, I pay attention to what people need and want to help companies make better products and services.

It's a practice that I believe parallels that of gift giving. Understanding another person so deeply at their core that you can surprise and delight them. And while an insightful gift can be a physical item you love, it can be a product feature that makes your life easier.

It can be a gesture, a note, or something that someone says, at just the right moment. I believe giving someone an insightful gift is one of the most human-centric acts we can do. A meaningful gift can build connection, an emotional closeness. On the flip side, a less than thoughtful gift can leave one feeling misunderstood.

So, Kellogg graduates, I want to remind you of the transition that will take place once you leave this university. You will transition from a place of knowledge to a place where you must understand others in order to be successful, and understanding others is an emotional art. So how does one master an emotional art? Practice these three things.

Number one, boundless curiosity. Enter someone else's world and wonder without judgment. Don't get mad at people; get curious. People may not make sense to you, but they always make sense to themselves.

Number two, eager listening; don't argue, don't teach, don't sell. Listen to understand, not to reply, defend, or correct.

Number three, profound empathy. Find a personal connection that allows you to see the world from someone else's point of view. Advocate for them in a way you would want for yourself.

As for my ride that morning, my driver noticed my hesitation when we arrived at an unfamiliar neighborhood, not a soul in sight in the early morning, and she said to me, "I will wait here for you until you are safely in the building."

This was a gift I could not see or touch, but it was a gift that I could feel deeply. This was a gift of understanding. But that wasn't all.

Because we entered each other's worlds for that thirty-minute ride, we realized that we had more in common than just two people working early that morning. When she discovered I was a teacher, she happily announced that her son was graduating in a few weeks. When I asked from which school, she proudly replied, "Kellogg."

"I teach there," I exclaimed. She asked, "Will I see you at graduation?"

And I chuckled. "You probably will."

So, Yuberry, I know you're out there today, and I want to thank you. I want to thank you for giving me the gift of understanding. I want to thank you for leading with boundless curiosity, eager listening, and profound empathy.

And to these Kellogg graduates, I hope you will remember to enter other people's worlds and understand them. Your loved ones, your customers, even complete strangers. Remember to give the gift of understanding when you can, as often as you can. This is what makes us human. Thank you.

Gina's speech is a best-in-class example in narrative architecture. The IRS framework is there, even if you don't see it at first. And woven through IRS are the narrative tools that make each beat pulse with movement: scene, summary, and reflection.

Intriguing Beginning (I): She opens with immediacy and mystery—"Recently, on a rideshare to work, a complete stranger gave me a gift." It's specific, unexpected, and brief enough to spark curiosity. We want to know: What gift? From whom? Why? That intrigue is heightened by a scene—an unfamiliar neighborhood, an early morning commute, and the warm welcome of a driver who "practically sang my name." It's showing, not telling, and it hooks us immediately.

Riveting Middle (R): She builds that ride into a vivid sequence: the pause of hesitation outside the building, the driver offering to wait until she's safely inside, the shared surprise at discovering their Kellogg connection. These are her scenes doing the heavy lifting—sensory detail, dialogue, emotion in motion. Punctuating these moments are summaries that give the story its structure: her three lessons on emotional art—boundless curiosity, eager listening, profound empathy. The summaries are concise and actionable, each one distilling the lived moment into something her audience can carry forward.

Satisfying End (S): She circles back to her driver by name—"So, Yuberry, I know you're out there today"—turning the story into both a public thank-you and a call to action for the graduates. This is where reflection takes center stage: Understanding others, she says, is "one of the most human-centric acts we can do," and it's worth practicing with loved ones, customers, and strangers alike. It's a truth earned through the scene and made portable through the summary.

Seen this way, Gina's five-minute address is a blueprint for how scene, summary, and reflection can animate the IRS structure. The scene pulls us in, the summary orients us, and the reflection makes us care and elevates the story into something bigger than the speech itself.

FROM GATHERING VOICES TO FINDING THE THREAD

It might feel like a pivot—and maybe even a contradiction—to spend nine chapters championing the role of the guide on the side only to now focus on telling master-level stories from the front of the room.

But scene, summary, and reflection are in fact leadership tools disguised as storytelling craft.

Yes, they make a story compelling—that's purpose number one. But there's a second, equally important, purpose: They sharpen the very mindsets that make facilitative leadership possible. To build a scene worth telling, you have to notice details others might overlook. To summarize well, you have to distill what matters most to others, not just to you. To reflect meaningfully, you have to step outside yourself and see the experience from multiple points of view.

That means paying close attention. Being Other Centric. Being pragmatic, not dogmatic. Leading through curiosity and story discovery. In other words, the same habits and mindset you cultivated throughout this book, and especially since chapter 6, are the ones that will make you a better storyteller here. Scene, summary, and reflection simply give those habits a stage.

FIVE BASIC PLOTS IN BUSINESS COMMUNICATION

By now, you can see that scene, summary, and reflection train you to notice, listen, ask, and distill. And when you lead this way, you're going to uncover a lot: rich insights, sharp observations, raw data, unfiltered opinions.

That's the gift—and the challenge—of story facilitation. Divergent communication, as we explored in chapters 6, 7, and 8, opens the floodgates. It invites in more perspectives, more possibilities, more truths than you alone could generate. But you can't use everything you collect. At some point, you have to converge. You have to weave all that material into something coherent and compelling.

How do you do that?

You start looking for patterns. Patterns are what allow you to move from a swirl of inputs to a story worth telling. They show you what's essential, what's recurring, and—just as important—what's an outlier that reveals something that warrants extra attention from us. In business, certain story patterns appear again and again, and when you can spot them, you can shape them.

Patterns in business storytelling often show up as plots—recurring arcs of action and meaning that audiences instinctively recognize. A plot is the backbone of a story: the sequence that connects beginning to end, the container that makes all the details hold together.

In *Let the Story Do the Work*, I described the five basic plots I've seen emerge again and again in business contexts. They aren't formulas, and they certainly don't cover every story you'll ever tell. But once you recognize them, you'll start to notice them everywhere—in product launches, boardroom pitches, change initiatives, and team updates.

Here's the shorthand version:

1. **Origin:** How something began—your company, your project, your partnership. Often used to inspire or connect by showing the spark that started it all.
2. **Rags to Riches:** A rise from modest beginnings to success, growth, or influence. In business, it's not always about money—it could be market share, impact, or credibility.
3. **Rebirth** (or Turnaround): A dramatic renewal after a decline or setback. The focus is on reinvention and recovery.
4. **Overcoming the Monster:** Facing down a formidable challenge—whether it's a competitor, a market force, or a deeply entrenched internal problem.
5. **The Quest:** A sustained pursuit of a goal, marked by obstacles, allies, and lessons along the way.

You don't have to force your material into these molds, but once you recognize the patterns, you can use them to give shape to complexity—and to make your story instantly more familiar and engaging to your audience.[1]

NARRATIVE ECONOMICS: PATTERN + EMOTION = INFLUENCE

Picture a person riding an elephant. The rider represents our logical mind—feeble but deliberate, able to plan and reason. The elephant represents our emotions—massive, powerful, quick to react and move with force. Even without having been on such a ride, you can probably imagine that if the elephant decides to go one way and the rider wants another, who is going to win? This is the anchoring analogy in *The Happiness Hypothesis*, written by social psychologist Jonathan Haidt, who studies the foundations of ethics, emotion, and culture.

If Haidt's image helps us see how emotion can outmaneuver logic in an individual's choices, Robert Shiller's research shows what happens when that dynamic plays out across millions of people at once.

Shiller has spent decades studying what moves markets. He shared a Nobel Prize in economics with Eugene Fama and Lars Peter Hansen in asset pricing and is known for blending quantitative analysis with the psychology of investors, consumers, and everyday players in the marketplace. From his many influential works such as *Irrational Exuberance* and *Animal Spirits*, he shows how confidence, fear, optimism, and shared beliefs can influence markets alongside traditional indicators. In *Narrative Economics*, he furthered the thesis that widely shared stories—about machines, the wealthy and powerful, cryptotechnology, and more—circulate through societies and influence collective behaviors that ultimately drive larger economies themselves.

Shiller's core insight is that when a narrative resonates with people emotionally, it can move quickly through a population similar to the way a virus can. Once people "catch" the story, they begin to buy, invest, or prepare for the future as if there were an invisible conductor guiding their every action. Those investments or consumption choices accumulate, creating economic forces and conditions that, in turn, generate new stories with their own emotional charge.

You can see this dynamic surfacing again and again in economic narratives. The "machines are coming for your job" storyline has appeared with each major wave of automation since the Industrial Revolution. Real estate booms and busts cycle through decades, with new characters and settings but familiar tensions. In the age of extreme wealth gaps in many countries, the tension between frugality and conspicuous consumption becomes even more visible. These narratives adapt to their moments, lead "characters," and particular settings, but their underlying patterns and emotional triggers remain recognizable.

Leaders tell stories within an existing, albeit invisible, influence of cultural narratives. Whether through intention or habit, those stories can amplify what is already circulating, introduce a new frame, or slowly redirect the conversation. This is why emotional stewardship matters—shaping not only the content of a story but also how it feels to the people who hear it.

THE WORK OF AN EMOTIONAL CARTOGRAPHER

By the time Chuen Chuen Yeo and I had finished working on her keynote for the Women in Tech Global Summit in Osaka, Japan, we had gone through more than half a dozen drafts. I didn't expect that. She is a natural storyteller, a seasoned leadership coach, and an award-winning author. Yet each draft uncovered a new revelation about her theme, tone, sequencing, or emphasis. Thinking back, it makes sense. She had chosen to deliver a message that would be hard for many in the audience to accept.

Chuen Chuen is a Singapore-based executive coach whose work has reached leaders in more than forty countries. She has trained with me in story facilitation, achieving the highest level of certification. In April 2025, she stood onstage before more than 250 senior women in technology. In her thirteen years of coaching, she had rarely seen this particular message—about self-acceptance and executive presence—met with such energy. By the end, she had aroused the people in the room to their feet, calling her back onstage for an extended period of standing ovation.

WRITING THE SPEECH

She began where most people don't: at the end. Using the IRS technique we'd explored together in chapter 9 (start with an Intriguing Beginning, then leap to the Satisfying End), Chuen Chuen zeroed in on the one message she knew her audience needed, even if it would sound like a sudden, loud, and unwelcome thud out of nowhere.

It was a simple but difficult message: You do not need to change yourself to be liked, accepted, and ascend to the highest level possible.

In a summit devoted to women in technology—where the focus often circles around breaking external barriers—she aimed instead at the interior ones. Those invisible cages women build for themselves: self-perceptions, self-imposed ceilings, the constant editing of our own words before they leave our mouths. She knew this thesis would make some bristle, perhaps even drawing potential rebuke. But what she found in her own PhD dissertation research was that "self-belief" was the most potent and the most essential ingredient of executive presence. This contradiction is a simple but difficult reality, like having a blister: There's no avoiding the pain except to acknowledge its presence. This is the very place her story needed to press, not the conventional belief her audience had readily accepted, but where the point would feel very raw.

Early in her speech, instead of tiptoeing around the tension, she called it out. With deliberate pauses and a pacing that oscillated like a conversation leaning in and pulling back, Chuen Chuen acknowledged matter-of-factly that some in the room might disagree with her. That, in a sense, women can be their own worst enemies. The very act of saying aloud what many were already thinking loosened the grip of resistance. She went further, telling them she intended to deliver "the raw, hard truth," because in her experience, people respond to honesty—even the kind that feels politically incorrect—more than they do to the safety of agreeable platitudes.

She was also meticulous about the language she used to earn that response. In testing her material, she discovered how one word could tilt the entire emotional trajectory. Changing a phrase in her introduction from "fear of failure" to "leadership fears" dramatically cooled the temperature of the room. The first drew nods, follow-up questions, and an organic curiosity. The second opened the door to the Arctic North—people recoiled and they clipped short their conversation. For her, it was proof that words don't just describe a message—they carry it, color it, and determine whether it awakens or disappears. Paying attention to those microreactions became as essential as crafting the story itself.

PRIMING THE ROOM AND WORKING THE ROOM

Her speaking slot was the graveyard shift: 3:00 p.m., late in the conference, when minds wander and energy dips. By the time it was Chuen Chuen's turn, the audience had been sitting for hours, absorbing a carousel of speeches and panel discussions.

So before she ever stepped onstage, Chuen Chuen began elevating the atmosphere. She moved through clusters of attendees, syncing her own energy to theirs, picking up on laughter, eye contact, and body language. She asked the conference organizers to pump upbeat music into the hall as people trickled back from the coffee break. Then, when the emcee called her name, she strode up with a high five and a quick, almost playful skip to reset the room.

Once there, she stayed attuned to the smallest signals. She noticed when the room sighed with her as she spoke about the "lack of role models." She felt the wave of applause at phrases like "bringing more authenticity," "letting the criticisms come," and "being the beacon for women who come after." These were proof points that her message and their experience were in lockstep. Because she was fully present, she could ride those waves instead of missing them.

And she made it personal. At one point, she invited the audience to turn to the person next to them and say, "I feel your passion. I believe in your mission. And I have your back." The ripple of voices, laughter, and softened expressions created a rare moment in professional gatherings: direct, person-to-person connection. She believes it was one of the reasons the crowd rose to its feet at the end. It was a reminder that the right interactive experience engages as much as binds.

REFLECTING BACK

Before she was a leadership coach, Chuen Chuen was a math teacher. The pivot had brought her into boardrooms and onto stages, but even with decades of speaking under her belt, her heart still pounded as she waited backstage in Osaka. She smoothed her suit jacket one last time and centered her focus. Later, she told me she thinks of impostor syndrome as the gap between who you are and who you believe yourself to be. In her mind, she was still that cautious career changer, freshly departed from the classroom, trying to persuade large companies to trust her with their rising leaders.

Looking back, she credits the standing ovation to something far more fundamental than the cleverness of her sentences. "No one cares what they hear if they can't feel a connection with the speaker," she said. "When you're delivering a difficult message, the emotional connection with the room matters more than the precision of your words."

That observation is at the heart of what I call *narrative excellence*—the craft of shaping stories that convey a core message through a shared experience, discovered story, anchored in shared emotion. Chuen Chuen's success that afternoon—much like Gina's moving convocation address, Gregory's gift for sensing the hidden narratives in people, Ahmed, Tian, Anthony, Alessandra, Bernhard, Tina, Rissa, Jake, Gayla, KJ, Reena, Alex and Arlene and Tyson's striking and compelling leadership stories, and Chris's masterful story facilitation—was the result of intentional choices in how she sought, shaped, and shared her message so it deepened understanding, strengthened trust, and opened possibilities her audience hadn't considered.

What these stories show is narrative excellence in motion. Narrative excellence is the practice of sharpening how we seek, shape, and share stories so they deepen understanding, strengthen trust, and open possibilities that data alone cannot reach. Telling flawless stories isn't necessarily the ultimate goal every time. Instead, leaders find and propagate narratives that better reflect the changing picture—stories that carry a richer chorus of voices, a wider arc of perspectives, and a deeper measure of humanity than the version we began with.

Think of Dado, my former client and friend, whom you met in the introduction chapter. What he assumed to be résumé talk turned out to be a mirror—an invitation to look deeper, past outcomes to the impulses, blind spots, and costs that shaped them. That practice of discovery became his foundation, and years later, he realized the edge at the highest echelon in his profession wasn't intellectual horsepower but the small differences that compound—when to speak, when to hold back, how to let others shine. That is narrative excellence: curiosity made practical, attention made visible.

And here's the part leaders rarely expect: When you pursue narrative excellence, you're hitting two birds with one stone by stepping into T^2—*Transaction* × *Transformation.* Yes, you'll reach the immediate goal: delivering the keynote, landing that dream job, winning the client, clarifying the vision that's been stuck in your head. But the most durable change happens along the journey of pursuing your goal. You start to see differently. Speak differently. You find more meaning in what you do, and in how you do it.

That's the transformation. A client once told me, "Your training helped me discover something about myself I didn't even know I was capable of doing." Another said, "Storytelling became a way of being. It reshaped how I lead, how I listen, and how I connect."

Practiced well, narrative excellence changes how leaders make sense of the world and act within it. Cultures grow stronger. Companies grow more competitive. And leaders begin to notice opportunities others simply overlook. Where operational excellence aligns people, processes, and tools for peak performance, narrative excellence aligns curiosity, humility, and synthesis to illuminate a fuller picture of reality.

Narrative excellence begins with a reckoning.

What stories am I carrying—about myself, about others, about the way the world works? How often do I hold those stories up to the light and ask if they're still true? How open am I to a different telling? And when my story meets someone else's, do I listen as if theirs might hold equal weight—or do I reflexively rank mine above it?

The most skilled practitioners of narrative excellence learn to weave together even the stories that seem mutually exclusive. They begin with three assumptions: First, no single person can see the full picture alone. Second, other people—including the competitor who plays dirty, the politician you'd rather never hear from again, the colleague who tests your patience—hold a piece of that picture you cannot find without them. And third, you won't see the whole picture unless you are proactively looking for the missing pieces.

In practice, narrative excellence looks less like a onetime act and more like a way of moving through the world. It is the habit of staying relentlessly curious. Of listening with the willingness to be changed by what you hear. Of seeking stories far beyond your usual orbit—in books, in strangers, in those you don't agree with. It is asking sharper questions, not only of people but of the "truths" you've long taken for granted. It is embracing the discomfort of being wrong, then learning from it. It is fluency in the craft—the IRS framework, the five basic business plots, asking Crazy Good Questions, the art of reframing. And it is knowing the subtle but critical difference between proving and persuading, and when each, separately or together, is worth the effort.

Dado's life makes this plain. From scarcity to scale, from résumé talk to the mirror, from chasing credit to building community—his arc is what happens when narrative excellence becomes habit. The projects are larger now; the timelines tighter; the stakes higher. The practice is the same: refine attention, widen the lens, carry the mirror.

Just as operational excellence drives an organization toward continuous improvement in its systems, narrative excellence drives a leader toward continuous improvement in perception—a lifelong discipline of widening the lens until a fuller picture comes into view. When leaders choose that discipline, they embody the very premise of *Winning Without Persuading: A New Framework for Leading with Curiosity and Story Discovery.* They build a reality that better prepares them to lead, one conversation, one connection, one transformation at a time.

appendix

Ladder of Inference
Decide what to do
Take Action
Explain/ evaluate what's happening
Contexts Assumptions Values
Name what's happening
Paraphrase the data
Select data
Available Data

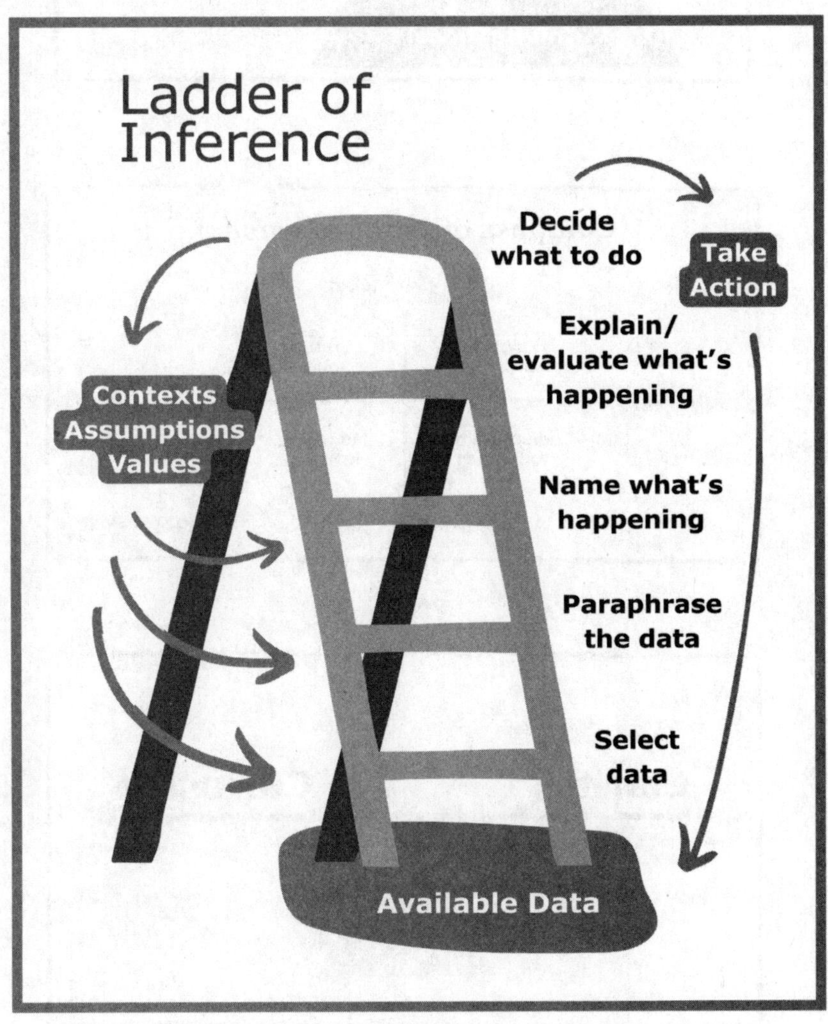

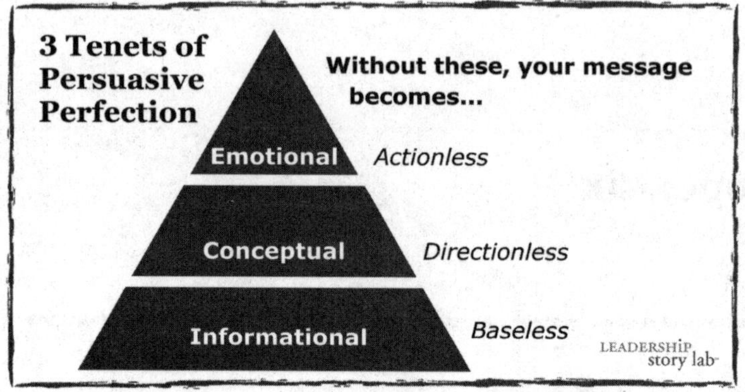
3 Tenets of Persuasive Perfection
Without these, your message becomes...
Emotional
Actionless
Conceptual
Directionless
Informational
Baseless
LEADERSHIP story lab

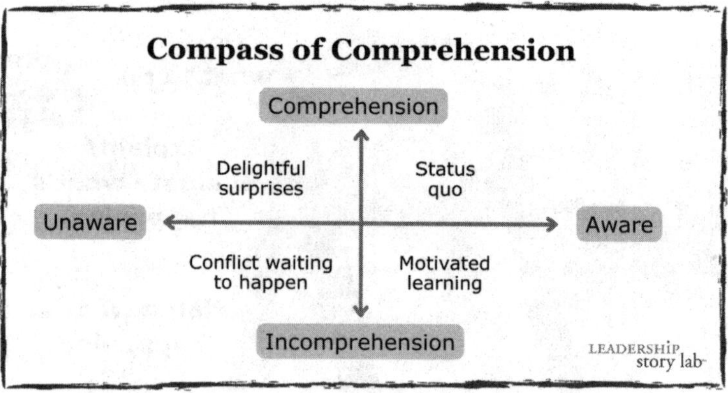
Compass of Comprehension
Comprehension
Delightful surprises
Status quo
Unaware
Aware
Conflict waiting to happen
Motivated learning
Incomprehension
LEADERSHIP story lab

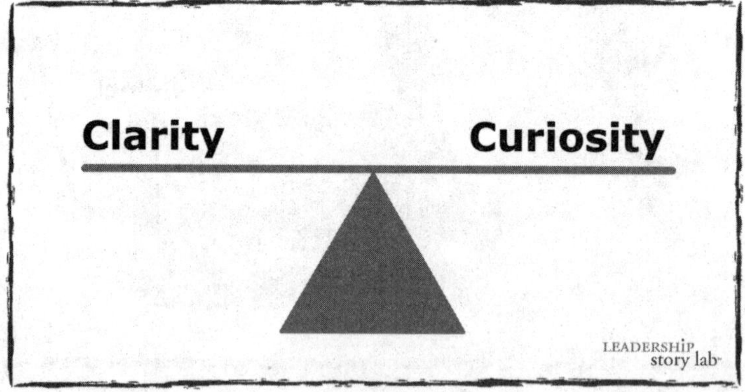
Clarity
Curiosity
LEADERSHIP story lab

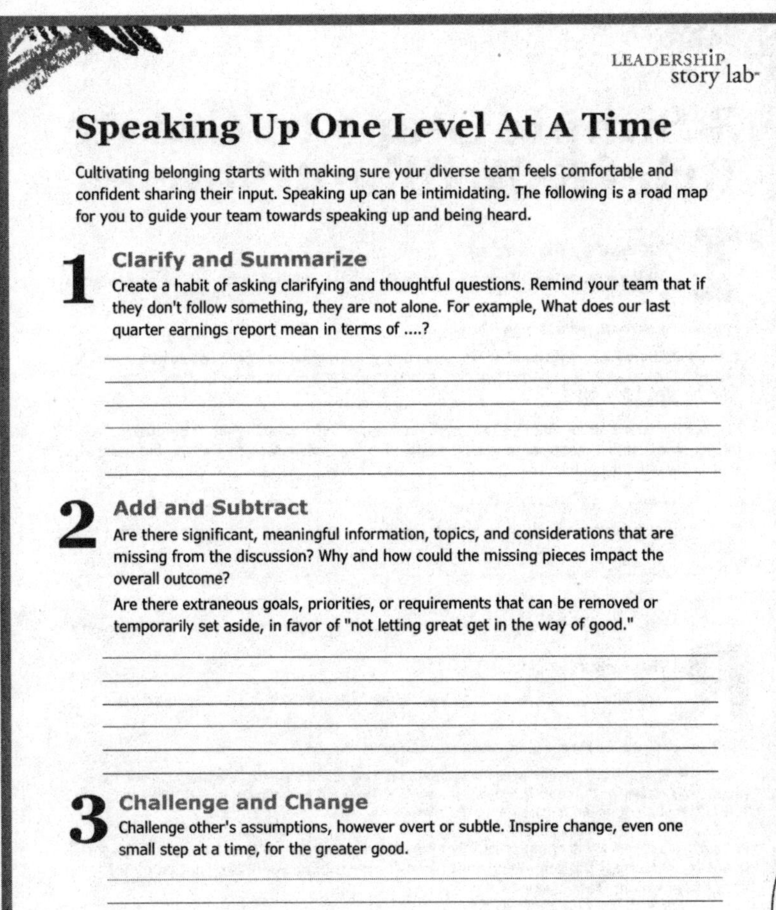

Speaking Up One Level At A Time

Cultivating belonging starts with making sure your diverse team feels comfortable and confident sharing their input. Speaking up can be intimidating. The following is a road map for you to guide your team towards speaking up and being heard.

1 Clarify and Summarize

Create a habit of asking clarifying and thoughtful questions. Remind your team that if they don't follow something, they are not alone. For example, What does our last quarter earnings report mean in terms of ....?

2 Add and Subtract

Are there significant, meaningful information, topics, and considerations that are missing from the discussion? Why and how could the missing pieces impact the overall outcome?

Are there extraneous goals, priorities, or requirements that can be removed or temporarily set aside, in favor of "not letting great get in the way of good."

3 Challenge and Change

Challenge other's assumptions, however overt or subtle. Inspire change, even one small step at a time, for the greater good.

LEADERSHIP
story lab™

3 Simple Steps to Create Brief & Brilliant Stories

I *Intriguing Beginning:*

Create a hook right from the start. How? Use conflict, contrast, or contradiction.

Start with a moment, not a résumé.

Instead of listing your background or explaining why you are speaking, invite us into a moment that matters. It could be small, unexpected, even strange. But it should stir curiosity. Make us wonder: Why this story? Why now?

Prompt: What's a small moment that became unexpectedly meaningful? Begin there. Create tension with conflict, contrast, or contradiction. Let the audience feel what you felt before they know what it means:

____

____

____

____

____

____

R *Riveting Middle:*

Tension is critical in moving your story. Tension is what gets you attention.

Don't just describe the event—show how it changed what you saw.

The middle is where the emotional or intellectual shift happens. It's where your story uncovers the insight, the stakes, or the conflict beneath the surface. What did the moment reveal? What tension did it hold? What question did it raise? What did it make you realize, even if just a little?

Prompt: What was the turning point in your story? Where was the tension—emotional, social, financial or internal? Did something shift (your understanding, your role, your emotion)? That's your insight. That's your "R."

____

____

____

____

____

____

LEADERSHiP
story lab™

3 Simple Steps to Create Brief & Brilliant Stories

S ***Satisfying End:***
Circle back — synthesize and reframe.

What makes a story satisfying to your audience? It doesn't just stop—it resonates. A strong ending circles back to where the story began, but with added depth. It synthesizes the insight in a way that feels earned. Whether it shifts perspective, reveals new connection, or offers a gentle next step, a good ending leaves your listener changed—even if just a little.

Prompt: How can you return to where you began—but with new understanding? What do you want your listener to carry forward? End there—with clarity, not closure.

"If challenge is the backbone of a story, change is the soul of it."

Let the Story Do the Work, Esther Choy

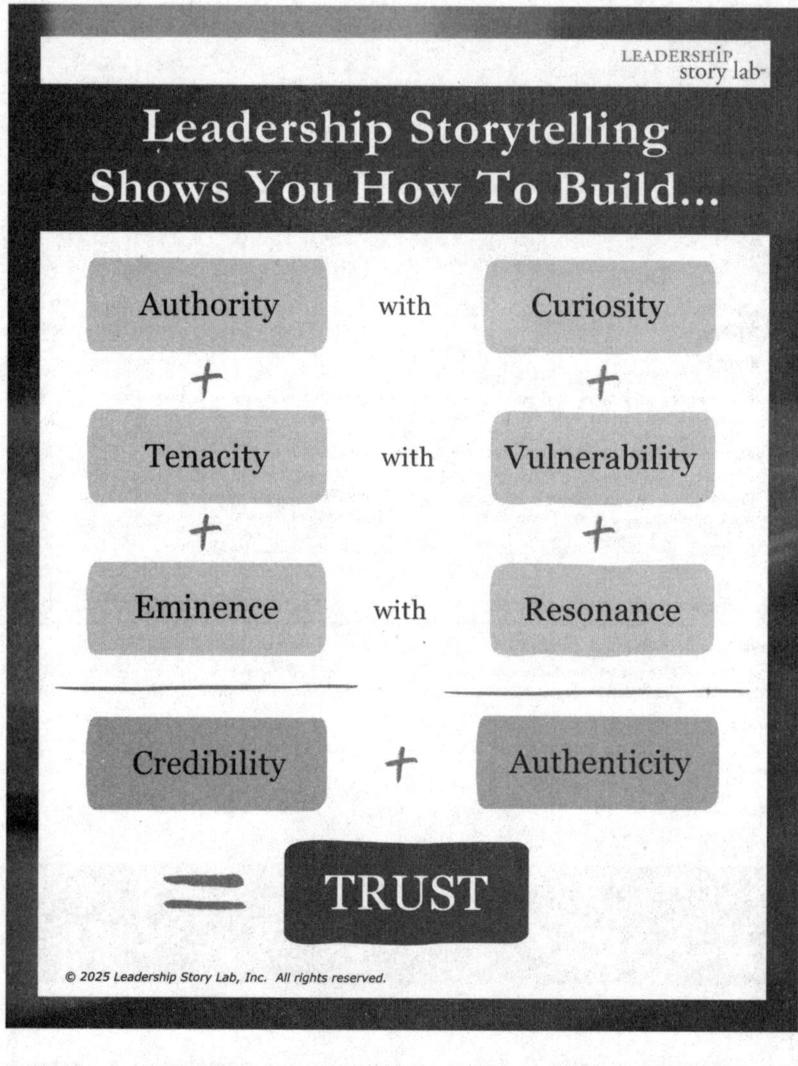
LEADERSHIP
story lab
Leadership Storytelling
Shows You How To Build...
Authority
with
Curiosity
+
+
Tenacity
with
Vulnerability
+
+
Eminence
with
Resonance
Credibility
+
Authenticity
=
TRUST
© 2025 Leadership Story Lab, Inc. All rights reserved.

acknowledgments

WHEN THE MENTEE BECOMES THE MENTOR

One chilly November morning, the Chicago sky was blanketed in a layer of gray clouds. My husband, working upstairs, heard a shriek from my office below. He ran down, fearing that someone we loved had died. But what he found instead was me—covering my face with my hands, tears spilling through my fingers as I pointed at my computer screen, urging him to read what had just arrived. It was an email from my longtime mentor, Don Norman.

> Esther, I started to write a thirty-word blurb. I couldn't. Instead, I wrote a three-hundred-word tribute . . .

DON'S REFLECTION

Esther Choy was an MBA student of mine at Northwestern University, where I taught design to the masters of management and manufacturing students earning joint degrees in design and business. They were brilliant, ambitious people—accustomed to having answers. But design, I told them, is about reframing problems and seeing through the eyes of the people who use what we create.

Many wanted PowerPoint slides in advance, bullet points, and "what's on the exam." I had no exams, only discussions and projects. My rule was simple: *no words on slides.* That frightened them. But Esther thrived.

Afterward, she told me she wanted to teach managers and executives how to tell stories. I encouraged her. Business people love numbers, I said, but numbers are abstract. Stories give context. Numbers reveal patterns; stories reveal people. Together, they reveal the truth.

Now, fifteen years later, with her company quite successful, she has written her second book. "Sure," I said when she asked me, "I'll write a blurb for you." But when I read the book, it wasn't at all what I expected. What I read instead was a book about people—about seeing colleagues and teams not as workers but as human beings with hopes, frustrations, lives beyond work, and insights to solve your problems.

One story stopped me cold: a woman who reversed a foundation's "no" on a grant, not by defending her proposal but by telling stories of those whose lives had changed because of past grants. She reframed the conversation from numbers to impact. The reviewer realized the decision wasn't wrong—the process was.

That story made me pause and examine my own work with the charity that bears my name. It rewards people and organizations doing social good. Why was I having so much difficulty fundraising? Because we had been telling an uninspiring story about methods and metrics when we should have been sharing the human stories that moved us to tears. I rewrote our proposal, focusing on those stories. The change was immense and immediate.

Thank you, Esther, superstar. The mentee has become the mentor.

—Don Norman
Don Norman Design Award (dnda.design)
Distinguished Professor Emeritus, University of California San Diego, author of *Design for a Better World*

My whole career is built around holding up a mirror for clients—like Dado, whose story opens this book. I've witnessed transformation happen again and again: times when they recognize their own reflection, their story, their truth. But this time, I was the one seeing myself through someone else's eyes. Don had held up the mirror for me.

I sat there, eyes swollen, the clock ticking toward my next client session, knowing I had five minutes to compose myself—but I didn't. For once, I let the mirror do its work for me.

Thank you, Don! I modeled my journey into storytelling after yours in human-centered design. My first book, *Let the Story Do the Work*, wouldn't be possible without your mentoring. Even now, you're giving me something I hadn't realized I needed—that my work has deep value and can impact people, even someone like you.

NOT A VILLAGE, BUT A NETWORK

Don's reflection reminded me that growth doesn't happen in isolation. Though the foundation of my journey has been shaped by his mentorship, I've also been lifted, inspired, and challenged by a web of people whose paths have intersected with mine in ever more lasting ways than I could describe. What carried this book to completion wasn't a single village gathered around me but a dynamic network that has stretched across years, continents, and communities.

Within this network, stories are the threads that hold everything together. I've always loved stories. Beyond the sheer joy of listening to and crafting them, storytelling has always been, for me, a means to something deeper: connection. Stories allow me to feel close to people—to form bonds that might otherwise be hard to build. Some people connect through sports, others by building companies, serving in the military, or cooking meals that bring people together. There are countless ways to bridge the distance between us; mine just happens to be through stories.

So it's only natural that if I love connecting with others through stories, I'd also want to create ways for people to share theirs with me. That's why storytelling—and story discovery—live so deeply in my bones.

I owe deep gratitude to the hundreds of coaching clients who have let me walk beside them as they discovered and shaped their stories. Through their openness, I've had the privilege of witnessing their journeys—reaching goals, uncovering new narratives, and transforming their leadership in the process.

In particular, I want to thank the following individuals once again for allowing me to share their stories in this book. Their openness made each lesson more vivid and memorable: Dado Slezak, Chris McAuley, Tyson Voelkel, Alex Kruzel, Arlene Milon, Rissa Reddan, Reena Kansal, Kennith Jackson, Jake Schlesinger, Gayla Braziel, Karla Trotman, Alessandra Rolff, Bernhard Krieg, Tina Peters, Anthony K. Do, Gregory Warner, Ahmed Abdulla Alfadhel, Gina Fong, and Chuen Chuen Yeo.

To everyone who has completed the Certified Story Facilitator program—you, too, have been an essential part of this journey. You believed in the power of curiosity and the value of discovering other people's stories as deeply as telling your own. Thank you for investing in yourselves so you can invest in others. Learning story facilitation with you has taught me as much as I have taught you.

To my unofficial book team—each of you played a vital role in turning ideas into pages, and pages into something that lives and breathes.

Alessandra Rolff: Is there anything in this world you *can't* find? I doubt it. No matter how absurd my questions were, you somehow uncovered research that was not only useful but inspirational.

Mandy Kaucher: Thank you for creating the clear, elegant visuals that bring abstract concepts to life. Your ability to make complexity look simple is a gift to every reader.

Sara Dennison: Your steadfast management of Leadership Story Lab's operations frees up my time and attention to focus on writing this book, an all-consuming project.

Reena Kansal: My only Kellogg classmate with whom I could commiserate about the elusive search for work-life balance. You've been my collaborator, business partner, confidant, and memory keeper of every client story. It's been an incredible journey working alongside you.

Tyson Voelkel: You've served our country courageously and our alma mater selflessly. You embody what it means to be elite without being elitist. Just when the pressure of finishing this manuscript felt overwhelming, you gave me perspective with one unforgettable line: "*Esther, no one is shooting at you. It's a first-world problem!*"

Gregory Warner: My fellow mirror-holder, you helped me see how my own story is the source of my "superpower." I count my blessings for our shared way of looking at people, situations, and the world from multiple perspectives—and for the brilliant foreword you wrote, capturing the essence of *Winning Without Persuading* better than I ever could.

To my HarperCollins Leadership team:

Tim Burgard, my editor—thank you for believing in the potential of this book from the very beginning. Your trust in me as an author and your steady editorial hand helped shape *Winning Without Persuading* into its strongest form.

Ron Huizinga, HarperCollins Leadership's brilliant art director—thank you for curating such remarkable talent, including **Irina Kiro**, who so beautifully captured the essence of the book's core concept in her book cover design.

And to **Jeff Farr** at Neuwirth and the entire **HarperCollins Leadership team**—your faith in this project, and your technical expertise, made this book the best it could be. I'm deeply grateful for your unwavering guidance and belief in its message.

Last but definitely not least is the heart and origin of my story:

To **Melia**—thank you for always asking such intelligent questions. You may not want to volunteer your stories, but your piercingly insightful observations push me to think deeper and harder. You remind me that curiosity itself is a form of storytelling.

To **Alina**—when I wavered, wondering whether I should even take on this book project, which would no doubt take time away from our family, you looked me in the eye and said, "*Mom, you HAVE to* *write this book.*" That moment anchored me more than you'll ever know.

And to **Bernhard**, my life partner and the very first mirror-holder for me—because of the way you saw me, I began to believe in myself, to trust that what I had to offer mattered, even when I felt differently. While launching your own venture, you carried the load at home so I could stay away to write. Thank you for being the "all gas and no brakes" person in our family and in my life.

This book exists because every story in it has shaped me—those shared by mentors, clients, students, collaborators, and loved ones who trust me with their truths. You are the network that sustains me, the mirrors that keep me honest, and the living proof of what storytelling can do: connect, transform, and remind us of our shared humanity. To all of you, and because of all of you, *Winning Without Persuading* found its voice.

notes

CHAPTER 1

1. "Is Ozempic as Magical as It Sounds?" Freakonomics Radio, episode 615, December 11, 2024, https://freakonomics.com/podcast/is-ozempic-as-magical-as-it-sounds/.

2. Lulu Garcia-Navarro, "The Interview: Rick Steves Refuses to Get Cynical About the World," *New York Times*, December 14, 2024, https://www.nytimes.com/2024/12/14/magazine/rick-steves-interview.html.

3. Jay Fitzgerald, "What Companies Want Most in a CEO: A Good Listener," *Working Knowledge*, October 16, 2021, https://www.library.hbs.edu/working-knowledge/what-companies-want-most-in-a-ceo-a-good-listener.

4. Esther K. Choy, "The Secret to Leading Effective, Happy and Healthy Teams at Work, *Forbes*, March 26, 2023, https://www.forbes.com/sites/estherchoy/2023/03/26/the-secret-to-leading-effective-happy-and-healthy-teams-at-work/.

5. *State of the Global Workplace*, Gallup, n.d., https://www.gallup.com/workplace/349484/state-of-the-global-workplace.aspx.

6. Ryan Pendell, "Employee Engagement Strategies: Fixing the World's $8.8 Trillion Problem," Gallup, June 13, 2022 (updated September 11, 2023), https://www.gallup.com/workplace/393497/world-trillion-workplace-problem.aspx.

7. Tait D. Shanafelt, Grace Gorringe, Ronald Menaker, Kristin A. Storz, David Reeves, Steven J. Buskirk, Jeff A. Sloan, and Stephen J. Swensen, "Impact of Organizational Leadership on Physician Burnout and

Satisfaction," *Mayo Clinic Proceedings* 90, no. 4 (2015): 432–440, https://www.sciencedirect.com/science/article/abs/pii/S0025619615000713.

8. Nicholas Epley, *Mindwise: How We Understand What Others Think, Believe, Feel, and Want*, https://www.nicholasepley.com/content/book.
9. James R. Detert and Ethan Burris, "Can Your Employees Really Speak Freely?" *Harvard Business Review*, January–February 2016, https://hbr.org/2016/01/can-your-employees-really-speak-freely.
10. *Academy of Management Journal* 50, no. 4 (2007): 869–884.
11. "The Most Popular TED Talks of All Time," playlist, n.d., https://www.ted.com/playlists/171/the_most_popular_ted_talks_of_all_time.
12. https://anthro.vancouver.wsu.edu/media/documents/garfield_et_al_2019.pdf.
13. "The Ladder of Inference," *Systems Thinker*, vol. 10, 2018, https://thesystemsthinker.com/the-ladder-of-inference/.
14. David Marchese, "The Interview: This World-Renowned Negotiator Says Trump's Secret Weapon Is Empathy," *New York Times*, August 16, 2025, https://www.nytimes.com/2025/08/16/magazine/chris-voss-interview.html.
15. Lisa C. Walsh, Julia K. Boehm, and Sonja Lyubomirsky, "Does Happiness Promote Career Success? Revisiting the Evidence," *Journal of Career Assessment* 26, no. 2 (2018), 199–219, https://doi.org/10.1177/1069072717751441.

CHAPTER 2

1. If you notice a lot of exclamation marks in her speaking note, that's because it's very reflective of Arlene's energy and passion for her work.
2. Daniel Kahneman, "The Riddle of Experience vs. Memory," TED Talk, February 2010, https://www.ted.com/talks/daniel_kahneman_the_riddle_of_experience_vs_memory.

CHAPTER 3

1. "The Tallest Poppy," Women of Influence, n.d., https://www.womenofinfluence.ca/tps/.

2. Thomas Gilovich, Victoria Husted Medvec, and Kenneth Savitsky, "The Spotlight Effect in Social Judgment: An Egocentric Bias in Estimates of the Salience of One's Own Actions and Appearance," *Journal of Personality and Social Psychology* 78, no. 2 (2000): 211–222. https://doi.org/10.1037//0022-3514.78.2.211.

3. Thomas Gilovich, Victoria Husted Medvec, and Kenneth Savitsky, "The Spotlight Effect in Social Judgment."

4. Thomas Gilovich and Kenneth Savitsky, "The Spotlight Effect and the Illusion of Transparency: Egocentric Assessments of How We Are Seen by Others," *Current Directions in Psychological Science* 8, no. 6 (1999): 165–168, https://doi.org/10.1111/1467-8721.00039.

5. Dan Pilat and Sekoul Krastev, "Why Do We Feel Like We Stand Out More Than We Really Do?" The Decision Lab, n.d., https://thedecisionlab.com/biases/spotlight-effect.

6. Weixi Kang, Kreisha Lou Guzman, and Antonio Malvaso, "Big Five Personality Traits in the Workplace: Investigating Personality Differences Between Employees, Supervisors, Managers, and Entrepreneurs," *Frontiers in Psychology* 14 (2023), https://doi:10.3389/fpsyg.2023.976022.

7. Timothy A. Judge, Joyce E. Bono, Remus Ilies, and Megan W. Gerhardt, "Personality and Leadership: A Qualitative and Quantitative Review," *Journal of Applied Psychology* 87, no. 4 (2002): 765–780, https://doi:10.1037/0021-9010.87.4.765.

8. Against this institutional and cultural backdrop, I give my client counterparts extra kudos for calling in a storytelling trainer/consultant like me.

9. Marian N. Ruderman and Cathleen Clerkin, "Developing Leadership by Building Psychological Capital," Center for Creative Leadership, 2015, https://cclinnovation.org/wp-content/uploads/2021/03/developing-leadership-by-building-psychological-capital.pdf.

10. *Becoming Visible*, Smithsonian Women's History Museum, n.d., https://www.becomingvisible.si.edu.

11. Esther K. Choy, "Women in Leadership: Astonishing but Hidden. Why It Matters Now," *Forbes*, March 9, 2025, https://www.forbes.com/sites/estherchoy/2025/03/09/astonishing-but-hidden-why-womens-leadership-stories-matter-now/.

12. "Uncovering Talent: A New Model of Inclusion," Deloitte, 2019, https://www2.deloitte.com/content/dam/Deloitte/us/Documents/about-deloitte/us-about-deloitte-uncovering-talent-a-new-model-of-inclusion.pdf.

CHAPTER 4

1. Sa'iliemanu Lilomaiava-Doktor, "Oral Traditions, Cultural Significance of Storytelling, and Samoan Understandings of Place or Fanua," *Native American and Indigenous Studies* 7, no. 1 (Spring 2020): 121–151, https://www.jstor.org/stable/10.5749/natiindistudj.7.1.0121.

2. "The Benefits of Holy Basil (Tulsi)," Cleveland Clinic, n.d., https://health.clevelandclinic.org/benefits-of-holy-basil.

3. "Story of Tulsi," Devshoppe, n.d., https://www.devshoppe.com/en-us/blogs/articles/story-of-tulsi.

4. "The Benefits of Holy Basil (Tulsi)."

5. "Salvatore Piparo: Reviving a Lost Art," Frontline World, 2011, https://www.pbs.org/frontlineworld/stories/italy801/interview/piparo.html.

6. Kimberley Watson, "'Calypso Is We!' Life Lessons in the Music of Trinidad and Tobago," Smithsonian Center for Folklife and Cultural Heritage, March 22, 2023, https://folklife.si.edu/magazine/calypso-music-trinidad-and-tobago.

7. Wayne E. Croft Sr., "The Soul of Black Preaching," *Theology Today* 81, no. 1 (2024): 35–39.

8. "Manifest Destiny," History.com, April 5, 2010, https://www.history.com/articles/manifest-destiny.

9. "Emperor Qin Shi Huang Biography," Biography Online, April 2015 (updated March 2018), https://biographyonline.net/military/emperor-qin-shi-huang-biography.html.

10. Sultan Alamer, "The Saudi 'Founding Day' and the Death of Wahhabism," Arab Gulf States Institute, n.d., https://agsi.org/analysis/the-saudi-founding-day-and-the-death-of-wahhabism/.

CHAPTER 5

1. "Communication Barriers to the Modern Workplace," A report from the Economist Intelligence Unit, sponsored by Lucidchart.
2. Krysten Crawford, "Study Finds Hybrid Work Benefits Companies and Employees," *Stanford Report*, n.d., https://news.stanford.edu/stories/2024/06/hybrid-work-is-a-win-win-win-for-companies-workers.
3. "A Guide to Hybrid Work and Managing a Remote Team," Gallup, n.d., https://www.gallup.com/workplace/316313/understanding-and-managing-remote-workers.aspx.
4. Jesse Stanchek, "A Guide to Leading an Effective Multi-Generational Workforce," SHRM Business, July 26, 2024, https://www.shrm.org/enterprise-solutions/insights/guide-to-leading-multi-generational-workforce.
5. Leonid Rozenblit and Frank Keil, "The Misunderstood Limits of Folk Science: An Illusion of Explanatory Depth," *Cognitive Science* 26, no. 5 (2002): 521–562, https://doi:10.1207/s15516709cog2605_1.
6. Olga Lainidi, Mimmi Kheddache Jendeby, Anthony Montgomery, Christos Mouratidis, Konstantina Paitaridou, Clare Cook, Judith Johnson, and Eirini Karakasidou, "An Integrative Systematic Review of Employee Silence and Voice in Healthcare: What Are We Really Measuring?" *Frontiers in Psychiatry* (2023), https://doi:10.3389/fpsyt.2023.1111579.
7. Elizabeth Wolfe Morrison, "Employee Voice and Silence: Taking Stock a Decade Later," *Annual Review of Organizational Psychology and Organizational Behavior* 10 (2023): 79–107, https://doi.org/10.1146/annurev-orgpsych-120920-054654.
8. Omar Durrah, Wafa Rashid Alalyani, Kamaal Allil, Ayman Al Shehab, Shooq Al Rawas, Ali Hubais, and Souzan Hannawi, "The Price of Silence, Isolation, and Cynicism: The Impact on Occupational

Frustration," *Heliyon* 9 (2023), https://pmc.ncbi.nlm.nih.gov/articles/PMC10679494/pdf/main.pdf.

CHAPTER 6

1. If you find the video version of this photo online, you will likely see, for a second maybe at the end, a man getting up from the floor filming this spontaneous Cirque du Soleil act. That's Anthony!
2. To treat yourself with more insights from Ann's journey and lessons, read her book: *Relearning to Read: Adventures in Not Knowing* (Renard Press, 2025).
3. John Vervaeke, "Four Kinds of Knowing and Personality, Formal Cause, and Purpose with Sam Tideman," YouTube video, uploaded December 20, 2023, https://www.youtube.com/watch?v=TrW3DOIkP78.
4. Evelyn Brister, "Disciplinary Capture and Epistemological Obstacles to Interdisciplinary Research: Lessons from Central African Conservation Disputes," *Studies in History and Philosophy of Biological and Biomedical Sciences* 56 (2016): 82–91, https://doi.org/10.1016/j.shpsc.2015.11.001.
5. David Goldman, "America Won the War on Inflation. You Still Think the Economy Stinks," CNN Business, October 31, 2024, https://www.cnn.com/2024/10/31/economy/inflation-economy-perceptions.

CHAPTER 7

1. I'm a Gen-Xer; I use proper punctuation when I text.
2. There are other forms of public, or not so public, speaking, of course. Keynoting, pitching, coaching, to name a few. I choose teaching and presenting as the two most encompassing genres of speaking.
3. Guy Itzchakov, Avraham Kluger, and Dotan Castro, "I Am Aware of My Inconsistencies but Can Tolerate Them: The Effect of High Quality Listening on Speakers' Attitude Ambivalence," *Personality and Social Psychology Bulletin* 43, no. 1 (2016): 105–120, https://doi.org/10.1177/0146167216675339.

4. Ángel López Gutiérrez and Juan José Arroyo Paniagua, "An Exploration of Silence in Communication," *European Public & Social Innovation Review* 9 (2024): 1–18, https://doi.org/10.31637/epsir-2024-610.

5. "The Year in Wisdom," podcast, *New York Times*, December 31, 2024, https://www.nytimes.com/2024/12/31/podcasts/the-daily/2024-best-advice.html.

6. Marie Gould and Alexandra Hawson, "Cooley and the Looking Glass Self," EBSCO, 2021, https://www.ebsco.com/research-starters/history/cooley-and-looking-glass-self.

7. Jennifer Kretchmar, "George Herbert Mead: Taking the Role of the Other," EBSCO, 2021, https://www.ebsco.com/research-starters/social-sciences-and-humanities/george-herbert-mead-taking-role-other.

8. Namkje Koudenburg, Jolanda Jetten, Karalyn F. Enz, and S. Alexander Haslam, "The Social Grounds of Personal Self: Interactions That Build a Sense of 'We' Help Clarify Who 'I' Am," *European Journal of Social Psychology* 54 (2024): 1153–1167, https://doi.org/10.1002/ejsp.3070.

9. Charlotte Nickerson, "Looking-Glass Self: Theory, Definition & Examples," *Simply Psychology*, updated September 22, 2023, https://www.simplypsychology.org/charles-cooleys-looking-glass-self.html.

10. Jennifer Porter, "Why You Should Make Time for Self-Reflection (Even If You Hate Doing It)," *Harvard Business Review*, March 21, 2017, https://hbr.org/2017/03/why-you-should-make-time-for-self-reflection-even-if-you-hate-doing-it.

11. Sound familiar? If not, refer to chapter 5, the section on curiosity.

12. Payam Soleimani-Nouri, Olivia Holtermann Entwistle, Matyas Fehervari, and Duncan Spalding, "A Novel Framework for Surgical Reflection," *Annals of Laparoscopic and Endoscopic Surgery* 8 (2023), https://ales.amegroups.org/article/view/9207/html.

13. Julian L. Stone, Emma-Louise Aveling, Molly Frean, Morgan C. Shields, Cameron Wright, Francesca Gino, Thoralf M. Sundt, and Sara J. Singer, "Effective Leadership of Surgical Teams: A Mixed Methods Study of Surgeon Behaviors and Functions," *Annals of Thoracic Surgery* 104, no. 2 (2017): 530–537, https://doi.org/10.1016/j.athoracsur.2017.01.021.

14. Timothy William Gray and Christopher John Coombs, "Developing Professional Judgement in Surgical Trainees: The Role of Critical Reflection," *Australasian Journal of Plastic Surgery* 1, no. 1 (2018), https://doi.org/10.34239/ajops.v1i1.34.

15. "Nick Enfield: Language vs. Reality," *Brain Inspired* podcast 166, May 9, 2023, https://www.youtube.com/watch?v=7miCG29sBc0.

16. Ron Carucci, "Why Senior Leaders Should Stop Having So Many One-on-Ones," *Harvard Business Review*, July 8, 2025, https://hbr.org/2025/07/why-senior-leaders-should-stop-having-so-many-one-on-ones.

17. "Chimamanda Ngozi Adichie: The Danger of a Single Story," TED Talk, October 17, 2009, https://www.youtube.com/watch?v=D9Ihs241zeg.

18. You can hear plenty of these examples in his podcast *Rough Translation*.

CHAPTER 8

1. Dave Whorton with Bo Burlingham, *Another Way: Building Companies That Last . . . and Last . . . and Last*, https://www.tugboatinstitute.com/anotherway/.

2. Jack Stack, of SRC Holdings, had built a thriving enterprise using precisely that self-funded, radically transparent approach.

3. Jim Detert, "What You Still Can't Say at Work," *MIT Sloan Management Review*, October 14, 2024, https://sloanreview.mit.edu/article/what-you-still-cant-say-at-work/.

4. "Nudging the World Toward Smarter Public Policy: An Interview with Richard Thaler," *McKinsey Quarterly*, June 1, 2011, https://www.mckinsey.com/industries/public-sector/our-insights/nudging-the-world-toward-smarter-public-policy-an-interview-with-richard-thaler.

5. Why questions don't have to even contain the word *why*. These questions simply point to hidden reasons that yearn to be brought forward.

CHAPTER 10

1. If you'd like to go deeper—and have the templates and examples I created to help you jump-start your own business stories—*Let the Story Do the Work* is still available on all major online bookselling platforms.

index

Abdul-Wahhab, Muhammad ibn, 60
adding what is missing, 82
Adichie, Chimamanda Ngozi, 136
adversaries, 11–12
advice, 124
African American preaching, 59–60
agreeableness, 40, 41
Alfadhel, Ahmed, 169–70, 172–76
Annals of Laparoscopic and Endoscopic Surgery, 130
Another Way (Whorton), 144–45
Argyris, Chris, 152
Arroyo Paniagua, Juan José, 122–23
artificial intelligence, 138
The Art of War (Sun), 139
assumptions, 125, 140–46, 143–44
Atomic Habits, 125
attention
  in beginning of story, 167–68, 177
  giving and getting, 5, 123–24
  in listening, 118
  in middle of stories, 170–71
  and pitch preparation, 101–3
  and spotlight effect, 38–40
attunement, 48
awareness, 150–53

balance, 13
Bankman-Fried, Sam, 138
Becoming Visible exhibition, 44–46
beginning of stories, 167–70. *see also* IRS storytelling model
Berry, Dorothy, 45
Biesenbach, Rob, 13
Big Five Personality Traits, 40
Björnsson, Hafþór Júlíus, 90–91, 167
blind spots, 144–45
Bloom, Nick, 76
Boehn, Julia, 15
Brain Inspired, 133
brainstorming, 123
Braziel, Gayla, 67, 67–70, 94
Brister, Evelyn, 106
Brooks, David, 14, 108
Burgard, Tim, 113, 114
Burris, Ethan, 9–10

calypso, 57–58
Campbell, Joseph, 166
capability meetings, 134–35
Carter, Jimmy, 67, 69, 70
Carucci, Ron, 134, 135
Castro, Dotan R., 118

Central Africa, rainforest
conservation in, 105–6
challenging others, 82–83
character
of others, accessing, 83–87
in storytelling, 165
clarity, 81–82, 170–72, 185
closure, 174
cognitive biases, 130
communication
business, plots in, 190–91
Compass of Comprehension in, 150–53
and human-centered design, 92–94
language, 133
silence in, 122–23
Three Levels of Speaking Up, 81–88
3 Tenets of Persuasive Perfection, 135–36
in the workplace, 72–73
see also specific aspects, e.g.: listening
compare and contrast questions, 159
Compass of Comprehension, 150–53, 205
competence, 86
comprehension, 150–53
concept, 135
concrete objects in story, 184
conditions for surfacing of stories, 48–49
confidence, 43
conflict
in beginning of stories, 169
in Compass of Comprehension, 150–52, 152–53
in middle of stories, 173–74
stories underpinned by, 155–56
transformed into informed decisions, 75–76
connection, 6, 26, 54, 57–58
conscientiousness, 40, 41
contradiction, 156, 169, 173–74
contrast, 156, 169, 173–74
convergent thinking, 131
Cooley. Charles, 128
Coren, Ashleigh, 45–46
covering, 47–48
Crazy Good Questions, 95, 146, 148, 157–61. *see also* questions
credentials, 86
credibility, 43
culture(s)
and deference to authority and work, 96–97
and hidden stories, 35–38
and silence, 122
traditional storytelling in, 54–60
cunto, 56–57
curiosity
in bridging ways of knowing, 107
core elements of, 100
as embracing incomprehension, 97–103
of facilitators, 95
in middle of stories, 170–72
power of, 3–15
value of, 18–19

Dalai Lama, 11
dance, 62–63
"The Danger of a Single Story" (Adichie), 136
data, 11, 12
deep rules, 148–49, 152–53
The Design of Everyday Things (Norman), 92–93
design thinking, 91–94

Detert, James, 9–10, 148, 149, 152, 153
Dhammapada, 124
dialogue, 184
different path questions, 160
disappearing ink, stories written in, 44–47
discomfort, tolerance for, 100
discoverability, 93
divergent thinking, 131
Do, Anthony K., 89–91, 166–67
"Does Happiness Promote Career Success?" (Boehm and Lyubomirsky), 15
dogmatism, 107
Dubner, Stephen, 52

echoing, 126
egocentric bias, 39–40
elitism, 4–5
Emanuel, Ezekiel, 3, 4
emotion
  in creating conditions for transformation, 183–99
  in motion, 184
  in narrative economics, 192–93
  positive, 15
  surprise and suspense, 147–48
  in 3 Tenets of Persuasive Perfection, 135
emotional awareness, 43
emotional carefulness, 41
emotional cartographers, 87–88, 193–94
empathy, 9, 12–13, 13, 118
endings of stories, 174–76. *see also* IRS storytelling model
Enfield, Nick, 133
engagement
  of employees, 7
  facilitation for, 94–95
  in middle of stories, 171, 174
engagement-facilitating behaviors, 130
engaging leaders, 10
environment, being at odds with, 139–40
Epley, Nick, 9
erased stories, 44–47
Evergreen philosophy, 144
everyday moments, stories from, 21–22
explanatory depth, illusion of, 76–78
"An Exploration of Silence in Communication" (Gutiérrez and Paniagua), 122–23
extraversion, 40, 41

facilitation, 89–109
  design thinking for, 91–94
  facilitative leaders, 95
  as relentless initiative, 108–9
  silence in, 123
  strategic edge of, 107–9
  and ways of knowing, 103–8
facilitators, 111–40
  listening by, 116–24
  qualities of, 95–107
  reflecting by, 124–31
  synthesizing with reframing by, 131–39
  teachers or presenters vs., 115–17
fear, silence driven by, 148
Fellows, Hazel, 44
finding compelling stories, 17–32
fitting in, 36–38
flexibility, 102
Fong, Gina, 20, 183–84, 186–89
Ford, Jamie, 131
Four Ps of knowing, 104–5

framing, synthesizing with, 131–39
Fronsdal, Gil, 124
FTX, 138
Fuller, Joseph, 5

Galanes, Philip, 123–24
Gibran, Khalil, 91
goal driven habit formation, 125
Golden Circle, 10, 85
The Good Life (Schulz), 5
greatest . . . questions, 160
griot, 59
guide on the side
  emotional cartographers as, 87–88
  leaders as both sage and, 3–15, 31
  recognition by, 74, 75, 78
  see also facilitation

habit formation, 125–26
Haidt, Jonathan, 192
happiness, 15
The Happiness Hypothesis (Haidt), 192
Harmon, Liz, 46–47
Harvard, 5–6
healing, 56
hero's journey, 166–67
The Hero with a Thousand Faces (Campbell), 166
Hibi, Hisako, 44–45
hidden stories, 33–49
  cultural elements in, 35–38
  and personality, 35–36, 40–41
  and professional culture, 36, 41–43
  psychological factors in, 35, 38–40
  questions to awaken, 153–57
  recognizing, *see* recognition
  structural factors in, 36, 44–48
history, 132
Ho, Melissa, 45
The Hotel on the Corner of Bitter and Sweet (Ford), 131
how, order of *why*, *what*, and, 85–86
How to Know a Person (Brooks), 14
How to Tell a Story, 13
human-centered design, 92–94
humility, 100

identity
  behind goals, 126
  covering, 47–48
  professional, 42–43
  social nature of, 127–28
  that doesn't fit dominant narrative, 46, 48
identity driven habit formation, 125–26
illusion of explanatory depth, 76–78
improvisational storytelling, 56–57
incomprehension, embracing, 97–103
Incomprehension Workshop, 98–100
India
  kathak in, 62–63
  storytelling in, 55–56
information, 135
informed decisions, 75–76
initiative, 108–9
inspiring leaders, 10
internal maps, 149–50
Irisumi, Toshihiko, 96–97
IRS storytelling model, 86, 165–80, 203
  elements bringing life to, 184–89
  intriguing beginning in, 167–70
  logistics of, 176–80
  riveting middle in, 170–74

satisfying end in, 174–76
Italy, storytelling in, 56–57
Itzchakov, Guy, 118

Kahneman, Daniel, 29–30
Kansal, Reena, 63
kathak, 62–63
Keckly, Elizabeth, 45
Kim, Greg, 144
Kluger, Avraham N., 118
Knight, Margaret, 45–46
knowing, 103–8
Krieg, Bernhard, 125–26
Krieg, Uwe, 55–56
Kruzel, Alex, 24

Ladder of Inference, 11–12, 204
language, 133
Language vs. Reality (Enfield), 133
leaders, 11
as both sage and guide, 3–15, 31
as emotional cartographers, 87–88
facilitative, 92, 95, 116, *see also* facilitators
great, qualities of, 4–5
hidden skills of, 67–88
inspiring and engaging, 10
recognition of others' stories by, 73–74, *see also* recognition
learning, 150, 151
Leguizamo, John, 48
Leonardo da Vinci, 123
Let the Story Do the Work (Choy), 13, 31, 52, 191
Lincoln, Mary Todd, 45
listening
empathetic, 9
by facilitators, 116–24
public speaking or negotiation vs., 117
reflecting vs., 127
location of story, 184
looking glass self, 128
López Gutiérrez, Ángel, 122–23
Lucas, George, 166
Lyubomirsky, Sonja, 15

Mandate of Heaven, 60
Manifest Destiny, 60
Margolis, Emily, 44
Mayo Clinic Proceedings, 7
McAuley, Chris, 14
Mead, George Herbert, 128
meaning making, 129
meaning-seeking questions, 159–60
Medvec, Vicki, 179
meetings, 134–35
mental maps, 143
mental models, 125
middle of stories, 170–74. *see also* IRS storytelling model
Milon, Arlene, 26–29
mind, filtering done by the, 124
mind reading, 9
mindset, facilitative, 89–109
mini-IRS, 178–79
mirrors, facilitators as, 126–27
Monkey King, 53
monomyth, 166–67
Morgan, Ann, 98–100
Morgan, Isabel, 46

naïve realism, 34
narrative economics, 192–93
Narrative Economics (Shiller), 192
narrative excellence, 196–99
navigational skill, 100
nested structure, 176, 178–79
neuroticism, 40, 41
Never Split the Difference (Voss), 13
New Year's resolutions, 125
Ngọc Lan, 74–75

nonjudgment, 118, 127–28
Norman, Don, 92–93
Norman Doors, 92–93

one-on-one meetings, 134
open-book management, 145–46
openness, 40, 41, 118
opportunities
  missed, 67, 71–72
  for recognizing stories, 70, *see also* recognition
  between what is said and what is meant, 92, 93
origin questions, 158
origin stories, 191
Other Centricity, 95–97, 107, 140, 190
Ott, Katherine, 46
outsiderness, 29–30
overcoming the monster stories, 191

Paired Introduction, 14, 85–87
participatory knowing, 104–7
Passion DNA, 14
patterns, 190–93
personality, storytelling and, 35–36, 40–41
perspectival knowing, 104–7
perspective gap studies, 9
perspectives, 125
persuasion
  listening vs., 118
  proving something vs., 77–78
  storytelling's power of, 52
  3 Tenets of Persuasive Perfection, 135
  winning without, 72, 111–40
Peters, Tina, 136–37
Peters, Winston "Gypsy," 58
Piparo, Salvatore, 57
place, in stories, 169
plots, in business communication, 190–91
Plummer, Denyse, 58
Porter, Jennifer, 129
positive emotions, 15
pragmatism, 107, 190
preaching, 59–60
presence, 19, 21–22, 195
presenters, facilitators vs., 115–17
priming the room, 195–96
procedural knowing, 104–7
professional culture, 36, 41–43, 47–48
The Prophet (Gibran), 91
proportion, in story structure, 176–77
propositional knowing, 104–7
proving, persuading vs., 77–78
psychological factors, in hidden stories, 35, 38–40
psychological safety, 118, 153

Qin Shi Huang, 60
questions, 143–61
  about assumptions, 140
  asked by facilitators, 95, 99–103
  to break deep rules, 152–53
  Crazy Good Questions, 95, 146, 148, 157–61
  great, 148, 149, 152
  for self-reflection, 129
  that awaken story, 153–57
quest stories, 191

rags to riches stories, 191
rebirth stories, 191
recognition, 67–88
  of hidden stories, 33–49
  nudging others to speak up, 78–88
  of others' voices, 73–81

spotting and snatching stories, 17–32
story discovery as, 13
storytelling as, 31–32
of untold but needed stories, 70–72
of what is effective, 72–74
recording stories, 23
Redden, Rissa, 83–85
reflection
by facilitators, 124–28
as narrative tool, 184, 186–90
psychological safety for, 118
self-, 128–30
reframing, synthesizing with, 131–39
relationships, 5, 7–8, 10–11
reluctance to tell stories, 33–35, 61. *see also* hidden stories
role-taking, 128
Rolffs, Alessandra, 125–26
Rough Translation, 30, 112

Sadun, Raffaella, 5
sage on the stage
emotional cartographers as, 87–88
leaders as both guide and, 3–15, 31
transformative opportunity missed by, 73
Salk, Jonas, 46
Samoa, storytelling in, 54–55
Saud, Mohammed Ibn, 60
scene, 184–90
Schlesinger, Jake, 68–70, 94
Schulz, Marc, 5–7
self-consciousness, 39
self-efficacy, 43
self-identity, 127–28
self questions, 160–61
self-reflection, 128–30
sequence, 176, 179–80
sermons, 59–60
Shah, Reena, 62–63
Sheeran, Ed, 90–91
Shiller, Robert, 192
silence, 78–81, 118–23, 148
Silicon Valley Bank, 138
Sinek, Simon, 10, 85
single-story trap, 137–39
Slezak, David (Dado), 186, 197, 199
small moments, 87
Smith, Marion Roach, 186
Smithsonian American Women's History Museum, 44
social feedback, 127–28
Social Q's column, 123–24
song, 57–58
sources of compelling stories, 17–32
Sparrow, 58
speaking up
nudging to encourage, 78–80
Three Levels of, 81–88, 202
spotlight effect, 38–40
spotting and snatching stories, 17–32
Srisuwan, Tian, 168–69, 172–75
SRV Holdings, 145–46
Stack, Jack, 145–46
Stanton, Andrew, 168, 171
Start with Why (Sinek), 85
State of the Global Workplace (Gallup), 7
status quo, 150–52
stereotypes, 136
Steves, Rick, 3–4
stories, 164–65
getting to the heart of, 86–87
hidden, 33–49, 153–57
as mandates for power, 60–61
of, but not about, yourself, 26–29

stories (*cont'd*)
purpose of, 61
spotting and snatching, 17–32, *see also* recognition
structure of, 163–81
unquestioned, 137–39
see also storytelling
story discovery, 87–88
facilitation enabling, 92, *see also* facilitation
power of, 3–15, 52
see also recognition
story facilitation, 13, 146. *see also* facilitation
story library, building, 23
storytelling, 165
in business, 73
connection through, 54
in habit formation, 125–26
as recognition, 31–32, *see also* recognition
recounting events vs., 85
reluctance for, 33–35, 61
self-promotion in, 13
traditional, 51–64
structural barriers for storytelling, 36, 44–48
structure of stories, 163–81
hero's journey, 166–67
IRS model, 86, 165–80
subtracting what's misaligned, 82
summarizing information, 81–82
summary, 184–90
Sun Tzu, 139
Sun Wukong, 53
surgical reflection, 130
surprise
in Compass of Comprehension, 150
in middle of stories, 171
suspense vs., 147–48
surprise questions, 159
suspense
in middle of stories, 171
surprise vs., 147–48
Swift, Taylor, 37–38
synthesizing with reframing, 131–39
system driven habit formation, 125

tactical empathy, 12–13
takeaway questions, 160–61
Tall Poppy Syndrome, 37–38
teachers, facilitators vs., 115–17
teams
accessing character of, 83–87
Compass of Comprehension for, 150–53
cross-cultural, 123
highly productive, 74–75
surgical, reflection by, 130
telling, crafting vs., 176, 179–80
Telling Time (Willard), 149
tell me more questions, 159
tension, in stories, 170, 171, 173
Thaler, Richard, 157–58
This Versus That, 77–78
Three Levels of Speaking Up, 81–88
3 Tenets of Persuasive Perfection, 135–36, 205
time, in stories, 169
tolerance for discomfort, 100
tone-setting, 130
traditional storytelling, 51–64
around the world, 54–60
and power, 60–61
revival of, 51–52
through dance, 62–63
transformation
brought about by reflection, 131
of conflicting viewpoints into informed decisions, 75–76

creating conditions for, 183–99
missing opportunities for, 73
transformational leaders, 43
Trinidad and Tobago, storytelling in, 57–58
Trotman, Karla, 74, 75
trust, building, 26–29, 201
Tugboat Institute, 144
tulsi plant (holy basil), 56
turnaround stories, 191

United States-Japan Foundation, 67–70
Unleash the Power of Storytelling (Biesenbach), 13
unquestioned stories, 137–39
the unspoken, detecting, 8, 33–49
US economy, perceptions of, 106–7

values, divergent, 74–75
Vervaeke, John, 104–5
viewpoints, conflicting, 75–76
Voekel, Tyson, 4
Voss, Chris, 12–13

Wallace, David Foster, 124–25
Warner, Gregory, 30, 111–15, 139–40
wasting talent, 18
West, Kanye, 37
what, order of *why, how,* and, 85–86
the *who,* 10–11
Whorton, Dave, 144–46, 149
why, order of *how, what,* and, 85–86
"why" questions, 158
"Why Senior Leaders Should Stop Having So Many One-on-Ones" (Carucci), 134
"Why You Should Make time for Self-Reflection (Even If You Hate Doing It)" (Porter), 129
Willard, Nancy, 149
Winfrey, Oprah, 19–20
winning without persuading, 72, 111–40
wisdom, 105, 186
working the room, 195–96

A Year of Reading the World (Morgan), 99
Yeo, Chuen Chuen, 193–96
Yoshino, Kenji, 47
yourself, stories of but not about, 26–29

about the author

Esther K. Choy is the CEO and chief story facilitator at Leadership Story Lab, where she helps leaders across industries harness the power of story to build trust, ignite change, and inspire action. The author of *Let the Story Do the Work* and a top contributor to *Forbes*' Leadership Strategy channel, her thought leadership has also been featured in *Harvard Business Review*, *Entrepreneur* magazine, and *The New York Times*. With her MBA from Northwestern University's Kellogg School of Management and her MFA in creative writing at DePaul University (in progress), Esther blends business rigor with narrative craft to redefine leadership as an act of discovery and transformation.

Esther lives in Chicago with her husband and two daughters. She begins her Mondays with a one-thousand-meter swim and a raw jalapeño.